THE RETRIAL OF

RÉGINE PERNOUD

THE RETRIAL OF JOAN OF ARC

The Evidence for Her Vindication

Translated by J. M. Cohen

Foreword by Katherine Anne Porter

IGNATIUS PRESS   SAN FRANCISCO

First Edition:
The Retrial of Joan of Arc:
The Evidence at the Trial for Her Rehabilitation, 1450–1456
Harcourt, Brace and World
Copyright © 1955 by Harcourt, Brace and Company, Inc.
and renewed 1983 by J. M. Cohen
Published by arrangement with Harcourt, Inc.

Cover art: *The Execution of Joan of Arc*
Les Vigils de Charles VII, by Martial de Paris
(called d'Auvergne), fifteenth-century French manuscript
Bibliotheque Nationale, Paris
© Bridgeman-Giraudon / Art Resource

Cover design by Roxanne Mei Lum

Reprinted in 2007 Ignatius Press, San Francisco
All rights reserved
ISBN 978-1-58617-178-0
Library of Congress Control Number 2006936324
Printed in the United States of America ∞

CONTENTS

Foreword *by Katherine Anne Porter*	vii
Preface	xi
Introduction *Before the Rehabilitation*	3
1. The Examination of the Trial	47
2. The Witnesses on Her Childhood	68
3. The Traveling Companions	95
4. The Arrival at Chinon and the Poitiers Judges	104
5. Orléans	126
6. The Witnesses on Her Daily Life	150
7. The First Imprisonment	191
8. The Rouen Witnesses	197
9. The Trial of the Judges	255
10. The Upright Souls	271
11. The Last Act	284
Appendix A: *The First Interrogatory*	291
Appendix B: *The Second Interrogatory*	294
Appendix C: *The Interrogatory Taken in Lorraine*	299
Appendix D: *List of Witnesses at Orléans*	301
Bibliography	303

FOREWORD

In the many hundreds of books in French about the condemnation and retrial of Joan of Arc, the authors invariably base their criticism of the first trial on the evidence given by witnesses in the second. None of these books has been translated into English. The French seem to write them for each other, or perhaps even at this late day the English reader does not enjoy seeing his nation put so soundly and irreparably in the poorest light of its history. Whatever the reason, this is the first book based firmly on the retrial of Joan of Arc to be translated into English, and the whole tremendous history is told again, this time by her childhood playmates and relatives, her royal and noble friends, her confessor, her valet, her squires and heralds, and her fellow soldiers. There are a few of the old enemies of the first court still in Rouen, but they can do her no more harm: and indeed their presence here perhaps lends even a more powerful authenticity to this story than if we heard only from her friends.

It is indeed a beautiful book, well translated, with the speed and symmetry and direction of the life it celebrates; and besides its merit as a work of scholarship, there is warmth and sanity in it, often absent from books about Joan of Arc, who inspires strange fervors and theories. In my small collection, out of the hundreds, there is one that proves to the hilt that Joan was a Catharist, that outcropping of ancient Manichaeism in medieval Provence; another, that she and her fellow captain, Gilles de Laval, Sire de Rais, were sorcerers, adept in Black Magic. The fact that Joan's first trial has been exposed in its falseness over and over has no effect on these infatuated minds; nor that Gilles de Rais, though proved a man of bad morals, still was tried and condemned by a court as corrupt as that which condemned Joan. Still a third book has been published to prove that Joan was a by-blow of the blood royal, and that the "secret" she whispered to the Dauphin in proof of her mission was that she was his half-sister, bastard daughter of his father King Charles VI, the virgin sent to save France after France had been betrayed by a woman.

The woman who had betrayed France was the infamous Isabeau of Bavaria who disavowed her son the Dauphin to make way for Henry VI of England; she had riddled the royal family with bastardy in so many directions, it is possible she may not have been certain which of her many children were legitimate. There is still a small school of thought in France, more Royalist than any king, which holds that only royal blood could have given Joan her splendor of courage and faith. There is not a word anywhere in the records of either trial to support a claim of royal blood, yet from time to time it is put forth again with passionate lunatic arguments.

The people of Domremy knew exactly who Joan was. Her old friends, neighbors, former playmates, godmothers and godfathers, confessors, and "uncles" by marriage in a distant connection—each in turn tells us something about her, with great freshness of feeling and speech. Remembering her tragedy during all those years when they were silenced by the fact that she was a condemned heretic, now that the Inquisition had lifted its ban, and they were free to say what they really thought, they claimed her for their own. When they said, "She was just like us", they meant to say also,

"We are like her; she is one of the family; we never thought her so unusual; there were many others like her." They never denied her superiority in all the general virtues, but admired it and wished to borrow virtue from her; and indeed, what happened is so gently and Christianly true—she borrowed virtue from them, in turn. As they shed light on her childhood and young girlhood among them, by their love and remembrance saving her true story for us, so she shed glory on them. There is a nimbus around every humble country figure, "good Catholics, as those farming people are", said Dunois, who came forward to speak for her before the papal commissioners who were—remotely at the request of King Charles VII, directly by permission from the Pope and the heads of the Inquisition itself—preparing a retrial for her, nearly twenty years after her death. After five centuries, they stand there in the pure light of day, in their breathing bodies, and we hear their voices raised in their natural speech: "When Joan left her father's house, I saw her pass before the house with her uncle, Durand Laxart. Joan said to her father then, 'Good-bye, I am going to Vaucouleurs.' . . ." She was on horseback, wearing the customary farm woman's dress of coarse red wool. We do not know how tall she was, nor how she looked, but every one of her witnesses who spoke of the matter at all had one word for her: she was beautiful. Joan's uncle was taking her to Lord Robert de Baudricourt, where she was going to ask to be taken to the King, or rather as she called him properly, the Dauphin, whom she was to cause to become King Charles VII of France. She had promised her uncle that she would help his wife in her coming childbirth if he would escort her to Lord Robert. This gentleman, on first sight of her, began her career, and the most tremendous event in French history, by advising her uncle to give her a good slapping and take her home. After talking with her, he gave her a safe-conduct to the Duke of Lorraine. And she was on her splendid way to Orléans, to Rheims, to Compiègne, to the stake at Rouen.

All attempts to account rationally for Joan of Arc's life end no better than those that try to shape it to fit some fantastic theory. She is unique, and a mystery, and as you read about her and think about her life, you are led up to a threshold beyond which she eludes you, you cannot cross it. Madame Régine Pernoud has the reassuring ground of firm Catholic belief in the practical efficacy of divine inspiration, and as you follow her attentively through her remarkably clear, detailed tracing of this history told by living tongues, netting the testimonies together with her learned, perfectly placed notes, you begin to share with her the experience of those men who were making the investigation— little by little, one step at a time, one bit of evidence added to another, or compared, they were arriving at Truth beyond the truth they had hoped to find; her method, so direct and knowledgeable, so dedicated to the discovery and presentation of the mystical truth that inheres in the accumulated, eagerly honest, spoken and recorded testimony, simply leads the way to that truth. Of all the books I have read on this subject, this is my choice, and the last, profoundly satisfying word for me, for any time to come.

—KATHERINE ANNE PORTER

PREFACE

In 1839, that learned scholar Vallet de Viriville assessed the number of works devoted to Joan of Arc at five hundred; fifty years later the figure had increased fivefold. Yet the interest she aroused in the nineteenth century is as nothing compared with the interest she has aroused since then. In France, her day has become both a religious and a national festival, Church and state finding themselves at one in raising her likeness on the altar and in the public square. More important, Joan has assumed for our age a living reality unimaginable a hundred years ago.

This being so, it is strange that a document of cardinal importance in Joan's story has been neglected. The detailed record of the trial in which Joan was condemned has been several times published and translated and is familiar in outline even to the general public; one cannot say the same of the record of the proceedings that led to her rehabilitation. This record is well known to specialists and has been much drawn upon by historians—generally at second hand—but the only edition today available is a transcription of the Latin version prepared by Jules Quicherat. It is an admirable work, but it has been unprocurable for many years, not only in the bookshops but also in the majority of libraries. As for translations, there is only the very fragmentary one made by Eugene O'Reilly[1] and used

---

[1] This was, of course, a translation into French.

by Joseph Fabre, dating from 1868 and 1888 respectively;[2] and it is, moreover, stiff reading.

That is all that we have of the only great document—except the account of her trial and condemnation—that throws on Joan, her personality, and her times the direct light of living men's evidence, reflected by no distorting mirror of chronicle or tale. What is more, the account of her condemnation, though it gives the drama at Rouen, leaves the details of Joan's life in shadow, whereas the record of her rehabilitation presents all the stages and essential episodes, one by one, from her baptism in the parish church of Domremy to her burning. (It also shows the impression she made on the crowds.) And it is her childhood friends, her comrades in arms, her former judges, who come, one after another, to evoke her memory; those same persons who had been the actors, or at least the supernumeraries, in the drama of which she was the heroine.

What is more, this rehabilitation suit, staged a bare twenty years after Joan's execution, in itself forms a strange enough page in history; it dealt with events still recent and tinged with the miraculous, events of which men were then free to measure the repercussions. For if we are in a better position than her contemporaries to analyze their effect on the structure of Europe, there was not, on the other hand, a single peasant or townsman in France whose life would not have been changed, to a greater or lesser extent, by the outcome of those battles that decided whether France should remain attached to England or be free. Finally, the case that was being argued was a singularly moving one: a victim, a woman, a mere girl had been burnt alive by judicial decree, and the question was whether that victim

[2] For these works, see the Bibliography.

was a heroine or a simple visionary—that is to say, a dangerous heretic.

The majority of historians have, inexplicably, failed to recognize the importance of the case. Many, looking through entirely modern spectacles, have been unable to see what it revealed to contemporaries. They have assumed the knowledge at that time of certain truths that, in fact, could not have come to light but for the suit for Joan's rehabilitation. It is, however, indisputable that the details, both of her career and her condemnation, were unknown to the great majority: the details of her heroism to people who had lived in the occupied zone, the details of her trial to the former inhabitants of free France. Facts that are absolutely familiar to us—the falsification or omission of certain documents in her trial—were totally unknown to those very men who undertook her rehabilitation. Finally, it is beyond doubt that public opinion, whether for or against Joan, was only inaccurately informed about her story, and that it was the suit that brought the truth to light. Some historians have even thought it possible to regard the whole rehabilitation suit as a cleverly staged play, put on either by the Church or the King. But if one takes the trouble to follow the stages of this affair, the development of which took no less than seven years and called together people from every district of France and from all social classes, it is clear that a piece of mummery on such a scale would have been difficult to carry through.

It will be up to the reader, in any case, to judge the facts from the documents of the case, which we intend to put before him in a translation as close as possible to the original text. There could be no question of publishing the complete record of the trial. With the account of each hearing and such legal documents as writs and summonses, it fills no less than 855 octavo pages in Quicherat's edition—and even so he omitted the majority of the preliminary reports (nineteen in all) drawn up in preparation for the case, and likewise the *Recollectio*, or general résumé of the whole proceedings made by Jean Bréhal (the Inquisitor entrusted with its conduct), which alone takes up a whole volume. We have extracted only the parts that are to us most alive and most valuable—that is to say, the statements of the witnesses—suppressing only repetitions that would have made the book bulkier without adding anything new. We have, in addition, put back into the first person those statements that the scribe had transposed into the third on translating them into Latin—"The witness says that ... , etc."—in which he followed the habitual procedure in ecclesiastical courts.

—RÉGINE PERNOUD

THE RETRIAL OF JOAN OF ARC

INTRODUCTION

Before the Rehabilitation

JOAN AND PUBLIC OPINION

On December 10, 1449, King Charles VII made a solemn entry into his city of Rouen, which had just been liberated after thirty years of foreign occupation, and throughout his kingdom, the bells were rung in token of rejoicing at the news of this decisive step in what historians were subsequently to call the "recovery of Normandy".

A little while after this triumphal entry, the King addressed to one of his counselors, Master Guillaume Bouillé, former rector of the University of Paris and canon of Noyon Cathedral, a letter to this effect:

> "Whereas ... Joan the Maid was captured and taken prisoner by our ancient enemies and opponents the English; and whereas they set up a case against her by the agency of certain persons nominated and appointed by them; and committed such wrongs and abuses that as a result of this case and of the great hatred that our enemies had for her, they iniquitously, cruelly, and in defiance of all justice put her to death: we wish to know the truth of this matter and to learn the manner in

which the proceedings were conducted. We order, command, and expressly enjoin you, therefore, to inquire and inform yourself well and diligently concerning all that is said of the matter; and to bring the information you gather on this subject under cover and seal before us and the gentlemen of our Council ... and to do so we grant you power, authority, and special orders by virtue of this.... Given at Rouen, on the fifteenth day of February ..."

On February 15, 1450, the campaign in Normandy was no more than begun; towns such as Caen and Cherbourg were still in enemy hands, and only the surrender of Rouen, brought about, moreover, by a revolt of its inhabitants that had forced Somerset, the English governor, hurriedly to leave his residence in the Old Palace and take refuge in Caen, allowed the King to review a series of events that had taken place twenty—but only twenty—years before in the triangle formed by the three royal cities, Orléans, Rheims, and Rouen. It was a series of events that has not yet ceased to amaze historians. A young peasant girl from the borders of Lorraine had delivered the key city of the kingdom from an interminable siege, had led the Dauphin through the heart of the occupied zone to the city where the kings of France were anointed, and had then been captured, sold, and finally handed over to a heretic's death. And all within two years.

One may wonder what the figure of Joan of Arc stood for on that day in February 1450. How did contemporaries see a page of history that was already taking on the gilt of legend and has retained, through the centuries, the power of surprising schoolboys? Contemporaries, moreover, to whom it had been personal, as well as public, history.

Realistically and objectively, Joan was a heretic who had been duly condemned by an ecclesiastical court. She had performed some remarkable exploits, it is true, and her trial had been conducted under conditions that made the court's decision suspect. The conviction for heresy held, nevertheless. Joan, whom we are in the habit of considering the most unimpeachable of all the saints, had been condemned for an infamous crime. If one had any respect for the authorities, one had to think of her as an agitator who had spread disquieting doctrines; one had to compare her to John Huss, whose followers had become so numerous that there had been attempts to start a crusade against them or to those Lollards whom the late King of England had just recently punished.

It is very important to note that what the King ordered, once he was in possession of that city of Rouen, which had been the scene of the last and most solemn stage in Joan's history, was not an expiatory ceremony or an act of reparation, but an inquiry. Certainly his own mind was made up, and the preamble to his letter conveys as much: Joan had been the victim of his "ancient enemies and opponents". However, in the first place, what he demanded, for himself and for public opinion, was "to know the truth of this matter". As long as Rouen had remained in enemy hands, nothing useful could be undertaken; it was at Rouen that a veil had been thrown over the truth of the story, that victory had been turned into defeat and the heroine into a child of the devil, a relapsed heretic. Only at Rouen could light be shed on the matter, and that was what the King wanted.

Popular opinion, on the whole, echoed the King's. To the people, it was clear that Joan had been an emissary of Heaven and the instrument of God's justice, that she had been unjustly condemned by the enemies of France, on false accusations, and that hers had been a martyr's death. Popular feeling, the feeling of the little man, knows no hesitations; and this will, as we shall see, lend valuable support to the actual rehabilitation. Joan had her witnesses also, and her martyrs; not only the mendicant friar Pierre Bosquier, sentenced to jail for evincing doubts about the honesty of the judges who had sent her to the stake (and that only a few weeks after her execution), but first among them all that unknown heroine Perrinaïc, condemned to the stake in Paris for having dared to sing her praises.

There are some curious shades in this popular enthusiasm—curious at least to us who look from a distance of five hundred years on events that are familiar yet distorted by habits of mind, errors of vision, pious exaggerations, or stubborn prejudices. At the time, they were easily explicable, these various degrees of popular veneration that will be unconsciously echoed by the witnesses in the rehabilitation suit.

At Rouen, for instance, the people knew Joan in the character of a martyr, of a young prisoner who had aroused their curiosity ("Everybody wanted to see her", two witnesses will say, Pierre Daron and Laurent Guesdon); of a heroine whom they saw one day led to the stake by a host of men at arms, "uttering such pious lamentations" that none of the spectators, even the English, could hold back his tears. In the midst of the flames, she had not ceased to call on the name of Jesus, and when she gave her last sigh, a dove was seen to fly away in the direction of France. Furthermore, the executioner could not reduce her heart to ashes. As for the men who had condemned her, they were well known, and the finger of scorn was pointed at them in the city. They were benefice-hunters to a man, in English pay, and absolutely gorged with the places they had gained as a price of their treason. Did not Cauchon, the chief of them, take his reward in the shape of a royal councilorship with a salary of a thousand pounds *tournois*, in addition to the seven hundred and sixty-five pounds he received for his services in going to claim the Maid on behalf of the King of England? But God's hand had fallen on them: "All those who were guilty of her death died most shamefully." The three principal malefactors met tragic ends. Cauchon died suddenly while a barber was trimming his beard; d'Estivet, his intimate friend and the prime mover in the case, disappeared most mysteriously, and his body was discovered in a gutter; and finally, their right-hand man, Nicolas Midy, was stricken with leprosy some time after the trial, had to resign the benefices that his "devotion" had won him, and went into a leper house, there to die consumed by his disease.

All this had been repeated from mouth to mouth during the twenty years of occupation that Rouen had undergone between Joan's burning and the King's entry. And the story had served to sustain a sort of clandestine resistance movement from the moment in 1432 when the audacious Ricarville seized the castle of Rouen at the head of three hundred companions, all of whom paid for their exploit with their lives, to that October day in 1449 when the English governor was finally forced to flee from the revolt of the inhabitants and abandon the place to the royal armies.

At Orléans, they seem, intentionally, to have preserved only memories of Joan in her glory. Every year, beginning indeed in 1435, the people had flocked to the procession of May 8, and enthusiastically celebrated the anniversary of their deliverance by Joan. There too Joan's mother and brothers lived, on pensions from the burghers. The fulfillment of one of the Maid's prophecies had been noted, with a display of great emotion, when Duke Charles returned from

England in 1440 after a captivity that had lasted for twenty-five years. And the news of Joan's death had with difficulty been accepted as true; people seem to have refused to believe it. In fact, they seem to have been within an ace of expecting that she would return in triumph "as if she were an angel of God"—to quote the words of one of the Orléans men who gave evidence in the rehabilitation suit—an angel before whom the enemy would melt away, as once they had done at Jargeau and at Patay. Things had gone so far that an adventuress was able to exploit her resemblance to Joan and pass herself off on the dazzled inhabitants as the Maid herself. They were far from averse to the idea of a miracle!

Inevitably, elements of superstition were mingled with this popular excitement. Prophecies were repeated and passed from mouth to mouth: the prophecy of Marie d'Avignon, who had seen the armor that was to be worn by a young woman when riding to the kingdom's rescue; Merlin's prophecy, in which he spoke of a Maid who would trample on the backs of archers (and it was well known that archers formed the main body of the English armies); and that prediction, too, that spoke of a virgin coming from Bois Chenu. One has a dim feeling that all these prophecies had a respectable foundation, and that even the theologians must have taken them seriously. Were they not all based, more or less, on that Christian belief, so real to the medieval mind, in the redemptive power of woman, of a virgin? We are dealing with an age in which above the doors of the cathedrals stood the image of a virgin. From the troubadours' songs to the romances of chivalry, the age of feudalism had devoted to Woman a veritable cult. It is from this cult, indeed, that chivalry itself was born. Something of this still survived into Joan's day. Indeed, she was expected by her age; men's minds were prepared for that astounding phenomenon.

But in everyday life, such ideas, however exalted they may be, are easily adulterated; there was no lack of false miracle-workers and false visionaries in that troubled age, when, for almost three-quarters of a century, wars, famines, epidemics, and the train of misery that followed them had come one after another. How, at first sight, could one distinguish a Joan of Arc from a Catherine of la Rochelle, or from that wretch Guillaume, the shepherd of Guévaudan, of whom no less a man than Regnault of Chartres, the anointing archbishop, had said that he "performed neither more nor less than Joan the Maid": an assertion that was soon belied by the sad end of the tale, which followed close on its beginning but which clearly shows the confusion then obtaining. In all good faith, men who refused blindly to follow the popular impulse could find doubtful elements in this story of Joan.

And perhaps there was some element of disapproval mingling with their doubts: this virago in men's clothes, riding among the soldiers, hardly corresponded to the generally accepted idea of a Christian virgin. That, however, is the picture of Joan that very many people would have retained, especially in the occupied territories, where nothing was known except by hearsay and where, moreover, English opinion had had its influence.

Besides, not all her predictions had been fulfilled. Certainly Paris had been retaken in 1436, and the Duke of Orléans freed four years later; but she had prophesied that all the English would be "pushed out of France", and now, almost twenty years later, they were still masters of Guienne, while the "recovery of Normandy", which was taking shape, was only just beginning to shake the minds of skeptics. Twenty years—not long when viewed from a distance, but, in a man's lifetime, what a test for the impatient!

What is more, one could always ask what the justification was for these fratricidal struggles that were tearing apart two kingdoms traditionally united. What about legal rights? What about justice? Had not Normandy been the fief of the English kings for two centuries and more? Whether it was the Bastard or the Plantagenet, had they not legitimate jurisdiction over a whole quarter of France between the Seine and the Pyrénées? It is true that they recognized the King's sovereignty over these territories and paid him homage for them. But their subjects had nothing but praise for the English administration, as witness the vine-growers and merchants around Bordeaux, whose fortunes England had made. And what justice was there in these dynastic quarrels that divided princes? Was Charles, who had been disavowed by his own mother, really the prince who should rule over the Lilies? A thousand contradictory rumors circulated among the people on this subject; some murmured, and would continue to do so long afterward, "He does not belong there". "He did not have the mark of the Lily flower on his breast at his birth, as the heir to the throne always has", etc.—little tales of no great importance that nevertheless go around. Even after his victory, Charles VII was to have the opportunity of pardoning a fellow who had repeated them in his cups and had been arrested in consequence by the royal sergeants—a proof that a certain amount of importance was attached to such rumors.

And that dazzling landing of King Henry V on the soil of France, his victory at Agincourt, where five thousand English archers—so it was said—had laid low the whole chivalry of France, six to one, was not that the will of Heaven? And had not his son Henry VI, born from his lawful marriage with a French princess, sole right to the title of King of France, which his grandfather Charles VI had acknowledged as his? Had not Joan come to combat a course of events that had been decreed by the judgment of God?

These doubts and many others divided public opinion—at least at such times as people had the leisure to think. For there was hardly a district in France where men were not constrained by dire necessity to face their most immediate needs without looking much further; daily life was for the majority the only question that demanded an urgent solution. The problem was one of drawing nourishment from a ravaged country where the amount of fallow land was increasing and where provisions no longer traveled on the main roads, which were a prey to men at arms. Food was a problem in the towns, and the cost of living was continually rising; while in the country the bands of freebooters spread panic, and not only in the battle areas. An adventurer like Rodrigo de Villandrando, the "king of the plunderers", could with ease hold the south of France to ransom, ravage the Albigeois, and render the royal officers powerless against his lawless soldiery. He could even terrorize the city magistrates—those of Bergerac for example—who openly paid ransom to these brigands. The very word "brigand", which comes from *brigandine*,[1] first appears in the language at this time: a sad legacy from years that are perhaps the darkest in French history, years in which brigandage was the effectual king, in which terrified peasants took refuge in their caves or dug themselves underground lairs, and in which people found themselves everywhere "consumed and oppressed". And as always

[1] A short coat of mail.

occurs, to the horrors of war were added those of epidemics: the plague, which had made its appearance in Europe a century before, had made terrifying reappearances during those dark years, and in 1439 had carried off fifty thousand victims in Paris alone.

To all these causes of confusion had been added, for many years now, the harrowing certainty that the royal authority could no longer be depended on. That prince who had been for so long the hopeless Dauphin, the ludicrous king of Bourges, the disavowed adolescent, and on whom there weighed in addition the terrible responsibility for the murder of Jean the Fearless, seemed immediately after Joan's triumphs to have fallen into an apathy; even after the liberation of Paris, he had taken eighteen months to decide to make his entry into a capital where everything awaited him. But at least each resumption of action in the last years had been marked by a victory.

Now amid all these miseries and confusions, one truth was clearly evident to contemporaries: Joan's fate was closely associated with that of King Charles; about that nobody was in any doubt. By pointing to him as "true heir to the throne", by causing him to be anointed at Rheims, she had allied her cause with her prince's. And no less clear was the feeling that efficacy is the true touchstone: a good tree yields good fruit; and for the immense majority, the good fruit was peace procured by the conclusive victory of one party over the other. Supporters of the English claim to both crowns and supporters of the King of France had more or less consciously associated the justice of their cause with the issue of this war.

The English had understood this from the beginning. They had delightedly presented the victory of Agincourt as a sign of divine favor; and they had passionately attempted, by the same token, to destroy the moral effect of Joan's victories. To bring them to an end was to bring Charles VII's progress to an end; but that was not enough. It was necessary to have her condemned as a pitiable adventuress, an obstinate heretic, a rebel against the holy laws of the Church. In that case, the royal cause would find itself forever compromised for having made use of an evildoer and a visionary. Indeed, this is what Master Guillaume Érard had called Joan, in his emphatic harangue on the famous day of her "recantation" in the cemetery of Saint Ouen: "O Royal House of France, you have never known such monsters till now. Today you are dishonored for having put your trust in this sorceress, this heretic, this creature of superstition." And Joan had quickly cut short this cunning speech with the brisk rejoinder, "Do not speak of my king. He is a good Christian."

The opportunists and politicians of all shades understood things in this sense too. With the King back in Rouen, Joan's cause appeared to them in a totally new light. The most deeply compromised had fled to England, and their possessions had been confiscated; as for the rest, a general amnesty had been decreed by Charles VII on his first entry on to Norman soil. But that did not prevent those who had made the wrong choice twenty years before from sweating still with apprehension. We shall see them piling up excuses and pretexts in their defense, alleging their fears, and the threats and pressure of the English—and giving, moreover, in many cases, only too true a picture of the facts.

There were, however, some who would not admit themselves beaten: all the clique of University men and Sorbonne doctors. To them the case had been quite clear before judgment was given. Certainly their personal attachment to the English party would have been enough to account for the resentment they felt; but it was not only because it was filled with Bedford's creatures that the Sorbonne displayed such fury against Joan as to claim the right of trying her as a privilege and seconded to Rouen at the time of her trial their most skillful judges, such as Guillaume Érard and Thomas de Courcelles. It is not only for that reason that a dull spite will still obtrude in the speeches of the surviving judges. It is also, perhaps principally, because Joan's very personality—"her deeds and her words", her speech and her behavior—hurled a straight defiance at the wisdom of these sages: a simple woman who proved more expert in war than a captain; an ignorant peasant girl who behaved as if she knew more than these doctors who held the keys of knowledge; a young girl under twenty who stated that she trusted more in her visions than in the light of their knowledge, than in them, the lights of the Church, who were soon to take on themselves the power of deposing a Pope. Not even fear could make these men forget such presumption; even their defeat did not make them change their minds. The most moderate—and among them some who had not been implicated in the affair—always remained skeptical when there was talk of Joan's mission. If only she had not made so much fuss about her visions. But to speak of miracles and cite the evidence of visions without the authority of the only valid authority, that of the Sorbonne—what unbearable presumption!

THE ROYAL INQUIRY

This was more or less the state of mind prevailing at the moment when Charles VII opened his inquiry. The event must have produced a certain stir in the town. Guillaume Bouillé, who was in charge, appeared very well qualified to fulfill his task. For a long time head of the College of Beauvais in Paris, some time after the liberation of the town he had been appointed rector of a purged University. Charles VII had chosen him as one of the members of his Great Council. He was, strange to say, a disinterested person and was later voluntarily to renounce the benefices that his office had brought him. Later still he was to request the executors of his will to bury him without any pomp. Finally—and this last fact, more than all the rest, justifies the King's choice of him—he had personally displayed a lively interest in Joan's posthumous cause, since before being charged with the inquiry, it was he who had compiled the first in date of the written memoranda contesting the validity of the Rouen trial. He was certainly the man of the moment, the man everything pointed to as the fittest to lay the first stone of the monument of her rehabilitation.

He showed this immediately by the choice of witnesses he summoned to appear, as well as by the promptness with which he called them and heard them. Twenty days had not passed since the King's letter when, on March 4, 1450, the first witness made his deposition.

This was Master Guillaume Manchon, a person of primary importance in the case because he had been the principal scribe and had taken down all the proceedings from beginning to end. No one could give a better account than he of the way in which the discussions had been conducted. So it was that his examination occupied the whole of March 4, while the six other witnesses were heard the next day. Four of these were Dominican friars, all belonging to the convent of Saint Jacques at Rouen. Two of them, Friar Martin Ladvenu and Friar Isambart de la Pierre, had played principal roles—the former had been Joan's confessor and both had continually ministered to her up to her last day. The other two, Friar Guillaume Duval and Friar Jean Toutmouillé, had been present at some hearings toward the close of the trial, and the former had accompanied Friar Martin Ladvenu when he had given Joan the last sacraments. These were all witnesses of her last moments, the men best able to testify to Joan's behavior in her final hour, which might have been that of the recantation her judges counted on. If Cauchon had stayed there till the last moment, if, contrary to custom, Joan had not been gagged, was it not because they expected from her a public retraction that would have definitely destroyed all belief in her mission and, furthermore, have wrecked the royal cause?

Finally, two other persons had been summoned by Guillaume Bouillé: one the very antithesis of the other. The first was Jean Massieu, a priest of doubtful morals, twice sentenced for scandalous behavior, who had performed the duties of usher in the case—which means that he had gone to fetch Joan and escorted her in her passage between prison and the court room. Now this miserable creature had shown himself susceptible to pity, and no doubt even then he had been piling up the details that might show him under a favorable light. But he seems in any case to have been sincerely affected by Joan's fate, and in her last moments, he was the only one besides Ladvenu and Isambart who dared to assist her to the extent of his powers. The second, Jean Beaupère, had been one of the judges in the condemnatory trial. He was a University doctor, puffed up with learning and logic, a very important prelate who had distinguished himself throughout the interminable Council of Basel by the fervor he displayed, at the head of the Anglo-French University clique, in attacking papal power. But he was a man who could never be susceptible to any feelings of pity: he was certain that he possessed the truth, and this certainty was enough for him. There was only one sort of feeling in him: spite. He had frequently examined Joan, and it was to him that she had made some of her finest answers— the one, for instance, concerning the state of grace: "If I am in it, may God keep me in it, and if I am not, may it be God's will to put me in it." To be thus put in his place by an ignorant girl was something that he could not forgive; and his answers, now that it was his turn to be examined, were full of spleen: "She was very subtle, with a woman's subtlety." Let us add, so that nothing shall be missing from the picture, that he was in his avarice a worthy rival to Cauchon. It had been to defend his claim to his canonical prebendary that Beaupère had come to Rouen from his home in Besançon, just in time to be called as a witness.

Such were the men whom Guillaume Bouillé questioned on March 4 and 5, 1450. Those seven were enough, both the men themselves and the information that they were able to supply, to recall the atmosphere of Joan's trial and to bring back forcibly memories of her features at the time of her sentence and burning. Now it became abundantly evident that the trial, which had condemned her while preserving, in appearance, all the rules of law and procedure, had really been marked by grave irregularities of a judicial kind; that it was fundamentally vitiated by the evident partiality of the judges; and that pressure had been exerted even on the scribes of the court. In the last resort, Joan's entire condemnation rested on her reassumption of male clothing, after she had given it up. But the witnesses attested that she had resumed this male costume to which the judges pretended to attach such importance only in order to save herself from the violence of her jailers.

In fact, this whole trial had been nothing but a sinister comedy staged to discredit the cause Joan had embraced and to cut short her victories. So much the King could observe when he was brought, in letters under cover and seal, the results of the inquiry he had ordered. His feelings had not deceived him; that the trial which had condemned her was invalid sprang clearly to light. And not less clear to him was the fact that it was the King of France's cause that the prosecutors had been trying to strike at and dishonor through Joan.

Henceforth he possessed, in the shape of seven pieces of evidence emanating from persons intimately concerned with the case, all the elements necessary for Joan's condemnation to be considered null and void. However, the enterprise was far from concluded. The King found himself, in fact, totally incapable of having her sentence officially annulled. It was beyond the competence of his courts to undo what an ecclesiastical court had done. Joan had been found guilty by the Inquisition; she was under conviction for heresy, and from that conviction, only the Church could release her. The inquiry of 1450 remained, therefore, semi-official and without real efficacy; but it moved public opinion, refocused attention on the most remarkable act of that interminable war, and opened a way toward the rehabilitation suit proper.

FRANCE AND CHRISTENDOM AT THE TIME OF THE REHABILITATION

Now this same year 1450 was to be a decisive year both for France and for Christendom.

In the first place, it saw the completion of the "recovery of Normandy" with a rapidity that could never have been foreseen. At the very moment when the summoned witnesses appeared before Guillaume Bouillé, on March 4 and 5, Henry VI, disturbed at the turn that military events were taking, was making preparations for the landing of a new army intended to stop the French advance and to rescue Somerset, who had been on the defensive at Caen ever since the revolt at Rouen. It was necessary to strike a heavy blow. The King of England saw his strength in Normandy crumbling away; for the last six months, towns had been falling, one after another. First it had been Fougères; then Verneuil, where Dunois and Talbot had found themselves face to face, as once before at Patay—but Talbot had not even given battle; then Pont l'Évêque and Pont Audemer; Bishop Thomas Basin had himself opened the city gates at Lisieux to the French and negotiated the surrender; all over the place his colleagues were imitating him; already the enemy were in occupation of Coutances, Granville, and Saint Lô.

Henry VI, whose finances were then in a bad way, decided to make the greatest effort of his reign and pledged the crown jewels. He entrusted the landing and the leadership of the expedition to Thomas Kyriel, who disembarked at Cherbourg on March 15 and advanced as far as Formigny, where the Count de Clermont's forces compelled him to entrench himself. Kyriel was self-confident and prepared to wait there for Somerset, who was to leave Caen and effect a junction with the newly landed troops. But Richemont arrived unexpectedly and swept this expensively equipped army away. The battle of Formigny, on April 15, 1450, was another Agincourt in reverse. The official figures assessed the number of dead on the English side at 3,774, and the prisoners at fourteen hundred, among whom was Thomas Kyriel himself.

The recovery of Normandy was to continue with the fall of Caen and the capture of Somerset on June 24, and then with the fall of Cherbourg on August 12. Normandy, and with it the whole of northern France, had become French once more. And Mont Saint Michel, the only place that had remained obstinately loyal to the French king, found itself rewarded for a resistance that had lasted for more than thirty years. Its magnificent isolation was ended, and, strangely enough, the man who had been in charge of this impregnable fortress' defense for the greater part of the time was the brother of the prelate who was to take up Joan of Arc's case and achieve her rehabilitation.

Guillaume d'Estouteville was then at Rome, where he had, some time before, been appointed titular cardinal of San Martino ai Monti in that city. He was a Benedictine who had entered the priory of Saint Martin des Champs and there attained the degree of doctor in canon law before becoming one of the mainstays of Pope Eugenius IV during one of the most disturbed papal reigns in history. As a Norman and a near relative of Charles VII (a cousin-german, his maternal grandmother being the sister of King Charles V), he must have followed with great attention the events that were taking place in his own country.

At that moment, however, Rome was entirely taken up with the celebration of the Jubilee year, amid an influx of pilgrims and an excess of ardor that surprised the ecclesiastical authorities themselves. To give one example, the town of Danzig alone saw the departure of more than two thousand pilgrims for Rome.

Now the papacy had scarcely emerged from the long crisis into which it had been plunged by the errors and exigences of the Council of Basel, as an immediate sequel to the Great [Western] Schism. Nicolas V, who was elected

Pope in 1447, was reaping the fruits of the firmness of his predecessor, the astonishing Eugenius IV, whose whole term of office had been marked by dramatic incidents; besieged in Rome by the Colonna family, he had had to face simultaneously the disorders of a population barricaded in the city, the defection of his troops, and conspiracies hatched even in the Castel Sant'Angelo—all this hardly more than a few weeks after his election, and, incidentally, at the very moment when Joan's case was being tried at Rouen (March to May, 1431). Stricken with paralysis three months later, in August 1431, sick and partially crippled, he had nevertheless put up a successful resistance for sixteen years against the Fathers of the Council of Basel: against the faction that wished to put the papacy into wardship and that was led by precisely those men who had just condemned Joan—by Jean Beaupère, Thomas de Courcelles, Nicolas Midy, Guillaume Érard, and the rest, the whole of the pro-English University of Paris. He had even prepared the abdication of the antipope elected by the Council, that Felix V who was just a lay nobleman and, incidentally, the father of nine children— Amadeus VIII, Duke of Savoy—when the Fathers, in the full fury of revolt, came to fetch him [the Duke] from his castle of Ripaille, on the shores of the Lake of Geneva, to put him in the place of the Pontiff who dared to resist them. The King of France had played an active role in that abdication, and, by a curious coincidence, one of the envoys whom he sent to the anti-pope to persuade him to give in was none other than Dunois, Joan's comrade in arms.

Confronted with the disorders of this assembly of Basel, with the conceit of these University doctors, and the avarice of the politicians who were its members, the Christian people themselves underwent an extraordinary rebirth of faith and piety, which this holy year of 1450 gave them an opportunity to display. After the religious setback at the opening of the century, this marked an unexpected revival, stimulated in particular by the mendicant friars—Franciscans and Dominicans—whose preaching moved the crowds. Ever since Joan's own times, two famous preachers had been moving great waves of mankind, and their personal piety—as much as their proselytizing zeal—was to win them canonization a short time after their deaths. These were Saint Vincent Ferrier, nicknamed the Angel of the Judgment, who had been asked to advise on a way of ending the Great Schism, and the astonishing Bernard of Siena, who fascinated crowds by a reputation that he owed both to his exceptional beauty and his absolute chastity. It was perhaps the impetus of influences like theirs that assembled enthusiastic crowds in Rome in 1450, crowds whose presence seemed to ratify the still quite recent victory of the papacy over the bad shepherds.

So a series of circumstances seems to favor the successive stages in Joan's rehabilitation: the strengthening of the French crown, the strengthening of the papal power; and, as Charles VII had always sincerely supported the latter against the Basel dissidents and their anti-pope, the ways were made singularly easy for the solution of a case that could not be opened except on the initiative of the Church.

No less than six years, however, were to elapse between the first and the last stages of the rehabilitation, between Guillaume Bouillé's semi-official inquiry in March 1450 and the official ceremonies on July 7, 1456, that were to mark Joan's greatest victory, her triumph over her judges: slow-moving years of history that formed the Shakespearean background of this suit for her rehabilitation.

The first thing they witnessed was the fulfillment of Joan's prophecies. The campaign in Guienne, begun in 1449, was concluded when on October 19, Bordeaux, a city that was more than half English, was restored to the King of France; the last English troops left the place, and as they passed they offered a sad salute to the Cordouan tower, which their Black Prince had erected at the mouth of the Gironde. The English found themselves "pushed out of France" by a series of French victories sufficient to shake the most skeptical. Talbot himself—the famous Talbot, Joan's opponent whom she had once taken prisoner on the field of Patay—had met his death at the battle of Castillon on July 17, 1453. What an astonishing revenge for the former King of Bourges, the timid youth reduced to misery and solitude whose treasurer—as was to be told during the trial—"had not then four crowns, either of the King's or his own!" Charles of Orléans,[2] who knew better than any what these victories signified, could well exclaim:

> Rejoice, free kingdom of France,
> For now God fights on your side....

And his voice raised a curious echo to the last verses written by Christine de Pisan,[3] who had just survived to hear, shortly before her death, the news of the relief of Orléans, and to whom we owe the only French poem addressed to Joan in her lifetime:

> In the year fourteen hundred and twenty-nine,
> Once more the sun began to shine ...
> For you, most fortunate of Maids,
> Have loosed the cord that held the land
> Of France as in an iron band.

---

[2] Charles of Orléans (1391–1465), nobleman and poet, for a long time a prisoner in England.
[3] Christine de Pisan (c. 1363–c. 1430), poetess.

At last released from his doubts, Charles ordered the mint of Paris to strike a number of commemorative medals, the inscriptions on which display a note of triumph: "Glory and peace to you, King Charles, and perpetual praise. The fury of the enemy has been conquered, and by your energies. Thanks to Christ's counsel and the aid of the law, the Kingdom, after being shaken by so long a crisis, has been rebuilt."

At this same time, terrible news arrived to distress Christendom: the Turks had captured Constantinople. Christendom's last bastion in the East had collapsed under Ottoman pressure, after a heroic resistance, on the morning of May 29, 1453; among the dead in battle had been found the body of the last Byzantine emperor, Constantine Dragases, and the pitiless invader had had his head embalmed to pass it as a trophy from one to another of the principal cities of his new empire. In the intoxication of victory, Mahomet II had ordered the women and children who had taken refuge in the Church of Santa Sophia to be slaughtered and had immediately had this citadel of Christendom transformed into a mosque by the recitation in front of the altar of verses from the Qur'an. This was a tragic answer to the appeals that the sovereign popes had been making to Christian princes for more than a century, without hope of success. Their only reaction to this catastrophe was to be a banquet held a year later at the court of Burgundy: the famous feast of the "Pheasant Oath", at which, with a great display of silver plate, precious cloths, and elaborate dishes, a pheasant was brought to the table, "alive and with a very rich gold collar round its neck, most richly garnished with pearls and precious stones", upon which Philip the Good swore, yet again, his empty oath to take up the Cross. The princes of the West would never really understand until they saw the

Crescent beneath the walls of Vienna. Only the papacy, it seems, realized how irreparable the cleavage was between East and West, for it occurred at a moment when one might have thought that the often projected union between the Orthodox and the Roman Churches might have been effected. Indeed, under Eugenius IV, it seemed quite close, though at that same moment the prelates of the Basel Council, completely oblivious to the interests of the universal Church, were attempting to engineer a new schism. The great rupture of 1453 was to render final and definite the throwing back of the East upon itself.

FIRST STAGE TOWARD THE REHABILITATION: THE ECCLESIASTICAL INQUIRY

Astounding though it may be, these vast happenings, which endangered the Church and Christianity itself, had their repercussions on Joan's suit. It was primarily because he was aware of the imminence of the Turkish threat that Nicolas V, returning once more to plans for a crusade, attempted to make peace between the Christian princes and therefore decided on August 13, 1451, to send Guillaume d'Estouteville to France as his legate. This legate had quickly come to the conclusion that there was one open question that he must solve at all costs: the case of Joan of Arc, which had, in fact, been an attempt to cast doubts on the legitimacy of the French king's cause. By all accounts, Charles VII was anxious for a revision of the case to be made because he was himself concerned in it, his fortunes being closely bound up with Joan's.

There are many historians who conclude from this that henceforth the rehabilitation suit was a purely political affair.

Some go further and see in the whole matter nothing but pure opportunism: the Church condemns Joan when the English king's cause seems to prevail, and hurriedly rehabilitates her when the French king wins.

These views appear very perfunctory when one begins to examine the details of the suit. There is no doubt that the King was very anxious for Joan's rehabilitation. It redounds very much to his honor—and there are not so many actions in his life that do, so we should not pass over this one in silence—that he did everything in his power to undertake it at the very first possible moment, indeed less than two months after the liberation of Rouen.[4] He himself undertook to bear the costs of the suit. But this was, in fact, the least thing he could do. Did he really exert pressure on its development, however? Did he really direct the questionings from afar or exert influence on the judges? Can one in any way compare his actions with those of a Warwick, the King of England's governor—to cite only one example? If so, we must be surprised at his powerlessness. Why did it require six years to revise a case that had taken only three months to try? And how did it happen that when some of the original judges were examined in this rehabilitation suit they persisted in denying the blessedness of Joan's revelations? One must assume that in their case the royal "directives" did not go very far, no further indeed than his attempts to speed up the delays of the court at Rome.

As for the Church, her behavior certainly gives no impression of her "being in a hurry" to please the King. One has rather the contrary impression, of delays that seem from a

---

[4] His letter to Guillaume Bouillé is dated, as we have seen, February 15, 1450, that is, six days after the death of Agnes Sorel, and we know how much the King wept for his "Beauteous Lady". Therefore we can assume that he had already been thinking for a long time of staging this inquiry.

distance surprising in a case that appears to us so easy to decide. It must further be observed that at the moment when the rehabilitation suit was started, the English in France were still masters of all Guienne, and there was nothing to make it predictable, after all, that the French king's cause was definitely won. What is more, it was at that very moment in 1453 when the victory of Castillon put the enemy to flight that the case began to mark time. Two years went by without any progress being made.

If it is reasonable to think that Charles VII gave the case its first impetus—which was, after all, his role and, setting aside his personal interest, constituted an act of elementary reparation—it seems that one can just as reasonably grant the examiners and judges of the rehabilitation the credit for entire good faith and a real freedom of decision. Perhaps Guillaume d'Estouteville undertook his task only to please the King. But one can assume that the personal feelings of a Norman of old stock corresponded pretty closely to the King's, and also to that of the people, who undoubtedly saw Joan as "the good woman from Lorraine". If he showed devotion in his service to her cause, it was perhaps not only out of base flattery. Besides, as the case develops, we shall see on more than one occasion the inquirers overwhelmed by their inquiry and themselves astonished at what it brought to their eyes.

But be that as it may, Guillaume d'Estouteville was received by the King at Tours in February 1452, and two months later took the road to Rouen.

The case that condemned Joan had been tried by a court of the Inquisition. Now no appeal could be made from the Inquisition. Only the Inquisition itself could take the initiative in proceedings to annul the former trial. Guillaume d'Estouteville, therefore, got in touch with the General Inquisitor of France.

He probably had no difficulty in interesting the Inquisitor in the case. Jean Bréhal, the Dominican who had just been chosen to fill this high office, was, like him, a Norman; and all that we know of his life and character point to vigor of action and deep moral qualities. Without giving up his office, he was appointed by his brothers prior of the convent of Saint Jacques at Paris (that "Jacobin" convent that was in the future to have its hour of celebrity), and a great deal later, toward the end of his life, it was he who was entrusted with the duty of reforming the convent of Évreux, where he had, years ago, taken his vows.

For us, his life is principally important for the two cases he was able to carry through, simultaneously, with an equal display of assiduity in each: that of Joan's rehabilitation and that on behalf of the mendicant orders. Two cases in which he confronted the same enemy—the University of Paris—and which contributed, in addition, toward throwing the doctors of the Sorbonne into a disrepute from which the Renaissance scholars were later to profit. It is well known that for two centuries the secular priests of the University had been attempting, with varying success, to prevent the mendicant friars—Dominicans, Franciscans, Carmelites, and Augustinians—from teaching, and even from hearing confessions. Disturbances, which were sometimes bloody, and strikes, which had dragged on for whole years, had marked the phases of a struggle that had just been revived by a Bull of Nicolas V. This Bull of 1448 confirmed the apostolic letters delivered in the previous year by Eugenius IV to the mendicant friars, whom the papacy had always supported in their claims. Its presentation let loose storms, which Jean Bréhal, in his character of mendicant and Inquisitor, confronted with equal skill and boldness. He was able to interest in their cause no less a person than the Constable Arthur de Richemont and, in conclusion of the whole matter, the Pope in 1457 once more overruled the decisions of the University of Paris, and the friars were completely reestablished in their privileges. One can imagine that Jean Beaupère, Thomas de Courcelles, and the rest, Joan's old judges, the pillars of the Sorbonne and enemies of the papacy, did not hold him in the odor of sanctity.

However that may be, it was with cheerful promptness that Jean Bréhal complied with Guillaume d'Estouteville's request at the end of April 1452. And we see him harness himself to a cause, to the fulfillment of which he was personally to devote himself from beginning to end: the cause of Joan's rehabilitation.

In order that the case might be opened in due form, it was necessary that an inquiry should first be conducted into the causes and circumstances of her condemnation. Failing a formal accusation or denunciation, every case before the Inquisition had to be based on such a preliminary inquiry. As Guillaume Bouillé's inquiry had not been conducted by an ecclesiastical court and according to the prescribed formalities, no notice could be taken of it. Nevertheless the prelates sent for it, and also for the documents in the Rouen trial. Guillaume d'Estouteville had brought to France with him two Roman canon lawyers, Paul Pontanus and Theodore de Leliis, the one as secretary, the other as consultant to the legation; and when they passed through Rouen they made acquaintance with these same documents. They were later to include their opinion of them in the file of rehabilitation documents.

The ecclesiastical inquiry opened without delay on May 2, 1452. This time the examinations were to be conducted in due form. It was not to be a matter, as it had been in the royal inquiry two years before, of collecting reminiscences, but of elucidating the causes and circumstances of a condemnation made twenty years earlier. Therefore, as is still done today in official courts, a questionnaire was drawn up to which the witnesses summoned were called on to supply their answers. The task of the two priests in drawing up this questionnaire was to make an examination of the trial, and then to take up the principal points of the charges in order to examine their validity.

What exactly were the reasons why Joan had been found guilty of heresy? The judicial sentence enumerated twelve, which can be reduced to the following conclusions:

1. Joan pretends to have had visions: that Saint Michael, Saint Catherine, and Saint Margaret appeared to her in the flesh, and that their revelations enabled her to know the future.

2. She wears male clothing and has taken part in wars and battles.

3. She claims to be in a state of grace and certain of her salvation.

4. She refuses to submit her acts and beliefs to the jurisdiction of the Church Militant.

In other words, in the eyes of the judges who condemned her, Joan was guilty of errors of faith, of blasphemy, and of rebellion against the Church. Moreover, after having admitted and abjured her error, she had relapsed into it, and it was as a "relapsed heretic" that she had suffered the pains of fire.

The questionnaire drawn up for the inquiry of 1452 had to make it possible for these charges to be refuted. In it one can easily recognize the hand of Guillaume Bouillé, for it concentrates largely on the irregularities and the causes of invalidity that his own inquiry had brought to light.

This first questionnaire contains a dozen heads,[5] intended to bring out:

1. The fundamental defects in the original case; the partiality of the judges, arising both from their personal feelings and from their collusion, proved by the facts, with the English party.

2. The defects in procedure, in particular, the fact that Joan, although prosecuted and sentenced by an ecclesiastical court, was kept in a secular prison; also the fact of Cauchon's incompetence, he having claimed the right to try the case as Bishop of Beauvais on the pretext that Compiègne, where Joan had been made prisoner, was in the diocese of Beauvais. But according to the provisions of canon law, Joan could be tried for heresy only by the bishop of the diocese in which she was born, or of that place where she had committed heresy.

3. Joan's innocence of the accusations against her; her personal piety and her humility toward Church and Pope.

4. The pretext resorted to in order to condemn her as relapsed, or the reasons that had decided her to reassume male clothing.

5. Finally, the last point and the one most typical of the medieval mentality, the notoriety of each one of these facts.

It is one of the specific features of the Middle Ages, at least in their heyday—and something of this lasted on into Joan's times—to place in the spoken word a trust that we

---

[5] Several historians have insisted on the similarity between the twelve articles of the accusation and the twelve articles of the rehabilitation. But, as we shall see, in fact, little use was made of this twelve-point questionnaire. It was used for only two days. The questionnaire that really served as a basis for the rehabilitation suit, both for the preliminary inquiry and for the case itself, contains twenty-seven articles.

place only in writings. One could almost explain the difference between medieval and classical times by the fact that the ancient world possessed a literary civilization the exact opposite of the verbal civilization that flowered in the age of feudalism. Be that as it may, men continued in that age, and especially in the ecclesiastical courts, which were more conservative than the secular, to attach great importance to public belief, to the *vox populi*, to hearsay. So it was that all cases before the Inquisition were preceded by an *inquisitio famae*, an inquiry bearing specially on the reputation that the accused enjoyed in the places where he had lived. Here, therefore, one of the points of the questionnaire was framed to establish whether "all and each one of the said things, to wit, Joan's condemnation, the inordinate hatred and partiality of the judges, were and are publicly notorious and commonly affirmed, notoriously spoken of and well known in the city and diocese of Rouen and throughout the whole kingdom of France".

On May 2 and 3, five witnesses were examined on this questionnaire in the presence of Guillaume d'Estouteville and Jean Bréhal. Three of them, Guillaume Manchon, the notary; Martin Ladvenu, the confessor; and Isambart de la Pierre had already appeared before Guillaume Bouillé, but with them were summoned one of the assessors of the first case, Pierre Miget or Migier; also a simple citizen of Rouen, the mason Pierre Cusquel—who had had access to the castle of Rouen, thanks to his master "Jean Son" (Johnson), the overseer, that is to say, the architect or masonry contractor—and he is a fair representative of the popular voice in this matter ("everybody pitied her"; "people said that the only reason why she had been condemned was because she had put on men's clothes again").

At this point, Guillaume d'Estouteville, being obliged to leave Rouen and go to Paris, appointed the treasurer of the cathedral, Philippe de la Rose, to continue the interrogations in his place and on his behalf. It was with him that Jean Bréhal was to complete the inquiry he had begun with d'Estouteville.

On May 4, he dispatched seventeen new summonses to appear, and the witnesses were called for the Monday following, May 8. But in the interval, considering no doubt that the questionnaire in its condensed form was inadequate, the two churchmen expanded it into twenty-seven articles, which remained thenceforth the basis of the whole rehabilitation suit.

These twenty-seven articles sum up the essential points of the original questionnaire, laying special stress on certain of them and taking notice, in addition, of some matters that had so far passed unnoticed. They particularly bring out the following:

— the English hatred of Joan; and the resultant constraint on the judges, who were under close English supervision;
— in particular, the threats and pressure exerted on the officers of the court;
— the lack of a defending counsel, which was contrary to the law;
— Joan's detention in a secular prison, which was also illegal;
— the underhand methods employed to incite her into opposition to the Church;
— the manner in which the interrogations were conducted;
— Joan's real feelings: her piety and her submissiveness toward Pope and Church;

—the subterfuge employed by the judges in omitting to explain to Joan the meaning of the term "the Church Militant", of which she was ignorant;
—the lack of agreement between the Latin and the French texts of the proceedings;
—the incompetence of the judges;
—the surprising anomaly of their granting a heretic, or one adjudged so, the last sacraments;
—the default of a secular sentence before the execution;
—Joan's attitude in her last moments;
—the real motive of the case, or the wish to discredit the French king; and
—finally, the public notoriety of each one of these facts.

When we compare these two questionnaires,[6] we can measure the immense effect that two days of hearings had had on the minds of the judges. The majority of the additional articles do no more, in fact, than formulate what the witnesses had stated on May 2 and 3, and herein lay arguments for an annulment that the inquirers had not thought of at first. So the threats and pressure exerted on the notaries, and even on the judges, in the condemnation trial, at such times as they had not shown all the requisite docility toward Cauchon, and the English desire to discredit the royal cause, now became the subject of Article 26. The whole text of the new questionnaire was framed in much more positive terms, as if the judges now considered, if not established, at least worthy of examination, various bases for annulment that had not struck them before. There were to emerge, in addition, during the course of the rehabilitation suit, a number of revelations all of which worked in Joan's favor. It is

---

[6] The texts are reproduced in the Appendix.

they that give the whole case its living charm. One has the impression of a constant advance toward the truth.

On this new basis, the hearing was duly resumed on May 8. The witnesses who had already been examined were recalled; and others were summoned, the majority of whom would plainly have given a great deal not to be there. These were the former assessors in the condemnatory case, who were not all equally guilty but who all cut a sorry figure.[7]

One will have some idea of the examiners' conclusions from the statements they heard when one learns that on passing through Orléans a month later, on June 9, Guillaume d'Estouteville, in his capacity of papal legate, granted indulgences to all who were to take part in the annual procession and ceremonies in Joan's honor, which were held in that city on May 8, the anniversary of the raising of the siege. Obviously he had already made up his mind.

At about the same date, Bréhal and Bouillé passed through Orléans, where they were enthusiastically received by the town council, which gave a banquet in their honor. Then, after holding conversations with d'Estouteville on their way through Paris, they went to the castle of Cissay, where the King was residing, to report to him the turn things were taking. He had already been officially apprised of their coming in a letter from the legate, dated May 22; and one must suppose that he was thoroughly satisfied with the progress of an inquiry that was in process of confirming the one

---

[7] We shall read their depositions in Chapter 8: "The Rouen Witnesses", page 197. The chief of them were the assessors Nicolas Caval, André Marguerie, Richard de Grouchet, Jean Fabri, and Guillaume du Désert, and the notary, Nicolas Faquel. A few of them, like Jean Favé, Jean Riquier, and Thomas Marie, had played no active part; and one of them, Nicolas de Houppeville, one of the judges, had been bold enough to oppose Cauchon and had been imprisoned for his courage.

that he had himself set going two years previously. He immediately ordered the sum of a hundred pounds to be paid to Jean Bréhal to cover the costs of the case, and a further indemnity of twenty-seven pounds for his traveling and other expenses, which was paid out a little later.

In these first days of July 1452, the King received Guillaume d'Estouteville in audience at the castle of Mehun; and the interview took place almost exactly a year before the famous battle of Castillon, which was to be fought on July 17 and in the course of which Joan's old opponent, Talbot, was to meet his death. The relationship between these two dates is curious.

When the inquiry was concluded, Joan's rehabilitation entered its second phase, which was chiefly a legal and theological one. The point was to discover what findings could be established by the light of canon and civil law, also of theology. It was then that Jean Bréhal drew up his *Summarium*, a digest of the case, for examination by the doctors and lawyers who were to give their opinions. This was the regular procedure in religious cases, and Cauchon himself had adhered to it, for he too had taken experts' opinion on Joan's statements. But the text with which he had provided them had been tampered with. "She alleges that she is in a state of grace ... she refuses to submit to the Church's judgment"; such was the corrupt form in which the prisoner's answers were presented.

In his *Summarium*, Bréhal went over the points of the charge one after the other; and for each one of them, he set out first the facts and then the answers relating to them, extracted from the report of the Rouen trial. Then he put one question: Ought the same conclusions to be drawn from those answers as were drawn by the Rouen judges and set out in the condemnatory judgment?

He next set about collecting expert opinions on this question. A great number of doctors and canon lawyers were consulted, and their opinions were added to the rehabilitation file. In addition to the two Roman jurists already spoken of, Paul Pontanus and Theodore de Leliis, particular mention should be made of Master Robert Cybole, former rector of the University and chancellor of Notre Dame in Paris; of Élie de Bourdeilles, a Franciscan who was then Bishop of Périgueux, and, more especially, of Thomas Basin, Bishop of Lisieux and the future biographer of Charles VII. Inquiries were also addressed to Master Pierre L'Hermyte, sub-dean of Saint Martin at Tours; to Guy de Vorseilles, also of Tours; and to Jean de Montigny, a canon lawyer of Paris University. Jean de Bréhal went so far as to consult foreign doctors, for example, Leonard of Brixenthal, a Dominican and professor at the University of Vienna.

Subsequently, the examiners went on to study the report of Jean Gerson, written as early as 1429, in Joan's favor, also that of the Archbishop of Embrun, Jacques Gélu, which dates from the same year. Then they proceeded to ask opinions of Martin Berruyer, Bishop of Le Mans, and of Jean Bochard, Bishop of Avranches. There was no famous canon lawyer who did not give his opinion of the case, and that is enough to prove how conscientiously it was examined.

As this point, toward the end of the year 1452, Guillaume d'Estouteville had returned from Rome, where he must have informed Nicolas V of his progress, for there is clearly a relationship of cause and effect between this enterprise of his and his nomination as Archbishop of Rouen, which dates from April 30, 1453.

The case, however, marked time, though not so much at the beginning of the year 1453, which was occupied, as we have seen, with the taking of legal opinions, as it did later on. The Roman curia had, truly enough, other preoccupations at that moment, for the news of the fall of Constantinople reached Rome on July 8 of that year. Historians have wondered at the delays that then befell the rehabilitation suit; and some have chosen to see in them a reflection of hesitations on the part of Nicolas V. But should one not, more simply, conclude that for the Pope this matter began to assume secondary importance compared with the vastness of events in the East? All the energy of the last years of his pontificate seems to have been consecrated to the promotion of a crusade against the Ottomans. To Guillaume d'Estouteville's entreaties, Charles VII had replied with a semblance of assent that was patently no more than a disguised refusal. But the court of Burgundy seemed disposed to make a contribution; Philip the Good had placed in the Church of Saint Donatian at Bruges a box intended to receive "alms for Turkey", and he was even to set out on a spectacular but fruitless crusade. And what could not be hoped, after all, of this prince, the "Grand Duke of the West" and incontestably the most powerful prince in Christendom? Would not the prospect of seeing his efforts succeed have been enough to explain why Nicolas V neglected everything that was not directly related to the crusade?

However that may be, the case does not seem to have advanced for about a year. On July 28, 1454, Guillaume d'Estouteville made his solemn entry into Rouen, where he was duly enthroned as archbishop. Almost at the same time, one learns, Jean Bréhal made a journey to Rome, and the accounts that mention his expenses expressly state that they were for "visiting our lord the Pope concerning the case of the late Joan the Maid".

It has been supposed—and the hypothesis does not appear to be baseless—that it was on this visit that Bréhal delivered to the sovereign Pontiff the text of the petition for the opening of the rehabilitation suit. In fact, only the Pope could take the decision; he had therefore to be officially apprised of a request to this effect. Jean de Montigny, one of the doctors consulted, had appended to his opinion, which was entirely favorable to Joan, the words: "Although many people might act as petitioning parties, since anyone prejudiced by the case has that right, and many people have been prejudiced by it, in general or personally, nevertheless for the present it seems to us that the close relatives of the deceased Maid should be given preference over the rest as plaintiffs in the matter of the injury done to one of them by the death and lamentable burning of the said Maid." Here a complete procedure was indicated, and it was this procedure that was wisely followed.

Joan's father, Jacques d'Arc, her elder brother Jacques, or Jacquemin, and her little sister Catherine were all three dead; but her mother, Isabelle Romée, and her two brothers Pierre and Jean were still alive. They lived at Orléans, and the municipality paid her mother a pension. Charles of Orléans, on his return from captivity, had made a gift to Pierre (who had since been ennobled together with his brother under the name of du Lys) of the Île aux Boeufs, situated on the Loire. To them was entrusted the role of petitioning parties, and this gives the whole rehabilitation suit a human interest that it might have lacked otherwise and that suited so well the simple and human figure that Joan was. The family was to choose as its counsel Master Pierre Maugier, doctor in canon law and former rector of the University, and, in the course of the case, nominated various attorneys to represent it at hearings that would have required too long a journey away from home. The principal and most assiduous of these attorneys was one Guillaume Prévosteau, a

Norman and counselor to the exchequer, whom Guillaume d'Estouteville had made promoter of the case in 1452.

We do not know exactly what stage the proceedings had reached when Nicolas V died, on March 24, 1455. It is probable, nevertheless, that they were progressing well, for his successor had scarcely been on the throne for two months when he delivered to Isabelle Romée and her sons, on June 11, 1455, the rescript authorizing them to open the suit. Calixtus III, who was previously Alfonso Borgia, was to be the Pope both of the rehabilitation and of the victory of the mendicant friars over the University. He was a vigorous person and had already shown himself to be such during the Great Schism and also afterward in reconciling to the Church his compatriot Gil Muños, the anti-pope of Peñiscola, who had for a short while worn the tiara under the name of Clement VII. Saint Vincent Ferrer had exercised a profound influence over him, and had long ago, at Valence, predicted his elevation to the papal throne.

The rescript of June 11 granted the petition of the d'Arc family and nominated three commissioners, whose charge was "in the final instance to pronounce a just verdict". The choice of the papacy was, as it turned out, particularly lucky. The three men were Jean Jouvenel des Ursins, Archbishop of Rheims and formerly Bishop of Beauvais, where he had been the immediate successor of Cauchon; Guillaume Chartier, Bishop of Paris and brother of Alain Chartier,[8] who had already celebrated Joan's exploits in an enthusiastic letter; and Richard Olivier, Bishop of Coutances and member of the cathedral chapter of Rouen—all three eminent churchmen and men who, both on account of their own characters and of the duties entrusted to them, would come

---

[8] Alain Chartier, poet (c. 1386–1449).

to take a living interest in Joan's cause. All three had in the past been resolute partisans of the King of France; and Richard Olivier had even taken an active part in Charles VII's return to Rouen.

The real case of Joan of Arc was about to open.

THE REHABILITATION SUIT

It opened with an extraordinarily moving scene. The first solemn session, after the inevitable delays to permit the various interested parties to make contact, had been fixed for November 7, 1455. It took place in Notre Dame in Paris. Into this holy place, on whose walls are inscribed almost all the great pages of French history, came on that morning the papal commissioners (with the exception of Richard Olivier, who was then on an embassy to the Duke of Burgundy), and with them Jean Bréhal, to occupy seats at the entrance to the great nave.

The next to enter was an old peasant woman, supported by her sons and surrounded by a whole group of priests and common people; this was Isabelle Romée with her sons Pierre and Jean (the official minutes mention only the former, but in their original form the presence of the second son Jean is also mentioned), escorted by a whole procession of people from Orléans. She bowed down "with great sighs and groans", and, "with pitiable plaints and mournful supplications", as she stated her request, handed to the commissioners the papal rescript, which one of the spectators read for her.

Now the announcement of this session had drawn into the cathedral a crowd that increased every minute. Isabelle's lamentations, which were taken up by the group around her, soon found an echo in that crowd filling the great nave. Once more Joan was rousing popular feeling; these crowds who had been witnesses, at Orléans, at Rheims, and at Rouen, of her deeds, her triumph, and her martyrdom, came once more to bear witness on her behalf at Notre Dame, in the heart of the kingdom. It is extraordinary to think of the power over the people's feelings that this daughter of the people can never have ceased to possess, both during her life and after her death. Every important act of her career moved crowds, and for five hundred years since, she has been honored by processions and guards of honor. It would be vain to search French annals for anyone to compare to her.

Be that as it may, the demonstrations became so violent that the priests found themselves overwhelmed. ("Everyone present shouted with her", run the minutes of the proceedings.) They had to take hasty refuge in the sacristy to avoid the turmoil and din, dragging with them Isabelle and her counselors. There they offered her words of consolation, asked her about herself and her daughter, and finally assured her of their solicitude and that of the Holy See, declaring themselves ready to make every effort to establish Joan's innocence and the justice of her cause.

After that intensely moving day, the parties were summoned for November 17 to the great audience chamber of the Bishop of Paris. Isabelle Romée appeared once more with her sons, still accompanied by her friends from Orléans and by the family lawyer, Pierre Maugier. The attendance was imposing: around the Archbishop of Rheims, the Bishop of Paris, and the Inquisitor of France were grouped the abbots of all the great Paris abbeys—of Saint Denis, Saint Germain des Prés, and Saint Magloire—also the abbots of Saint Lô in the diocese of Coutances, of Saint Crépin in the diocese of Soissons, and of Cormeilles in the diocese of Lisieux. Guillaume Bouillé was there also; and, lastly, two scribes, who had previously been present at Notre Dame, took notes for the official account of the sessions. These were Denis Lecomte and François Ferrebouc, both graduates in canon law.

It is tempting to draw a comparison between that assembly and the one at Rouen twenty-four years earlier that had pronounced Joan guilty. Both were alike composed of prelates, abbots, and doctors. But at Rouen there had presided a bishop divorced from his see, one who, although a Frenchman, had twice fled, from Rheims and from Beauvais, before the approach of French armies. He had forsaken his diocese, like the promoter d'Estivet and like the judge Jean Jolivet, abbot of Mont Saint Michel, who had abandoned his glorious abbey. As for the vice-Inquisitor, he had only taken part in the proceedings—the evidence is unanimous on this point—under constraint and compulsion. It would be easy but superfluous to go on, for the case of Joan's judges has been tried long ago, whether it concerns creatures avowedly of the English party like Beaupère, Loiseleur, or Nicolas Midy, or benefice-hunters like Zanone de Castiglione, or dried-up University scholars like Thomas de Courcelles or Guillaume Érard, or simply cowards of the stamp of Pierre Miget or André Marguerie.

What is most remarkable is the difference of atmosphere; in Paris, the sessions are public and will all take place in the daylight, while at Rouen, judgment was given in a fortress and behind bars; there the accused had not even a lawyer to defend her, whereas Cauchon's heirs will be able to nominate a representative to claim for the Bishop's succession the benefit of the amnesty granted by Charles

VII on setting foot on Norman soil. Finally, and above all, in contrast to the threats and pressure exercised during the first trial, there is the liberty undeniably enjoyed by the witnesses wherever they were interrogated. Certain of them hurriedly turned their coats to cut a better figure. But that is a common occurrence and discredits nobody but themselves. It is impressive, however, that such a man as Nicolas Caval, who had been Cauchon's personal friend and had read his funeral service and acted as executor to his will, should have been able, in perfect tranquillity, to come and make his statement and to adhere to his old position without changing his view or retracting anything.

One circumstance, clearly, is more important than all the rest: the condemnatory trial had taken place at the height of a war, in a region shut in on itself, to which enemy occupation had brought its inevitable train of meannesses, treason, and stifling miseries, material and moral; the rehabilitation suit, on the other hand, benefited from a glorious peace in a country restored to itself, where communications had once more become easy, where prosperity was already returning, where the general amnesty had caused an immediate release of tension.

So hearings and depositions will go on, according to a smooth and well-ordered procedure. They will reexplore, by touching stages, the ways that Joan herself had followed and call one by one to the witness-rail the most surprising procession of priests and peasants, soldiers and lawyers, princes of the blood and ploughmen. All will have their word to say about Joan: sometimes a humble man's memories, from those to whose houses she came to spin in the evenings; sometimes tales of astounding feats of arms; and sometimes tragic accounts of prison and the stake. Each will speak his own language—the precise language of the jurist, the bluff language of the soldier, the laborious and rather monotonous language of the tiller of the soil—and all will contribute, by little touches, to the drawing of the most astonishing portrait in French history: that of a girl under twenty who did not know A from B, but who revived a kingdom and chose its king.

CHAPTER 1

The Examination of the Trial

We will give the first word to these witnesses in the rehabilitation suit. Nothing is more moving than to follow by way of their statements the progress of a truth that gradually dawned in the minds of the commissioners charged with the rehabilitation, to discover with them what was still unknown or dimly known to public opinion, and to see their suspicions transformed into convictions founded on the facts revealed to the court. Even in a case so well known as Joan of Arc's trial, a direct reading of the text differs from the best of spoken accounts as a picture differs from the best of reproductions.

The question that presented itself to the commissioners of the Holy See was then *Was Joan a heretic?* But for us now the question might rather be *How did anyone manage to make Joan look like a heretic?* The first hearings of the rehabilitation suit answer both questions by revealing the background of the original trial, which only a very small number of witnesses knew.

These hearings took place at Rouen, for it had been decided that the case for her rehabilitation should be tried in the same city that had been the scene of her condemnation. The papal commissioners moved there; Isabelle Romée and her sons appointed attorneys to represent them there, and all interested parties were cited to appear between December 12 and 20. Notices were posted on the church doors, and proclamations were read in the streets, as was usual in such cases.

The principal witnesses called also received personal summonses, which led, at Beauvais for example, to a strange scene: Master Jean de Frocourt, a canon of the cathedral who was entrusted with the presentation of the summonses to the respective successors of the principal actors in the case, Cauchon, d'Estivet, and the vice-Inquisitor Jean Lemaître, made his way to the episcopal palace, where he chanced to find, walking together in a gallery of the palace, the three men he had to bring together: Guillaume de Heilande, then Bishop of Beauvais; Master Réginald Bredouille, the promoter of the diocese who had succeeded Jean d'Estivet in that office; and with them the prior of the Dominicans of the town, Brother Germain de Morlaines. But when he read them the summons, all three of them immediately protested that they were not compelled to answer for their predecessors.

So far as the Dominican prior was concerned, the position was delicate. He was in effect being asked to call the vice-Inquisitor Jean Lemaître as witness. But he declared that he knew no vice-Inquisitor of his order, either at Beauvais or in the diocese. Was Lemaître still alive? It is doubtful. His existence on January 1452 is vouched for, but after that date there is no further trace of him. Perhaps he was hiding his shame and remorse in the obscurity of some convent. Beyond any doubt, he had tried to conceal himself before, and it had only been by a special order of derogation, moreover, that he had taken part in the trial. For his office was only effective under the Archbishop of Rouen, and Cauchon was Bishop of Beauvais. But Cauchon absolutely

THE EXAMINATION OF THE TRIAL 49

needed a representative of the Inquisition to legalize the case. Anyhow, if Lemaître was still alive, he was not at Beauvais.

A very important hearing took place on December 15, 1455, in the great hall of the archiepiscopal palace of Rouen, and it was then that Master Simon Chapitault, licentiate in canon law, was chosen to perform the functions of prosecutor. It was then also that Guillaume Manchon, who had been clerk of the court in the trial that had condemned Joan, was picked out from among the spectators and requested to place in the court's hands all the documents he still had.

It is the deposition of the notary Guillaume Manchon, made either in the course of the preliminary inquiries already mentioned or in the course of the suit itself (particularly on December 17, 1455, a day almost entirely given up to individual examinations), that best allows us to follow the stages of the "examination of the trial" and to observe the judges' methods of laying traps for Joan, into which she was bound to fall, as well as the perversions of the procedure practiced by Cauchon and his accomplices.

At the time when he appeared at Rouen before the apostolic commissioners, Manchon was still fulfilling the duties of clerk to the ecclesiastical court of that city. He was also priest of the parish of Saint Nicolas le Paincteur, and canon's prebendary in the collegiate Church of Notre Dame d'Andely. Clearly an honest man; his honesty had earned him the dislike of the English, as Jean Favé, one of the witnesses, will later attest: "I have heard it said that the English were displeased with Master Guillaume Manchon, the notary in this case; and that they considered him suspect and favorable to Joan because he came reluctantly and did not offer them slavish obedience...."

At the time of the rehabilitation, Manchon was about fifty. Here is his explanation of the duties he performed:

Guillaume Manchon

I was notary throughout the whole of Joan's case, and with me was Master Guillaume Colles, called Boisguillaume. . . . In taking notes of the case, I was often rebuked by my lord of Beauvais, and by the judges, who tried to compel me to write things down according to their interpretation and not as Joan meant them. When there was something that they did not like, they ordered me not to put it down, on the excuse that it had nothing to do with the case; but in my writing I followed only my own understanding and conscience.

Now unspeakable means were employed to extort false confessions from Joan and to get them attested.

In my opinion [this is still Manchon speaking] both those in charge of the conduct of the case, that is to say, my lord of Beauvais and the lawyers whom they summoned from Paris for the purpose,[1] and also the English at whose instance the case was started, acted out of hatred and contempt for the King of France, as is clear from the following statements:

First, a certain Master Nicolas Loiseleur, who was a favorite of the Bishop of Beauvais and a particular adherent of the English party (for once, when the King was besieging Chartres,[2] he called on the King of England to raise the siege), pretended to be a man from the Maid's country and so succeeded in getting writings, conversation, and confidences from her (in prison) by giving her

---

[1] The lawyers sent by the University of Paris: Jean Beaupère, Thomas de Courcelles, Nicolas Midy, Jacques de Touraine, Pierre Maurice, and Gérard Feuillet.

[2] Allusion to the siege of Chartres in 1421, which was raised by Henry V of England. It was then that Nicolas Loiseleur, canon of Chartres, crossed over to the English side. A little later he became a canon of Rouen and, with Beaupère and Midy, was one of the principal architects of the case, acting under Cauchon's instructions.

news from home, which was pleasing to her. What is more, he asked to be her confessor, and what she told him in private he found means of bringing to the ears of the notaries. In fact, at the beginning of the case, Boisguillaume and I, with witnesses, were secretly introduced into an adjoining room, in the wall of which was a hole that one could hear through. This was so that we should report what she said or admitted to this same Loiseleur. And I rather think that he communicated to us what the Maid said or communicated privately to him, and a report of this was drawn up as a cunning means of catching her out....

At the beginning of the case, during the five or six days when I was writing down the Maid's answers and excuses, the judges tried to compel me to alter my words in translating them into Latin, thereby changing the meaning of her statements into something different from my understanding of them. And two men, acting under my lord of Beauvais' instructions, were placed in a window near the judges' seats; and there was a serge curtain in front of that window so that they should not be seen. These men wrote down and reported everything that incriminated Joan and nothing that excused her. And I believe that it was Loiseleur (who was concealed there). And after the session, when a comparison was made with what these two had written, their account was quite different from ours and contained none of Joan's defense. My lord of Beauvais was greatly annoyed with me about this. And where the word *Nota* appears in the reports of the case, that was where there were differences of opinion, and where fresh questionings were necessary; and they found that what I had written was true.

In another part of his deposition, he comes back to this subject and reveals who the concealed men were—or at least one of them.

At the beginning of the case, when Joan was questioned, there were clerks hidden in a window, concealed by curtains so that no one saw them. I think that Master Nicolas Loiseleur was there with them and that he watched what these notaries wrote down; they wrote as they chose, omitting Joan's defense. I was sitting below the judges with Guillaume Colles and Master Jean de Beaupère's clerk, who also took notes. But there were such great differences between our accounts that lively arguments sprang up between us; and for that reason, as I have already said, where points were in doubt I wrote *Nota*, so that Joan should be questioned afresh on the subject.

The disgraceful part played by this Nicolas Loiseleur was confirmed by other witnesses, in particular by the man who was usher in the case.

Jean Massieu

I have heard it said that Nicolas Loiseleur, who pretended to be a Frenchman taken prisoner by the English, sometimes slipped secretly into Joan's cell and persuaded her not to submit to the Church's authority, or she would find herself deceived.

Another witness was Guillaume Colles, called Boisguillaume, who had been the second notary in the case.

Guillaume Colles

Master Nicolas Loiseleur, who pretended to be one of the French king's men from Lorraine, and a prisoner, sometimes went into Joan's prison and told her to put no trust in the churchmen, "for if you believe them you'll die." I think that the Bishop of Beauvais knew all about this. Otherwise this Loiseleur would not have dared to do such a thing. Also many who took part in the case murmured against this Loiseleur.

Indeed Pierre Miget, one of the assessors of that case, had protested.

Pierre Miget

I have heard that during the proceedings there were people hidden behind the curtains, and it was said that they wrote down some of Joan's admissions and statements. But exactly what was done I do not know. I heard this from Master Guillaume Manchon.... I complained to the judge, saying that this did not seem to me a proper course of action. Whatever may be the truth about these concealed notaries, I think it absolutely true that the notaries who signed the minutes of the case were honest and the contents of the report were honestly set down.

Careful man that he was, Guillaume Manchon had kept his minutes of the trial, written in French at the moment of the questioning. These he was requested to put in the hands of the court, and there were references to all the overwritings that they contained, especially to the frequent *Notas* that occurred in the margin. Manchon explained these all over again.

Guillaume Manchon

In the first days, during Joan's examination in the chapel of Rouen castle, there was great disorder, and almost every one of her words was interrupted. This was when she was speaking about her visions. For there were certain secretaries of the English king, two or three of them, who put down Joan's answers and depositions in their own way, omitting her explanations or anything that might be in her favor. I complained about this, saying that unless some other procedure were adopted I would no longer undertake the task of making the record. For that reason they changed the location next day, and we sat in a large court, near the great court of the castle; there were two Englishmen guarding the door. And as there were disputes at times about Joan's speeches and her answers, and as certain people said that she had not answered as I had written, wherever these disputes occurred I put down *Nota*, so that she should be questioned afresh on the point and the dispute cleared up. That is the reason for these *Notas* at the heads of the paragraphs.

He also possessed one of the authentic copies of the record in Latin, which he was asked to identify officially at the time when he presented it to the court.

I swear that this is the true record made during the trial, and I recognize my own signature and those of my colleagues. It contains the truth. I wrote it myself, and also the two other copies. One of them was given to my lord the Inquisitor, one to the King of England, and one to my lord Bishop of Beauvais. The text of this record follows the minutes in French that I gave to the judges and that were written in my own hand. These minutes were translated out of French into Latin by Master Thomas de Courcelles and myself, a long time after Joan's death and execution. In their present form, they are as good as we could make them and perfectly truthful.

So the definitive record, the official text of the proceedings, to which anyone would have turned if he had wished to study the case or examine the procedure, had not been drawn up until long after Joan's death, and it was Master

Thomas de Courcelles, one of the doctors sent to Rouen by the Sorbonne, who had been entrusted with the translation into Latin. This fact, as we shall see, was to take on a certain importance.

In the meantime, as everything demanded a careful checking, the commissioners submitted these texts to the other notaries in the condemnatory trial, who publicly vouched for their authenticity before the court. First came Guillaume Colles, called Boisguillaume, whom we have mentioned already. Like Manchon, he was a scribe to the ecclesiastical court of Rouen.

Guillaume Colles

> He is shown a copy of the report, at the end of which he recognizes his signature, and which he identifies as one of the original five copies that were made, upon which he says: There were two other notaries in this case, Master Guillaume Manchon and Master Nicolas Taquel, and they scrupulously set down the questions and answers as contained in this copy of the report. In the mornings we noted down the questions and answers, and after lunch we compared them together. And we notaries would not have altered a word for anything in the world, because we were not afraid of anybody.

This Nicolas Taquel next gives evidence. He had not been present at the first sittings of the court.

Nicolas Taquel

> I had knowledge of Joan during the case that was brought against her on the subject of her beliefs. I was one of the notaries in the case, though I was not present from the

beginning, as can be seen from my signatures. I was not there either on those days when the case was tried in the great court, but only from the date when it was tried in the prison. As far as I can see, my first appearance was on March 14, 1431, as is evident from my letter of instruction, which tallies with my memory. From then onward, I attended to take down the questions and Joan's answers, although I did not write myself. But I listened and referred to the two other notaries, that is to say, to Manchon and Boisguillaume, and especially to Manchon.

He was shown a copy of the text imprinted with his sign manual, and he recognized the signature, declaring that he had affixed his signature to this copy and certified its contents. He also recognized the signatures of Manchon and Boisguillaume. He declared that this text was composed in its present form a long time after Joan's death, but exactly when he did not know.

I received ten francs for my pains and labors, although I had been told that I should get twenty. These ten francs were given to me by a certain Benedicite,[3] but where the money came from I have no idea.

THE TWELVE ARTICLES OF CONDEMNATION

Now the examination of the documents thus presented to them and solemnly recognized by the various writers was to cause some surprises to the judicial bench.

In particular, the questions of the articles that had served as a basis for Joan's condemnation seemed to them to require some explanation. As a result of the questionings, Jean d'Estivet had extracted from Joan's replies seventy counts

[3] The nickname of Jean d'Estivet, the promoter.

on which the court's deliberations and sentence had to be based: a procedure absolutely regular in such cases. In trials before the Inquisition, the beliefs of the accused, as they emerged from his replies, were drawn up in this way, in the form of propositions, which were then submitted to the judges. But, strangely enough, instead of these seventy counts, it was a shortish statement containing only a dozen articles that had served as a basis for their deliberations and led to the final sentence. The commissioners turned to Manchon for explanations about the drawing-up of these twelve articles, and the following dialogue ensued:

> [Commissioners]: How is it that although the promoter drew up seventy counts against Joan, these counts were reduced at the end of the case to a dozen? Who drew up the twelve articles, and why were the articles drawn up by the promoter not inserted in the sentence?
>
> [Manchon]: Some time before the articles contained in the text had been drawn up, Joan had been several times interrogated and had made numerous answers. On her questions and answers, the promoter, with some advice from the court, drew up and based his articles. His purpose was to reduce to some order the random copies on which she had been interrogated. Then she was questioned afresh on each one of them, and it was decided by the counselors, especially by the gentlemen from Paris, that, according to custom, all these articles and answers must be reduced to a few short articles, covering the principal points, so that the matter could be presented briefly and so that the deliberations might be better and more swiftly concluded. That is the reason why the twelve articles were drawn up. But it was not I who made them, and I do not know who it was that composed or extracted them.
>
> How was it possible to reduce such a quantity of articles and answers to twelve counts and, what is more, to

put them in a shape so very different from what Joan admitted to? It is improbable that men of that consequence could have been willing to compose articles like those.

I believe that in the original report of the trial, made in French, I accurately recorded the questions and the articles drawn up by the promoter and the judges, also Joan's answers. As for the twelve articles, I refer you to the men who drew them up, whom neither my colleague nor I would have dared to contradict.

When these twelve articles were inserted, did you make a comparison of these counts and Joan's replies, to see whether they corresponded to what she had said?

I do not remember.

Manchon might have remembered. They immediately placed before him a paper written in his own hand taken from the bundle of documents that the d'Arc family's counsel and lawyers had collected. On that sheet, the notary had noted discrepancies between the counts and Joan's replies that sometimes amounted to a clear and straightforward contradiction. For instance, Joan's famous phrase in which she said that she submitted to the Church, "God shall be served first", became "She refuses to submit herself to the decisions of the Church Militant, but defers to God alone." The clerk had therefore, after comparing the articles with the answers contained in the text, proposed various additions and corrections. This memorandum, containing corrections in his own hand, was dated April 4, 1431—two months before the conclusion of the case. Now, no notice had been taken of this, and the articles had been submitted, without any corrections, for the opinions of the lawyers and theologians to whom Cauchon had referred, as he was obliged to do in such a case.

Manchon, Boisguillaume, and Taquel, the three notaries, were then called. They recognized Manchon's signature on the memorandum without any hesitation, and the questioning continued in these terms:

> Why were the articles not corrected? How was it that they had been inserted in the report in their original form? Were they, to your knowledge, sent to the judges, for their deliberations, corrected or uncorrected?

The Notaries

This memorandum was written in Manchon's hand. We do not know at all who made the twelve articles. It was said at the time that it was customary to draw up articles like those, extracting them from the admissions of those accused of heresy; and that this was the usual procedure of the masters and doctors of theology in Paris in cases involving heresy. In the matter of the corrections that should have been made to these articles, we believe that they were transcribed as they stand in this memorandum, which has been shown to us and which we have recognized. As to whether the corrections were added to the articles sent to Paris and elsewhere for discussion, we have no knowledge. We believe that they were not, for it is clear from another memorandum, written in the hand of Guillaume[4] d'Estivet, the promoter of the case, that they were sent off the next day by this same d'Estivet uncorrected. For the rest, one can refer to the text of the report.

Manchon was asked if he believed that the articles were composed in the spirit of truth, for there were great discrepancies between the articles and Joan's answers.

---

[4] Guillaume for Jean: copyist's error.

Manchon

> What stands in my report of the case is the truth. As for the articles, I leave it to those who made them, for it was not I that made them.
>
> Did the deliberations cover the whole case or only these twelve articles?
>
> I believe that the deliberations did not cover the whole case, for it had not yet been put into shape, and it was not put down in the shape in which it now is until after Joan's death. The deliberations were on the twelve articles.
>
> Were those twelve articles read to Joan?
>
> No.

One can imagine a silence in the court at that moment.

> Did you notice the differences between these articles and Joan's replies?
>
> I do not remember. The men who displayed them said that it was the custom to extract counts of this kind. My attention was not drawn to the matter, and besides I should not have dared to remonstrate with such important persons.
>
> He was shown the written sentence, signed by him and the other notaries, into which these articles had been inserted.
>
> Did you sign this, and why did you insert the twelve articles and not the promoter's version?
>
> I signed this sentence as did my colleagues. As to what the sentence says, I refer to the judges' speeches. As for the articles, that was the judges' pleasure. It pleased them to have it like that.

Boisguillaume, who was called to confirm these statements, remained evasive:

Boisguillaume

I know very well that there were twelve articles in the case. But who made them, and whether they differ from Joan's confessions, for that I refer to the proceedings. It was not I or the other notaries who invented them.

And Taquel declared himself ignorant too:

I heard the notaries talking about certain articles that were said to have been drawn up. But who drew them up I have no idea. I know that they were sent to Paris, but whether they were signed or not I do not remember. I do not believe that I signed them, because I do not remember having signed anything except the report and the sentence.

He was asked whether, after these articles were extracted and seen by the judges, any decision was made that they ought to be corrected.

I do not remember.

So, the twelve articles on which the whole condemnation rested were nothing but mendacious propositions that misrepresented Joan's thoughts, which they were alleged to reproduce, and that, furthermore, had never been shown to her. Who was responsible for these falsifications? The promoter Jean d'Estivet had drawn up the seventy articles, and Thomas de Courcelles was afterward to point to Nicolas Midy as the forger of the twelve mendacious articles—Nicolas Midy, the same man who preached Joan a last sermon at the foot of the scaffold. The clerk Boisguillaume repeated the popular impression when he gave the court the following opinion on those two personages:

Boisguillaume

This d'Estivet was the promoter, and for that reason was very zealous for the English, whom he tried very hard to please. He was a wicked man and tried all through the case to slander the clerks and anyone he saw acting in a just way, and he very often abused Joan, calling her a loose woman and a filthy creature. I believe that God punished him at the end of his days, for he came to a miserable end. He was found dead in a gutter outside the gates of Rouen. And I have heard it said that everyone who had a share in Joan's death came to a shameful end; Nicolas Midy himself, for instance, who was stricken with a leprosy a few days afterward, and the Bishop, who died suddenly while he was being shaved.

THE SCHEDULE OF ABJURATION

That was not all. Another trick, cleverer still, had been revealed by the examination of the documents in the case. The twelve articles enumerated Joan's *errors*, but these *errors* she had publicly abjured, and it is this abjuration that had laid her open to the punishment of the *relapsed*, of the heretic, that is, who falls back into the errors that he has forsworn. A whole performance had been staged to this end. Joan had been led to the cemetery of Saint Ouen where, in front of the crowd and in the presence of her judges, Guillaume Érard, one of the delegate masters from the Sorbonne, had read her a hortatory sermon. After this, Joan had been invited to abjure by signing a schedule prepared in advance, under threats that if she did not do so she would be condemned forthwith. Manchon describes the scene thus:

Manchon

It was decided that she must be preached to, and she was put on a little stand, and counseled by Master Nicolas Loiseleur, who said: "Joan, believe me, for if you are willing you shall be saved. Put on your own clothes, and do everything that you are ordered. If you do not, you will be in peril of death. But if you do what I tell you, you will be saved, and you will receive great benefits and no harm, and you will be reconciled to the Church." She was then led to a platform or tribune. And there were two sentences prepared, one of abjuration and the other of condemnation, which the Bishop had with him. And while the Bishop read the condemnation sentence, Master Nicolas Loiseleur told Joan to do as he had said and put on woman's clothing. And during the short interval that followed, one of the Englishmen present called the Bishop a traitor. The Bishop replied by calling him a liar. And in the meantime, Joan answered that she was ready to obey the Church. They then made her swear the abjuration which was read to her. But I do not know whether she repeated it after the reader, or whether as soon as it had been read to her she answered that she accepted it. She smiled. The executioner was close by with his tumbril, waiting for her to be handed over to him to be burnt. I did not see the letter of abjuration written. But this was done after the discussions were concluded and before they came to that place. I do not remember whether that letter of abjuration was ever explained to Joan, or if they told her its purport, or read it to her except at the moment when she made her abjuration. That first sermon, sentence, and abjuration took place on the Thursday before Pentecost, and the sentence condemned her to imprisonment for life.

What exactly had Joan abjured? The clerk Taquel gave the following details in his deposition:

Taquel

I was present at Saint Ouen when the first sermon was preached to her, but I was not on the platform with the other clerks. I was fairly near, however, at a spot from which I could observe all that was said and done. I remember very well seeing Joan when the schedule of abjuration was being read to her. It was Master Jean Massieu who read it, and there were about six lines of large writing. That letter of abjuration was in French and began with, "I, Joan," etc. After the abjuration she was sentenced to perpetual imprisonment and led off to the castle. Afterward I was supposed to question her—or so they said. But there was a disturbance, and I do not remember what was done about that.

Another witness was to declare for his part:

Guillaume de la Chambre

I was present at a sermon preached by Master Guillaume Érard. But I do not remember what was said in the sermon. I do remember well the abjuration that Joan made, although she had delayed a long time in making it. However, Guillaume Érard decided her to do so by telling her that if she did as she was advised she would be let out of prison. And it was on that condition and no other that she did it. After that she read a little schedule of six or seven lines written on a piece of paper folded in two. I was so near that I could easily see the lines and how they were arranged.

Obviously no one could testify better on this point than the usher Jean Massieu, the man who had read Joan the famous schedule. Here is how he describes it:

Jean Massieu

As for the abjuration, when the sermon was preached to her by Master Guillaume Érard at Saint Ouen, Érard had a schedule of abjuration in his hand and said to Joan, "You are to abjure and sign this schedule." Then the schedule was handed to me to read to her, and I read it to her. I well remember that in the schedule it was written that she must never carry arms again, or wear man's clothing, or cut her hair short, also a number of other things that I do not remember. And I am certain that this schedule was eight lines long and no more, and I am positive that it was not the one quoted in the report of the case. The one I read was different from the one set out in that report, and it is the former one that Joan signed.

A document as important as this schedule of abjuration should, indeed, obligatorily have been contained in the official text of proceedings. It was there, but, as Massieu said, in a form totally different from that described in the evidence. It was a very long abjuration in Latin, enumerating all sorts of errors of faith, blasphemies, and impieties, which Joan was alleged to have committed and which she was declared to have renounced. The key to the mystery was to be supplied by the questioning of Thomas de Courcelles, the University doctor who was entrusted with the translation of the proceedings into Latin.

Thomas de Courcelles

Who composed the schedule of abjuration contained in the report and beginning: "You, Joan"?[5]

I do not know, and I do not know either whether it was read to Joan or whether it was explained to her. A sermon was preached to her at Saint Ouen by Master Guillaume Érard. I was standing on the platform, behind

---

[5] Copyist's error. This should read "I, Joan".

the priests. I do not remember any of the preacher's words, however, except that he said, "The pride of this woman". Then the Bishop began to read the sentence. I do not remember what was said to Joan or what she replied. I do, however, remember well that Master Nicolas de Vendérès composed a schedule which began, "When the eye of the heart ...". But whether that was the one contained in the report I have no idea. I do not remember whether I saw this schedule in Master Nicolas' hands before or after the Maid's abjuration. But I think that it was before, and I have certainly heard it said that some of those present remonstrated with the Bishop of Beauvais for not applying the sentence and for accepting Joan's repentance. But as to what was said and who said it I do not remember.

The schedule inserted in the report begins, "*Quotiens humanae mentis oculus* ...", and that is certainly the one that Thomas de Courcelles had seen in Nicolas de Vendérès' hands, and the one that he had transcribed. It was not the one that was read to Joan in the cemetery of Saint Ouen and the one she signed. So the whole matter was being cleared up, and the promoter of the rehabilitation, Simon Chapitault, was able to exclaim that they were dealing with an "artificially fabricated" abjuration; one text had been substituted for the other, and the case of her relapse was based on a forgery.

This revelation threw a new light on the final scene of Joan's trial, the condemnation scene. When the matter of her relapse was argued, indeed, five days after the sinister comedy in the Saint Ouen cemetery, Cauchon called the lawyers together to explain to them that as Joan had resumed the errors that she had abjured, it was necessary to take a decision about her. Now of the forty judges who were present, thirty-six subscribed to the opinion of Gilles de Duremot, the abbot of Fécamp, who asked that the abjuration schedule should be read to her once more, to be certain that she had properly understood it and that she persisted in her errors. This put Master Cauchon into a strange state of embarrassment, and it is not surprising to find Master Nicolas de Venderès among the four who were of the opinion that Joan ought to be handed over to the secular arm without more ado, since it was he who had substituted a false schedule for the one that had actually been read. The Bishop ignored the majority opinion—which was obviously his only way of preventing the imposture from being discovered. So one can take it that of the forty lawyers who made up the tribunal only four were the real planners of the condemnation, which they achieved by a vile trick of which the others were not conscious.

What finally remained of the "fine case" of which Cauchon had once boasted? After the hearings of December 1455, the apostolic commissioners realized that, although apparently provided with all the guarantees that a regular procedure can offer, the record that had been put into their hands was nothing but a tissue of trickery and falsification. Joan's innocence stood out from that moment, amid all the plots employed to undo her.

All the same, they had not come to the end of their discoveries. Christmas, however, was drawing near and the tribunal broke up after hearing a first address from the promoter Simon Chapitault, who had no trouble in showing that the condemnatory trial had been corrupt both in its basis and in its procedure.

CHAPTER 2

The Witnesses on Her Childhood

Before departing to Paris for Christmas, the apostolic commissioners had settled the broad line on which the case was to run. At the request of the promoter Simon Chapitault, it had been decided that the first inquiry in the case proper should be conducted at Joan's native village of Domremy, a hamlet on the borders of Lorraine and the Barrois, where some forty years before (in the year 1412 most probably), on January 6, the feast of the Epiphany, a small girl, "like any other", had come into the world. There had already been three children in the home of her parents, Jacques d'Arc and Isabelle Romée: three boys, Jacques, Jean, and Pierre; and the year after Joan's birth another little daughter, Catherine, had been born. What had her behavior been, what had been her occupations and her pastimes during the sixteen or seventeen years that she had lived there, with her family, the quiet life of a peasant girl, neither rich nor poor? What education had she received? Had there been anything about her to reveal her miraculous vocation?

Moreover, some points remained obscure that could only be cleared up at Domremy: the question of the "Fairies'

Tree", for example. The condemnatory sentence read, "Joan said that she had often heard voices near a tree known as the 'Fairies' Tree'." Without explicitly stating anything, this amounted to an insinuation that, behind these alleged revelations, there might be some history of sorcery. Prosecutions for sorcery were still pretty rare at the beginning of the fifteenth century, but there is no doubt that fifty or a hundred years later it would have been for acts of witchcraft that she would have been condemned.

In addition, the articles of the sentence presented Joan as a rebellious and wayward daughter, the despair of her parents. This was one of the points on which the clerk Manchon had thought it useful to make one of his corrections, which have been mentioned in the previous chapter: "In the place where it is said that her parents were almost out of their minds with despair about her, correct and insert that they were displeased about her departure." It was necessary, therefore, to know Joan's attitude toward her parents and the circumstances of her departure.

Some attempt had also been made to cast doubt on Joan's behavior during the removal of Domremy's inhabitants to Neufchâteau, at the time of a skirmish between hostile soldiers that caused a short panic in the region. This episode took place in July 1428, two months after Joan's first approach to Baudricourt, and perhaps this alarm had some influence on the change of mind that the captain had undergone when Joan returned to the charge a little later. Baudricourt held the town of Vaucouleurs for the King of France, but was totally isolated.

Finally, the promoter Chapitault had come to the conclusion that, contrary to general belief, an inquiry had been conducted by Cauchon in Lorraine according to the regular procedure, but that, as this inquiry was too favorable to the accused, he had suppressed it. And this was not, as we shall see, the only matter he had omitted. The interrogatory[1] drawn up for the use of witnesses in Domremy and Vaucouleurs also aimed at gaining some information about this inquiry of 1431.

One can imagine the excitement that must have prevailed in this little village when proclamations were read from the pulpit and in the streets announcing the transfer of the tribunal to Domremy and summoning all those who had known "Joan the Maid" to come and give evidence. On the morning of Wednesday, January 28, some grave persons installed themselves in the prebendary of the little church dedicated to Saint Remy. There was the promoter Simon Chapitault, who had come from Paris to conduct the inquiry. But the other members were local worthies to whom the papal commissioners had delegated their powers, as was usual in such cases. There was the dean of Notre Dame in Vaucouleurs, Master Réginald Chichery, and a canon of the Toul cathedral, Wautrin Thierry. In addition, there was Dominique Dominici, a clerk of Toul, who performed the office of scribe.

The first witness called to testify was, in default of her close relatives, Joan's godfather. Her father Jacques d'Arc was then dead, as were her eldest brother and her younger sister Catherine. Her mother, Isabelle Romée, and her two brothers Jean and Pierre had constituted themselves the civil plaintiffs, and so could not testify. Now after the parents, the godfathers and godmothers were considered in that age the nearest kin and the most directly responsible for those whom they had held at the baptismal font. Every child had several godfathers and godmothers, first, to increase the feeling of protection around about him, and second, for practical reasons: because at a time when oral testimony was

---

[1] The text of this interrogatory for the Lorraine inquiry will be found in Appendix C, p. 299.

preferred to written evidence, when official records, and even parish registers, did not yet exist, it was safer to have a number of witnesses to testify to a person's identity, his baptism, and his age—which, by the way, no one ever worried about knowing exactly. The time-honored formula for a witness questioned about his age was to reply, such an age, or thereabouts.

JOAN'S GODFATHER

Jean Moreau

(Of Greux,[2] near Domremy, farmer—aged seventy or thereabouts)

Joan,[3] that you are asking me about, was born in Domremy and baptized in Saint Remy Church, the parish church hereabouts. Her father was called Jean d'Arc and her mother Isabelle. When they were alive, they were farmers at Domremy. To my own knowledge, they were good and pious Catholics and good farmers, of good reputation and honest way of life according to their state of farmers. For I had many talks with them. I myself was one of Joan's godfathers, and her godmothers were Étienne Royer's wife, and Béatrice, d'Estelin's widow, who lived in Domremy village, and Jeannette, Tiercelin de Viteau's widow, who lived in the town of Neufchâteau.

Joan, in her early days, was well and properly brought up in the faith and in sound morals, and she was such a good girl that almost everyone in Domremy loved her. And Joan knew her *Credo*, her *Pater noster* and the *Ave Maria* the way little girls of her age do.

---

[2] The hamlet of Greux is close beside Domremy. After the anointing, Joan asked the King for exemption from all taxes for both parishes, and this he granted her.

[3] The villagers refer to her as Jeannette and to her mother as Isabellette.

Joan was as well-behaved a girl as any one of her kind can be, for her parents were not very rich; and in her youth and up to the time that she left her father's house she used to go out ploughing and sometimes she looked after the cattle in the fields; and she did woman's work, spinning and all that.

Joan went gladly and often to church, and to the hermitage of Notre Dame de Bermont near the village of Domremy, when her parents thought she was at the plough, in the fields, or somewhere else. If she was in the fields and heard the bell rung for Mass, she would come to the village and go to church to hear the Mass, and I have seen her do so.

I have seen her make confession at Easter time and on other feast days. She used to confess to Messire Guillaume Front,[4] who was then vicar of the parish church of Saint Remy at Domremy.

As for the tree that was called the Ladies' Tree, I have sometimes heard that ladies who cast spells—*fairies* they used to call them—*used* to come in the old days and dance under that tree. But people do say that since they read the Gospel of Saint John there they do not come anymore. In our time, on the Sunday when they sing the introit *Laetare Jerusalem*,[5] in God's holy church (in our parts they call it Fountains Sunday) the young men and girls of Domremy go and dance under that tree (and sometimes in spring and summer too, on saints' days), and sometimes they eat their food there, and on their way back they go to the *Fontaine aux Raines*[6] (the Frogs' Spring), strolling and singing. They drink the water of that fountain and play around it and gather flowers. Joan

---

[4] He was dead by the time of the rehabilitation. The influence of this good priest, who was imbued with Franciscan ideas, is supposed to have been partially responsible for Joan's predilection for the mendicant orders.

[5] The fourth Sunday in Lent.

[6] Now the *Fontaine des Groseilliers*.

the Maid and the other girls went there sometimes, and she behaved just like the others. I have never heard that Joan went there alone, or for any other reason, either to the fountain or the tree—for the fountain is nearer to the village than the tree—except for a walk and to play with the other girls.

When Joan left her father's house, she went to Vaucouleurs two or three times, to talk to the captain. I have heard tell that my lord Charles, who was then Duke of Lorraine, wanted to see her, and gave her a horse with a black coat, as they said. And I cannot say anything more except that in that July I went to Châlons. For they said that the King was going to Rheims to be crowned, and there I found Joan, and she gave me a red suit that she wore.

When Joan was at Neufchâteau, she was always in her father's and mother's company, because of the soldiers. They stayed four days at Neufchâteau and then went back to Domremy. And that I know, because I was at Neufchâteau town with the rest, and I saw Joan there, and her mother and father.

ONE OF JOAN'S GODMOTHERS

Béatrice

(The widow of d'Estelin, a farmer of Domremy—aged eighty)

Joan was born at Domremy, the daughter of Jacques d'Arc and Isabelle, farmers, true and good Catholics, upright and brave, according to their powers, but not very rich; and Joan was baptized in the font of Saint Remy Church; and her godfathers were Jean Moreau of Greux and Jean le Langart, and the late Jean Rainguesson; and her godmothers were Jeannette, the widow of Tiercelin, the clerk, Jeannette, wife of Thévenin Royer; and myself.

Joan was well and properly instructed in the Catholic faith like other girls of her age. And from her childhood and her adolescence up to her leaving her father's house, she was brought up to good habits. She was chaste and well-mannered, and frequent and pious in her attendance at church and the holy shrines. And after the village of Domremy was burnt,[7] Joan always went on saints' days to hear the Mass in the village of Greux; she confessed gladly on the proper days, and especially on the most holy feast of Easter, or the Resurrection of our Lord Jesus Christ. In my opinion, there was not a better girl in the two villages. She applied herself to all the different jobs in her father's house, and sometimes she spun flax or wool, or went to the plough, or to the harvest fields, when it was time, and sometimes when it was her father's turn, she watched the village beasts or herds.

... That tree is called the Ladies' Tree, and I have been there sometimes, with the gentlemen and their ladies of the village, to stroll under the tree, because it is a fine tree. It is beside the main road that goes to Neufchâteau; and I have heard tell that in the olden days ladies that cast spells, who are called *fairies* in French, used to go under that tree. But because of their sins, as they say, they do not go there now. The young men and girls of Domremy go under that tree too, on *Laetare Jerusalem* Sunday, which is called Fountains Sunday, and in spring, and Joan used to go with them. And there they sing and dance rounds and eat their food, and on the way back they go to the *Fontaine aux Raines* and drink at that fountain. And when the vicar carries the Cross through the fields, on the vigil of the Ascension,[8] he goes under that tree too, and he recites the Gospel, and I have seen him do it. And that is all that I know about it.

---

[7] An allusion to the Burgundian attack in July 1428, in the course of which the church of Domremy, adjoining Jacques d'Arc's house, was burnt.

[8] Allusion to the Rogation ceremony.

... I have heard tell that there were some Friars Minor in the village to make inquiries about what people said. But I do not know anything more, for nobody asked me anything.

ANOTHER OF JOAN'S GODMOTHERS

Jeannette Royer

(Of Domremy—aged seventy)

That tree is called the Ladies' Tree; and I have heard tell that the ladies of Domremy used to go and walk under that tree in the olden times. And I believe that Dame Catherine de la Roche, Jean de Bourlemont's wife and lady of this manor, went and walked with her attendants under that tree.

THE THIRD GODMOTHER

Jeannette

(The widow of Tiercelin de Viteau—aged sixty)

About the tree that is called the Ladies' Tree, they do say that once upon a time a gentleman called Pierre Granier, knight and lord of Bourlemont, used to meet a lady called Fée[9] under that tree and that they used to walk together there. I have heard that read out of a romance. The lords and ladies of the manor of Domremy, that is to say Dame Béatrice, the wife of Messire Pierre de Bourlemont, with her ladies, and Messire Pierre himself, used sometimes to go, or so they say, to walk under that tree. And the young men and girls of the

---

[9] Fairy. An ex post facto explanation, this one.—*Trans.*

village go there every year, on *Laetare* Sunday, which they call Fountains Sunday, for a walk; and there they eat and dance and go to the *Fontaine aux Raines* to drink. But I do not remember whether Joan the Maid ever went under that tree. And I never heard that she had a bad reputation because of that tree.

In this inquiry, intended primarily to make certain of Joan's good behavior and Christian habits, particular attention was bound to be given to the testimony of the priests. In default of Guillaume Front, the vicar of Domremy in Joan's lifetime, here is the vicar of a neighboring parish, who knew her.

THE PRIEST OF RONCESSEY

Étienne de Sionne

(Vicar of Roncessey, near Neufchâteau—aged fifty-four)

I often heard from Guillaume Front, who was vicar of Domremy when he lived, that Joan, called the Maid, was a good and simple girl, so pious, well brought up, and God-fearing, that there was not a girl like her in the village. She often used to confess her sins to him, and he used to say that if Joan had had any money of her own, she would have given it to her priest for the singing of Masses. But I know nothing else about the contents of those articles, except by hearsay.

... I have been told by several people that Joan was at Neufchâteau, in the house of a decent woman called La Rousse, because of the soldiers; and she was always in the company of her father and of the others from the village who had fled there.

THE PRIEST OF A NEIGHBORING PARISH

Dominique Jacob

(Vicar of the parish of Montiers sur Saulx in the diocese of Toul—aged thirty-five)

Joan came from Domremy and, as I believe, she was baptized in the Church of Saint Remy, in that village; and her parents were Jacques d'Arc and Isabelle, man and wife, who were good Catholics and of a good reputation. I have always heard them well spoken of as such.

I could only attest to this by hearsay, for Joan was older than I.

I saw and knew Joan three or four years before she left her father's and mother's house. She was brought up to have good morals and good habits, and she often went to church. Sometimes when [the bells for] Compline were rung in the village church, she would go down on her knees; and I used to think that she said her prayers most devoutly.

... I know nothing except by hearsay of certain Friars Minor coming to these parts to make an inquiry. I do not know whether they did.

All the inhabitants of Domremy fled because of the soldiers and came to Neufchâteau; and among them came Joan with her father and mother, and she was always in their company; and she was with her father and mother when she left Neufchâteau.

A LOCAL PRIEST

Henri Arnoul

(Of Gondrecourt le Château—aged sixty-four)

Joan used to confess gladly and often. I confessed her four times myself, three times in Lent and once on a saint's day. She was a good, God-fearing girl. When she was at church, sometimes she would be bowed before the Cross, sometimes she would have her hands clasped and her eyes raised and her face turned to the Crucifix and the Blessed Virgin.

THE BEADLE OF DOMREMY

Perrin Drappier

(Of Domremy—aged sixty)

Joan the Maid was a good girl, chaste, simple, and modest, all the years of her youth until she left her father's house. She was a God-fearing girl and never took His name or His saints' names in vain. She went to church often and confessed often, and the reason I know that is because I was beadle of Domremy church at the time, and I often saw Joan come to church, to Mass and Compline. And when I did not ring for Compline, Joan used to ask me why and scold me, saying that it was wrong of me. And she even promised me a present of wool if I would be regular in ringing for Compline. And Joan often went with her sisters and others to the church and hermitage of Notre Dame de Bermont, founded in honor of the Blessed Virgin Mary. She gave liberal alms, and worked gladly, spinning and doing the other necessary tasks, and sometimes she went out ploughing, and took her turn guarding the cattle.

... That tree is called the Ladies' Tree; I have seen a lady of the manor, the wife of Messire Pierre de Bourlemont, with the mother of the same Pierre, go walking sometimes to that tree, and they used to take their attendants and the village girls with them, and take bread, wine, and eggs. In spring, and on *Laetare* Sunday, which they call Fountains Sunday, the young men and girls of the village have a custom of going to the tree and the fountain, and they take little loaves with them, which they eat under the tree, and as they walk there they sing and dance....

I think that an inquiry was made; however I did not see any signs to show whether it was or not.

CHILDHOOD FRIENDS

Colin

(The son of Jean Colin of Greux, farmer—aged fifty)

Joan, to my knowledge, was a good, simple, sweet girl, and well-behaved. She went gladly to church, as I have seen. For nearly every Saturday afternoon, Joan with her sister and some other women used to go to the hermitage of Notre Dame de Bermont, carrying candles. She was deeply devoted to God and the Blessed Virgin, so much so that some other lads and I—for I was young then—used to tease her for being so pious. She worked gladly, and looked after the cattle when they were grazing. She was always happy looking after the beasts on her father's farm, and she spun and did the household chores.... I have heard from Messire Guillaume Front, who used to be vicar of the parish, that she was as good a Catholic as he had ever seen, and that he had not a better one in his parish.

Simonin Musnier

(Farmer—aged forty-four)

I was brought up with Joan the Maid, in the house next door to her father's. I know that she was a good, simple, pious girl, who feared God and His saints. She went often and gladly to church and to the holy shrine. She tended the sick and gave alms to the poor. I have seen her do

> so, for I was ill myself when I was a child, and Joan came to comfort me....
>
> ... That tree is called the Ladies' Tree, as I have always heard. The *fairies*, as they call them in the common tongue, used to come under that tree in the olden times, as I have always heard, for I have never seen any sign of an evil spirit there myself.... I have been under that tree myself, when I was young, with Joan and other young people on Fountains Sunday, to play there and take a stroll as other local girls and boys do.

Hauviette

Ever since Péguy's *Joan of Arc*, Hauviette and Joan have been inseparably linked. At the moment when she gave evidence she was about forty-five. She had married a Domremy peasant, Gérard de Syonne.

> Ever since my childhood I had known Joan the Maid, who was born at Domremy, the daughter of Jacques d'Arc and Isabelle who were man and wife, honest farmers and true Catholics of good reputation. I know this because I was very often with Joan, and, being her friend, I went to her father's house. However I do not remember anything about her godfathers or godmothers, except by hearsay, for Joan was three or four years older than I, by what they said.
>
> ... Joan was a good, simple, sweet girl. She often and gladly went to church and the holy shrines, and she was often put to shame by what people said about her devotion as a churchgoer. I have heard the priest who was vicar in her time say that she confessed often. Joan worked just like other young girls. She did the household chores, and spun, and sometimes—I have seen her—she watched her father's flocks.

... That tree has been called the Ladies' Tree since olden times, and they say that long ago the ladies they call *fairies* went there. But I have never heard of anyone who saw one. The boys and girls of the village have a custom of going to that tree and to the *Fontaine aux Raines*, on *Laetare Jerusalem* Sunday, which is called Fountains Sunday, and they used to take bread with them.

I have been with Joan the Maid, who was my friend, and other girls and boys to the Fairies' Tree on Fountains Sunday. We used to eat there and dance and play. I have known them bring nuts to the tree and the fountains.

I did not know when Joan went away, but I cried very bitterly about her going. I loved her very dearly, you see, because she was so kind, and I was her friend....

... Joan was always with her father and mother when she was at Neufchâteau. I was at Neufchâteau too just then, and I saw her all the time.

Mengette

Joan's other friend. The third, Guillemette, did not appear. Either she was dead or she had left the district.

Mengette was about forty-six; she was the wife of Jean Joyart.

My father's house was almost next door to Joan's father's, and I knew Joan the Maid, because I often spun in her company and did the other household chores with her, both at night and by day. She was brought up as a good Christian and was a model of good behavior, as you could see. She liked going to church and went often. She gave alms out of her father's goods, and she was so good and simple and pious that the other girls and I used to tell her that she was too pious. She liked working and undertook all sorts of jobs. She spun and did the household chores and went out to harvest, and sometimes, when

> the time came round, she used to take her turn looking after the animals, and she spun all the time. She went willingly to confession. I have often seen her on her knees in front of the village priest.
>
> ... That tree is called the Ladies' Dwelling, and it is an ancient tree. Indeed, I have never heard that there was a time when that tree was not there.... I went there often with Joan. We used to eat there, and then we went to drink at the *Fontaine aux Raines*, and sometimes we spread a cloth under that tree and ate together there, and then we would play and dance as the young people still do today....
>
> When she went away, she said good-bye to me. Then she departed and prayed God to bless me, and set out for Vaucouleurs.

For one day they heard in the village that Joan had gone to Vaucouleurs. Up to that time she had no history; she was "just like the other girls". The phrase recurs with an almost irritating regularity. Was there really nothing to distinguish her from the others? One feature, however, is revealed to us by the word the scribe has translated as *libenter*, gladly, and which also recurs constantly. She spun, sewed, and did the other household chores gladly, she went to church gladly when the bells were rung, gladly she ... By means of this brief word, these simple people have revealed to us what is perhaps Joan's most precious trait; a good disposition, moral soundness, a sort of joy in life. Even the monotony of prison, her anguish and her distress, therefore, did not succeed in entirely destroying her fundamental gaiety, the evidence of good physical and mental balance.

But one day astonishing news spread through Domremy. Joan had gone off to Vaucouleurs. She wanted to have the King anointed. She had, however, attempted to confide in one of her friends, Michel Lebuin, as well as in a local peasant, Gérardin d'Épinal. But they had not understood her.

THE CONFIDANT

Michel Lebuin

(Of Domremy, farm laborer at Burey[10]—aged forty-four)

Joan went to church gladly and used to visit the holy shrines. I know that because, when I was young, I went on a pilgrimage with her to the hermitage of Notre Dame de Bermont. She went nearly every Saturday to that hermitage with her sister, and put candles there. She gave all the alms she could gladly for the love of God. She was active in working with the women and the other girls, and she worked well and properly. She often made confession. I know that because I was her friend, and I often saw her confess.

That tree is called the Ladies' Dwelling. I have heard that those creatures that are vulgarly called *fairies* used once upon a time to come under that tree. But I do not know whether they did, because they do not do so now. The boys and girls of Domremy go there every year. . . . When Joan was a girl she went to "do the fountains" like the other girls. But I do not think that she ever went there otherwise or for any other reason, for there was nothing about her that was not good.

All that I know is that once Joan told me herself, on the eve of Saint John the Baptist, that there was a maid between Coussey and Vaucouleurs who would have the King of France anointed within a year. And the very next year the King was anointed at Rheims. I do not know anything else.

---

[10] Burey is between Domremy and Vaucouleurs.

A FARMER

Gérardin

(Of Épinal—aged sixty)

That tree is called the Ladies' Tree. I have seen the lords and ladies of the manor of Domremy, once or twice in spring, bring bread and wine and go and eat under that tree, which is as pretty as the lilies at that time of year and spreads very wide. Its leaves and branches come down to the ground. On Fountains Sunday, the boys and girls of Domremy have a custom of going under that tree. Their mothers bake them loaves, and the young people go and "do the fountains" under that tree. They sing and dance there, and then they go to the *Fontaine aux Raines* and eat their bread and drink its waters, as I have seen. Joan went there with the other girls and did just like the rest.

... All I know is that when she was about to go away, she said to me: "Friend, if you were not a Burgundian, there is something I would tell you." But I thought it was something about a lad she wanted to marry. I saw her afterward at Châlons with four people from our village, and she said that she was afraid of nothing except treason.

A DOMREMY WOMAN

Isabellette

(The wife of Gérardin of Épinal—aged fifty)

She gave alms gladly and had the poor of the village gathered together, and she wanted to sleep beside the hearth and to let them lie in her bed. One never saw her hanging about the streets, but she stayed in church to pray. She did not dance, and often we other young people used to notice that and talk about it. She was always working and spinning and digging the ground with her father. She did the household chores, and she sometimes looked after the animals. She confessed gladly and often, as I have seen. For Joan the Maid was my friend, and she held my son Nicolas at the font when he was baptized. And I often went about with her, and I used to see her go and confess in church to Messire Guillaume, who was the vicar then....

... I always heard that tree called the Ladies' Dwelling. When the village castle was still standing, the lords and ladies of the manor used to go for a feast under that tree on *Laetare Jerusalem* Sunday, which was called Fountains Sunday, and sometimes in the summertime they would take some boys and girls with them. I know because I went once with Messire Pierre Bourlemont, the lord of the manor, and his wife, who came from France; and I often went with the village girls both in the spring and on Fountains Sunday....

I have heard Durand Laxart, the man who escorted her to my lord Robert de Baudricourt, say that she promised to ask her father if she could go and help his wife when she was in labor, so that he should take her to my lord Robert.

... Joan was at Neufchâteau with her father, her mother, her brothers, and her sister when they drove their cattle there because of the soldiers. But she did not stay there long and came back to Domremy with her father, as I saw. For she did not like living in those parts, but preferred to live at Domremy, as she said.

JOAN'S UNCLE

Durand Laxart

Durand Laxart, whom Isabelle has just mentioned, was Joan's "uncle" through his marriage to her mother's cousin Jeanne. He lived in one of the two hamlets called Burey that lie between Domremy and Vaucouleurs. He also is a simple "farmer", and he relates, laconically enough, a tale that he must have told a hundred times before.

> Joan was a relation of my wife Jeanne. I knew Joan's parents, Jacques d'Arc and Isabelle, very well. They were good and pious Catholics, of good reputation, and I believe that Joan was born in the village of Domremy and that she was baptized at the font of Saint Remy Church in that place.... Joan was well-behaved, pious, and patient. She went gladly to church, she confessed gladly, and she gave alms to the poor when she could, as I have seen, both in the village of Domremy and at Burey, in my house, where Joan stayed for six weeks. She worked gladly, and spun and followed the plough, and looked after the animals and did other tasks befitting to a woman, all gladly....
> ... I went myself to fetch Joan from her father's house and took her away with me, and she told me that she wanted to go to France, to the Dauphin, to have him crowned. She said, "Was it not said that France would be ruined through a woman, and afterward restored by a virgin?" And she also asked me to go to Robert de Baudricourt, to ask him to lead her to the place where my lord the Dauphin was. This Robert told me several times to give her a good slapping and take her back to her father; and when the Maid saw that Robert would not take her to the place where the Dauphin was, she handed me my cloak herself and said that she would go back. And on my way back I took her to Saint Nicolas;[11] and when she got there she went with a safe-conduct to my lord Charles, Duke of Lorraine;[12] and when my lord Charles saw her, he spoke to her and gave

---

[11] A place of pilgrimage then much visited, six miles from Nancy.
[12] It was Baudricourt who had sent Joan to the Duke of Lorraine, so that he could question her. For their interview, see Marguerite La Touroulde's testimony, on page 124.

her four francs, which she showed to me. Then Joan came back to Vaucouleurs, and the inhabitants of the town bought her men's clothing, breeches, gaiters, and all that she needed; and Jacques Alain of Vaucouleurs and I bought her a horse for the price of twelve francs, out of our own pockets. However, my lord Robert de Baudricourt had the money paid back to us afterward. And after that Jean de Metz, Bertrand de Poulengy, Colet de Vienne, and Richard Larcher, with two servants of Jean de Metz and de Bertrand, took Joan to the place where the Dauphin was. I do not know anything more, except that I saw her at Rheims, at the King's coronation.

Some of the Domremy people remember her leavetaking and describe her departure, Jean Waterin, for instance, who was more or less of the same age as Joan, and Gérard Guillemette.

A FARMER

Jean Waterin

(Of Domremy, living at Greux—aged forty-five)

I often saw Joan the Maid, and in my youth I often drove her father's plough with her. I have been in the fields and pastures with her and the other girls. Often when we were playing together, Joan would draw aside and speak with God, as it seemed to me; and I and the others made fun of her. She was good and simple, and went often to the churches and the holy shrines. When she was in the fields, she used to go down on her knees every time she heard the bell tolled; she worked gladly and sewed and did the work and the chores of the house, and went ploughing with her father; and sometimes, when it was her turn, she guarded the beasts. She confessed gladly, as the village priest said; and often she went on pilgrimage to Notre Dame de Bermont, carrying candles....

... I saw her when she left the village of Greux, and she said good-bye to the people. And I heard it said many times that she was to restore France and the blood royal.

ANOTHER FARMER

Gérard Guillemette

(Of Greux—aged forty)

I saw Joan once on *Laetare* Sunday with the girls of the village and did not see her afterward. The boys and girls of the village of Greux go to "do the fountains" at the Church of Notre Dame de Bermont.

... When Joan left her father's house, I saw her pass before the house with her uncle, Durand Laxart. Joan said to her father then: "Good-bye, I am going to Vaucouleurs." After that I heard that Joan had gone to France....

... I myself went to Neufchâteau with Joan, her father and her mother, and I always saw her with her father and her mother, except for three or four days when she helped her hostess with whom they were lodging. La Rousse was her name, a decent woman of that place. And Joan's father and mother were present all the time. I know for certain that they did not stay at Neufchâteau for more than four or five days, only until all the soldiers had gone. Then she went back to Domremy with her father and her mother.

The vicar of the parish of Domremy was, at the time of Joan's departure, a curate of Vaucouleurs. He heard Joan's confessions and saw her leave for Chinon.

THE WITNESSES ON HER CHILDHOOD

THE VICAR OF DOMREMY

Jean Colin[13]

(Vicar of the parish—aged sixty)

During the time that Joan was at Vaucouleurs, she came two or three times to confess to me. So I heard her confessions two or three times, and I can conscientiously say that she seemed to me a good girl, who showed every sign of being a good Catholic and a perfect Christian. She went to church gladly....

... I saw her at Vaucouleurs when she made up her mind to go to France; and I saw her mount her horse and ride away, and with her Bertrand de Poulengy, Jean de Metz, Colet de Vienne, all knights and servants of Robert de Baudricourt.

Another priest, Jean le Fumeux, had seen her at Vaucouleurs.

A CANON

Jean le Fumeux

(Canon of Notre Dame at Vaucouleurs, vicar of the parish of Ugny—aged thirty-eight)

All that I know is that Joan came to Vaucouleurs and said that she wanted to go to the Dauphin. I was a boy myself then, and beadle in the chapel of Notre Dame at Vaucouleurs. I often saw Joan the Maid enter that church most devoutly; she used to hear the morning Mass and stay behind a long time praying. I saw her kneeling before the Holy Virgin under the vault of that church,

---

[13] This is a different person from the Jean Colin, farmer, mentioned on p. 79 above.

sometimes with her face bowed and sometimes looking straight before her. I believe that she was a good and saintly girl.

THE INQUIRY OF 1431

And now we come to the question of the inquiry that Cauchon set going in Lorraine in 1431, at the time when the preparations for the case were going forward. The men charged with gathering the information were anxious not to arouse the attention of the people of Vaucouleurs, the only town north of the Loire except Tournai and Mont Saint Michel holding out for the King. And as the results were not to Cauchon's liking, he covered the inquiry up with equal discretion; none of the judges had any knowledge of it.

Some of the witnesses examined at Domremy remembered having seen the commissioners, in particular Joan's friend and confidant Michel Lebuin:

Michel Lebuin

When Joan was taken prisoner, I saw a man called Nicolas Bailly of Andelot, who came to Domremy with several others, and on the instructions of Messire Jean de Torcenay, then captain of Chaumont, held an inquiry in the name of the self-styled king of England and France about Joan's reputation and manner of life, or so they said. But in my opinion he dared not compel any man to speak on oath for fear of the men of Vaucouleurs. I think that Jean Bégot of that town was examined, for they lodged in his house. I believe too that when they made that inquiry they discovered nothing about Joan to her discredit. And that is all I know.

Jean Jaquard

(Son of Jean Guillemette, of Greux—aged forty-seven)

I saw Nicolas Bailly of Andelot and Guiot his servant with several others at Domremy, and it was said that they were making an inquiry about the case of the Maid. But in my opinion they did not compel anybody. During the inquiry they examined, I believe, Jean Moreau, Jean Guillemette, my father, and Jean Colin, all now living, and the late Jean Hannequin of Greux and several others. After that, these commissioners prudently retired, for they were afraid of the Vaucouleurs men. I believe that this inquiry for information was made on the instructions of the captain of Chaumont, who was on the side of the English and the Burgundians.

More complete details were given by the witness who had drawn the promoter Simon Chapitault's attention to this inquiry. This was a certain Jean Moreau, a merchant, and probably a traveling merchant, who had heard the business discussed by other merchants who had traveled with him from Lorraine to Rouen, where he was himself residing at the time of Joan's trial.

Jean Moreau

(Merchant—aged fifty-two)

I am a native of Viville[14] near La Motte en Bassigny, which is not very far from Domremy, where Joan came from. However, I never knew Joan or her parents. But the fact is that at the time when Joan was with the King

---

[14] This statement was made at Rouen, on May 10, 1456. This is a different Jean Moreau from the one whose testimony is given on pp. 71–73 above.

of France, two hardware merchants, Nicolas Saussart and Jean Chando, arrived in Rouen, and it was from them that I heard about Joan, and the tale of how she came from Lorraine. They said that Joan had gone to Jean [*sic*] de Baudricourt at Vaucouleurs to tell him to take her or have her taken to the King, and that he, therefore, had her taken to the King, who was then at Chinon. When she arrived, and before she had ever seen the King, she was told that one of the courtiers was he, but she said that he was not. In the end, after being examined by the clerks and the lawyers, she spoke to the King. I did not hear any more talk about Joan till the time when I saw her, when they preached two sermons to her, one at Saint Ouen and the other in the old market at Rouen.

I only know that at the time when they were building up a case against her, somebody important from Lorraine came to Rouen. As I came from the same country, I made his acquaintance. He told me that he had left Lorraine and come to Rouen because he had been specially commissioned to gather information in Joan's country of origin, to find out what reputation she had there. This he had done, and he had brought his information to my lord Bishop of Beauvais, expecting compensation for his labors and his expenses. But the Bishop had called him a traitor and a sinner and told him that he had not carried out his instructions properly. This man complained to me, because, to judge from what he said, he could not get payment of his fees since the information he brought did not seem to be of any use to the Bishop. He told me also that in the course of his inquiries he had learned nothing about Joan that he would not have liked to hear about his own sister, and this despite the fact that he had gathered information in five or six parishes near Domremy and in Domremy itself. He said that he had learned that Joan was most devout, and that she often went to a little chapel where it was her custom to hang garlands in front of the Virgin's statue, and that sometimes she kept her father's cattle.

One of the commissioners, Nicolas Bailly, was still alive and performing his duties of scrivener at Andelot in the diocese of Langres; he was summoned to Toul and invited to testify.

Nicolas Bailly

(Of Andelot in the diocese of Langres, scrivener royal and deputy magistrate in the borough of Andelot—aged sixty)

Joan was a native of Domremy and an inhabitant of that parish, and her father was Jacques d'Arc, a good and honest farmer, which I have seen and know him to be. I also know it by hearsay and on many men's report, for I was the scrivener chosen by Messire Jean de Torcenay, then the captain of Chaumont, who held his power from the so-called king of France and England, at the same time as one Gérard Petit, deceased, then provost of the town of Andelot, to make an inquiry as to the facts about Joan the Maid, who was then, so they said, lying in prison in the city of Rouen....

I saw Joan several times in her youth and up to her departure from her father's house. She was a good girl and well-behaved, a good Catholic who went gladly to church and to the holy shrines. She used to go on pilgrimage to the church at Bermont and made confession nearly every month, as I have heard many of the inhabitants of Domremy village say; and I found it to be so at the time of the inquiry I made about her with the provost of Andelot....

... I am the scrivener, as I have said already, who collected the information, in my time, as I was commissioned to do by Messire Jean de Torcenay, the captain of Chaumont, who had, as he said, letters of commission from the self-styled king of France and England. When Gérard, the late provost, and I collected this information about Joan, we did the job so thoroughly that we got twelve or fifteen witnesses to certify the information that we collected on the subject of Joan the Maid, before Simon de Thermes, squire, who acted as lieutenant to the captain of Chaumont, because we were under suspicion for not having falsified that information. These witnesses stated in front of the lieutenant that they had testified as they had testified and as their answers stood on the question sheet. Then the lieutenant wrote to Messire Jean, the captain of Chaumont, that what was written in that interrogatory, made by us the scrivener and the provost, was the truth. And when the captain saw the lieutenant's report, he said that we, the commissioners, were false Armagnacs.[15]

Nicolas Bailly was asked whether he still possessed that inquiry, or a copy of it. He said that he did not.

---

[15] The Armagnac faction were the supporters of the Dauphin.

CHAPTER 3

The Traveling Companions

On January 31, 1456, the tribunal moved to Vaucouleurs. Baudricourt was dead, and this deprives us of a testimony that would have been of first-rate interest. What went on in the mind of this captain and warrior who had assumed the impossible task of maintaining resistance at Vaucouleurs, the only town, as we have said, in the whole of northern France except Tournai and Mont Saint Michel to remain loyal? What were his thoughts when he gave an escort to a little peasant girl in a red bodice and skirt, to conduct her to the King—thus introducing the first act of the whole drama?

But in default of Baudricourt, the commissioners heard, on that January Saturday, the evidence of Jean de Novelonpont, and he was the first among the soldiers to believe in Joan. She literally conquered him. As he repeats them to us, Joan's words retain all their convincing fervor; he had thrown her a few ironic remarks, and her answer had conquered him. The scene that he revives for us here is worthy of the finest days of chivalry.

THE FRIEND ON THE FIRST DAY

Jean de Novelonpont, or de Metz

(He was ennobled by Charles VII in 1448; aged fifty-seven)

When Joan the Maid arrived at the town of Vaucouleurs in the diocese of Toul, I saw her dressed in poor clothing, in woman's clothing, and it was red. She lodged in the house of a certain Henri Le Royer of Vaucouleurs. I said to her, "What are you doing here, my dear? Is it not fated that the King shall be driven from his kingdom, and that we shall all turn English?" And the Maid answered me: "I have come here to the royal chamber to speak to Robert de Baudricourt, to ask him to escort me, or to have me escorted, to the King. But he pays no attention to me, or to what I say. But all the same, before mid-Lent I must be with the King, even if I have to wear my legs down to the knees. For there is no one on earth, be he king, or duke, or the King of Scotland's daughter,[1] or anyone else, who can restore the kingdom of France, and he will have no help except through me, although I would much prefer to stay with my poor mother and spin, for this is not my station. But I must go, and I must do it, for my Lord wishes me to perform this deed." I asked her who her lord was. She said that he was God. And then I, Jean, who testify to this, I promised the Maid, putting my hand in hers as a sign of faith,[2] that, with God's aid, I would lead her to the King. And I asked her when she wanted to go. She answered, "Rather today than tomorrow, and rather tomorrow than later." Then I asked her if she wanted to travel in those

---

[1] There were at this time discussions about the marriage of the Dauphin, the future Louis XI, to Margaret of Scotland. The marriage actually took place at Tours in 1436.

[2] This was truly a sign of faith, of feudal homage. The vassal who swore feudal homage put his hand in between his lord's as a sign of trust and fidelity. By this gesture Jean became Joan's liegeman.

clothes.³ She replied that she would rather have a man's clothes. Then I gave her a suit and breeches belonging to my servants, so that she could put them on. And after that some people of Vaucouleurs had a man's suit and breeches and everything else that was necessary made for her, and they gave her a horse, which cost about sixteen francs. When she was dressed and had a horse, together with a safe-conduct from my lord Charles,⁴ Duke of Lorraine, the Maid went to speak with that lord, and I went with her, as far as the city of Toul. And when she returned to Vaucouleurs, about Quadragesima Sunday⁵—it will be twenty-seven years ago, I think, next Quadragesima Sunday—I and Bertrand de Poulengy, and two of his servants, and Colet de Vienne, the King's messenger, and a certain Richard, an archer, escorted the Maid to the King, who was at Chinon, at my expense and Bertrand's. And after leaving the town of Vaucouleurs on our way to the King, for fear of the English and the Burgundians, who were everywhere on the road, we sometimes rode by night. And we were eleven days on the road, on our ride to the town of Chinon; and as I was riding with her, I asked her several times if she was going to do what she said; and the Maid always told us not to be afraid, since she was commanded to do this. For her brothers in Paradise told her what she had to do, and it was four or five years ago that her brothers in Paradise and her Lord—that is to say, God—had first told her that she would have to go to the war to restore the

---

³ This point is interesting in relation to the alleged reasons for her condemnation (because it was her resumption of male clothing that caused Joan to be considered a relapsed heretic). Far from being scandalized, Jean de Novelonpont seems to have found it quite natural that Joan should put on a man's garments for her ride; and it was the same with the people of Vaucouleurs, who went so far as to make a collection in order to give her a man's clothes.

⁴ This interview has already been mentioned in the previous chapter.

⁵ The first Sunday in Lent, February 13, 1429.

kingdom of France. On the way, both Bertrand and I slept each night with her. The Maid slept beside us without taking off her doublet and breeches; and as for me, I was in such awe of her that I would not have dared go near her; and I tell you on my oath that I never had any desire or carnal feelings for her.

... On the way she would very gladly have heard the Mass. For she often said to us: "If only we could hear a Mass it would be a grand thing." But, to my knowledge, we only heard the Mass twice on the way. And I had great trust in what the Maid said, and I was on fire with what she said, and with a love for her which was, as I believe, a divine love. I believe that she was sent by God. She never swore, she loved to hear the Mass, and crossed herself with the sign of the cross. And so we escorted her to the King, to the town of Chinon, as secretly as we could.

JOAN'S HOST AND HOSTESS AT VAUCOULEURS

Catherine Royer

(Of Vaucouleurs—aged fifty-four)

At the time when Joan decided to go away she had been in my house for three weeks, ... and it was then that she sent a message to Robert de Baudricourt asking him to escort her to the place where the Dauphin was. But my lord Robert refused. I saw Robert de Baudricourt, then captain of the town of Vaucouleurs, and Messire Jean Fournier[6] enter my house. I heard Joan say that this man, who was a priest, had brought a stole, and that he had exorcised her in front of the captain, saying that if there was any evil thing in her, let it begone away, and if

---

[6] Baudricourt had asked him to exorcise Joan, as a precaution, which he did, as we shall see, in Henri and Catherine Royer's house.

there was any good thing, let it come to them all. And Joan went up to the priest and fell down on her knees; and Joan said that this priest had done wrong, since he had heard her confession; and when Joan saw that Robert would not escort her, she said—I heard her say it—that she must go to the place where the Dauphin was: "Have you not heard the prophecy that France was to be ruined by a woman and restored by a virgin from the marches of Lorraine?" I remembered having heard that, and I was flabbergasted. Joan desired it ardently, and the time was as wearisome for her as for a pregnant woman, until she could be taken to the Dauphin. And after that I believed what she said, and so did many others, so much so that Jacques Alain and Durand Laxart agreed to escort her, and they did escort her as far as Saint Nicolas, and then returned to Vaucouleurs, because Joan said that this was not the way in which she ought to depart. When they came back, certain people of the town had a tunic, breeches, gaiters, spurs, a sword, and other necessary things got ready for her, and they bought her a horse and Jean de Metz [Jean de Novelonpont], Bertrand de Poulengy, Colet de Vienne, and three others led her to the place where the Dauphin was. I saw them mount their horses to go.

Henri Royer

(Husband of Catherine; aged sixty-four)

Joan used to say that she must go to the noble Dauphin, because her Lord, the King of Heaven, wanted her to go, and that, being thus instructed by the King of Heaven, even if she had to go there on her knees she must go. Joan came to my house; she was then dressed in woman's clothes, of red. Afterward she wore a man's coat and breeches and other things, and rode on horseback to the place where the Dauphin was, and she was escorted there by Jean de Metz, Bertrand de Poulengy and by their servants, Colet de Vienne and Richard Larcher; and I saw them depart, all together. When she decided to go, she was asked what she would do, seeing that there were so many soldiers about. She answered that she was not afraid of the soldiers, for her way was open; and if there were soldiers on her way, she had God, her Lord, who would clear a road for her to go to the lord Dauphin, and that for that she was born.

BAUDRICOURT'S COMPANIONS

Some knights of Robert de Baudricourt's company very well remembered Joan's stay at Vaucouleurs and her departure.

Geoffroy Dufay

(Nobleman—aged fifty)

I sometimes saw Joan the Maid come to Maxey sur Vayse. She came from Domremy, so they said. I did know her father and mother, but I do not know their names. I do know, however, that they were good Catholic Christians, as those farming people are, and I have never heard anyone say anything to the contrary....

... When Joan came to Maxey, she sometimes visited my house; I think that she was a good, simple, and pious girl....

I often heard the Maid speak. She said that she wanted to go to France. I knew that Jean de Metz, Bertrand de Poulengy, and Julien, who were squires, escorted the Maid to the King.

I did not see her at the time, but people told me that she was departing with them.

Albert d'Ourches

(Nobleman and knight—aged sixty)

I saw Joan at Vaucouleurs, when she asked to be escorted to the King. I heard her repeat several times that she wanted to go to the King, and that she wanted to be escorted there for the Dauphin's very great benefit. That Maid seemed to me a girl of very good morals; I should have liked to have a daughter as good as she was. I saw her later in the company of the soldiers. I saw the Maid confess to Brother Richard[7] before Senlis and receive the Blessed Host, with the Dukes of Clermont and Alençon, on two successive days, and it is my belief that she was a perfect Christian....

As I said above, she asked to be escorted to the King. That Maid spoke very beautifully. She was escorted to him later by Bertrand de Poulengy, Jean de Metz, and their servants.

JOAN'S SECOND COMPANION

Bertrand de Poulengy

(Squire to the King of France—aged sixty-three)

Joan came from Domremy, as they said, and her father was Jacques d'Arc of the same village. I do not know her mother's name. But I have often been in their house, and I know that they were good farming people....

I have seen that tree several times, and I had been there twelve years before I saw Joan. I have heard that

---

[7] This Brother Richard, a mendicant friar of the Order of the Hermits of Saint Augustine, a disciple of Saint Bernard of Siena, played a part of some importance in Joan's life, since it was he who was entrusted with the delivery of the letter that she addressed to the people of Troyes during the march on Rheims, the letter that won their surrender.

girls and boys of Domremy and other villages in that neighborhood go to walk and dance under that tree....

Joan the Maid came to Vaucouleurs at the time of our Lord's Ascension,[8] as far as I remember, and I saw her there, talking to Robert de Baudricourt, who was then town captain. She said that she had come to him, Robert, on behalf of her Lord, to ask him to send word to the Dauphin that he should stay still and not make war on his enemies, for the Lord would send him help before mid-Lent. Joan said that the kingdom did not belong to the Dauphin but to her Lord, and that her Lord wished the Dauphin to be made king, and that He would give him His kingdom to rule, and that He promised that the Dauphin would be made king in spite of his enemies, and that she herself would lead him to be anointed. Robert asked her who her lord was, and she answered, "The King of Heaven". After that she went back to her father's house with her "uncle", Durand Laxart of Burey le Petit. And after that, toward the beginning of Lent,[9] Joan came back to Vaucouleurs and asked for an escort to go and see the lord Dauphin; after Joan had been on a pilgrimage to Saint Nicolas and had been to my lord the Duke of Lorraine, who had wanted to see her and had sent her a safe-conduct, and had returned to Vaucouleurs, to Henri Royer's house, I, Bertrand, and Jean de Metz, with the help of some other people of Vaucouleurs, saw to it that she gave up her woman's clothes, which were red in color, and wore a tunic and a man's suit, spurs, gaiters, a sword, and all the rest. Also we had a horse got ready for her; and then, with Joan and with Julien, my servant, with Jean de Honecourt, Jean de Metz' servant, and with Colet de Vienne and Richard Larcher, we set out on the road to go and see the Dauphin.

---

[8] An allusion to Joan's first journey, in May 1428, when Baudricourt refused to listen to her.

[9] Next year, in 1429.

As we left Lorraine, on the first day, we were afraid because of the Burgundian and English soldiers who commanded the roads, and so we traveled by night. Joan the Maid said to me, and to Jean de Metz too and those who were riding with us, that it would be a grand thing if we could hear the Mass. But because of the war that was waging about the country we could not. We wanted to pass unnoticed. Each night she slept with Jean de Metz and me, keeping on her surcoat and her breeches laced and tied. I was young then, but all the same I had no desire or carnal urge to touch her as a woman, and I would not have dared to approach Joan, because of the great goodness I saw in her.

We were eleven days on the way,[10] riding to the King, who was then Dauphin, and we had plenty of alarms on the road. But Joan always told us not to fear, and that once we had reached the town of Chinon the Dauphin would welcome us. She never swore, and I was myself greatly encouraged by her voices, for she seemed to me to have been sent by God. And I never saw any badness in her. She was always such a virtuous girl that she seemed like a saint. And so, all together, without great difficulties, we rode to the town of Chinon where the King—then the Dauphin—was.

---

[10] From February 13 to 23.

CHAPTER 4

The Arrival at Chinon and the Poitiers Judges

The inquiry on Lorraine soil—at Domremy, Vaucouleurs, and Toul—had ended on February 11. Simon Chapitault went back to Rouen, where the resumption of sessions had been fixed for February 16. In the meantime, four witnesses had been called before the episcopal court in Paris. Two of them were the physicians, Jean Tiphaine and Guillaume de la Chambre, called to testify in particular as to the disease by which Joan had been attacked in prison, and also as to the case in general, in which they had taken part willy-nilly. Their depositions, dated January 10, will be given later. The two others had taken a more direct part in the case; they were Thomas de Courcelles and another judge, Jean de Mailly, Bishop of Noyon and Cauchon's most devoted friend.

On Monday, February 16, the promoter of Beauvais, Master Réginald Bredouille, presented himself before the commissioners, in his own name and as procurer to the bishop of the diocese. For him it was merely a matter of simple formality: to reply to the summonses, at the same time renouncing all desire to defend the cause of their predecessors. The prior of the Dominican convent at Évreux, Jacques Chaussetier, came in his turn to protest in the name of the convent at Beauvais against the summonses intended for the vice-Inquisitor.

The case was resumed next day, and the hundred and one articles alleged by the d'Arc family as grounds for the nullity of the first case were read at the bar; they had previously been laid before the tribunal on December 20 by Simon Chapitault. Master Réginald Bredouille was invited to contest them. But this was only another opportunity for him to declare that he had no intention of interfering in the case, and at the same time to deny, as his office made it obligatory for him to do, the truth of the accusations leveled against Cauchon.

Two further inquiries were then ordered, one at Orléans, the other at Paris, the latter intended to complete the depositions gathered there between January 10 and 15. The hundred and one articles presented by the promoter, and immediately taken up for discussion, were to serve as a basis for these inquiries.

Before passing over to the Orléans inquiry, it has seemed to us interesting to give a certain number of depositions concerning, particularly, Joan's arrival at Chinon and the examination to which she was put at Poitiers. They are to be found in evidence gathered in Paris in the months that followed, or at Orléans and at Rouen; but whatever their date, it is best to put them in their logical order, to place them where they belong in the development of Joan's story.

The little escort was, as we have seen, eleven days on the way; on February 23, toward noon, they arrived at Chinon. From one of the previous stages, Sainte Catherine de Fierbois, Joan had sent a letter to Charles VII to advise him of her coming. We know that, after long hesitations, the King agreed to receive her, and that she convinced him at their first interview that "he was the true heir of France and the King's son." However, he refused to put any trust in Joan until she had been examined by some clerics and theologians.

The examination took place at Poitiers, and the questionings must have occupied about three weeks of the month of March. The depositions that follow will furnish us with some details on this subject, but it will always be regretted that the text of the inquiry itself—the judges' questions and Joan's replies—has not been preserved. What a priceless document that would have been, enabling us to see Joan, interrogated in all good faith and replying with perfect assurance at the very moment when she felt her mission to be on the point of fulfillment! Some of her answers only have been preserved by Seguin Seguin, that excellent Dominican friar who was still alive at the time of the rehabilitation. We possess also a résumé of the opinion of the Poitiers doctors, but it gives no details except that "one can find no evil in her, but only goodness, humility, virginity, devoutness, honesty, and simplicity."

On several occasions during her condemnatory trial Joan was to refer her judges to that examination at Poitiers, which was certainly conducted in the most thorough fashion. Its purpose was to ferret out evidence of diabolical possession, fraud, or simulation, the marks of the false visionary that she might have been. Traps were laid for her, as they were to be at Rouen, though in quite another spirit, and her everyday behavior was closely watched. On the other hand, Queen Yolanda of Sicily, Charles VII's mother-in-law, assisted by some matrons and ladies of her train, examined Joan in private to see if she was a virgin; and, as we have just seen, the Poitiers judges did not omit to report the result of this examination in their conclusions. In actual fact, according to the thought of the times, Joan's virginity was something like a confirmation of the truth of her mission; if she declared herself to be God's instrument she must be His entirely. Besides, Joan had taken the name of "the Maid"; she knew that entire innocence was the reverse side of the medal of perfect charity. And the cult of the Virgin, which had, in the course of the Middle Ages, undergone the great development with which we are familiar, had accustomed men's minds to this idea of the importance of virginity in the consecrated life. Cauchon himself was to think no differently.

THE PRESIDENT OF THE CHAMBER OF ACCOUNTS

Simon Charles

One of the most important men in the kingdom, he was president of the Chamber of Accounts. In 1429, he had been no more than master of the Court of Requests, but a man devoted to the royal cause and enjoying Charles VII's confidence. It is perhaps he who most faithfully records the reactions of the King, with whom he was intimate. On reading him one feels that Joan's relations with the King were a perpetual struggle between belief and doubt. The contrast between this elusive man, a mass of hesitations and withdrawals, and the character of Joan, unshakable in her conviction and fidelity, is tragic from the start.

> The year when Joan went in search of the King, I had been sent by him on an embassy to Venice, and I returned about March, when I heard from Jean de Metz, who had brought her, that she was with the King. I know that when she arrived at Chinon there had been a discussion in the Council as to whether the King should entertain her or not. At first they asked her why she had come and what she wanted. She did not wish to say anything without having spoken to the King, but she

was pressed in the King's name to explain the reason for her mission. She said that she had two reasons, for which she had been sent by the King of Heaven: one was to raise the siege of Orléans, the other to lead the King to Rheims for his anointing and coronation. When they heard this, certain of the King's counselors said that he must put no trust whatever in Joan, and others said that since she claimed to have been sent by God and had something to say to the King, the King ought at least to hear her.

However, the King wanted her to be examined first by the clerks and churchmen; which was done. And finally, though with difficulty, it was decided that the King should hear her. When she entered the castle of Chinon to come into his presence, the King, on the advice of his principal courtiers, hesitated to speak to her until the moment when it was reported to him that Robert de Baudricourt had written him a letter, saying that he had sent a woman to him, that she had been escorted through the territory of the King's enemies, and that she had, almost miraculously, forded many rivers in order to come to the King. Because of that letter the King was impelled to hear her, and Joan was accorded an audience. When the King learned that she was approaching, he withdrew behind the others; Joan, however, recognized him perfectly, made him a bow, and spoke to him for some minutes. And after hearing her, the King appeared to be joyous. Then, still not wanting to do anything without the advice of the churchmen, he sent Joan off to Poitiers to be examined by the clerks of the University of Poitiers. When he learned that they had examined her, and was told that they had found nothing but good in her, the King had armor made for her and entrusted some soldiers to her, and she was put in command of the conduct of the war.

Joan was very simple in all her actions, except in the conduct of war, in which she was altogether an expert.

I have heard from the King's own lips some very high praise for Joan. That was at Saint Benoît sur Loire, where the King took pity on her for the hardships she endured and commanded her to take a rest. Then Joan burst into tears and said to the King that he must have no doubts and that he would have his whole kingdom and would be crowned within a short time. And she scolded the soldiers most severely when she saw them doing anything that she thought they ought not to do.

About the events at Orléans, I know nothing except by hearsay, for I was not present there. But there is one thing that I heard from Lord de Gaucourt about the time when she was at Orléans. On the day when they captured the Bastille des Augustins,[1] it had already been decided by the commanders of the King's army that any attack or charge was out of the question, and this same lord de Gaucourt was ordered to guard the gates and prevent anyone from breaking out. But Joan was dissatisfied with this decision. It was her opinion that the garrison and townsmen ought to rush out together and assault the bastille, and many of the soldiers and the men of Orléans were in agreement with her. Joan called the lord de Gaucourt a wicked man. "Whether you like it or not," she said, "the soldiers will charge, and they will win as they have done in other places." And despite the lord de Gaucourt, the soldiers who were in the town broke out and made an assault on the Bastille des Augustins, which they captured. And from what I have heard from this lord de Gaucourt, he was in great danger himself.

... Joan was with the King when he came to the city of Troyes, through which he had to pass on his way to Rheims to be crowned. But at the moment when he arrived before the city the soldiers saw that the provisions were exhausted, became dispirited, and were on

---

[1] May 6, 1429. See the following chapter, beginning on p. 126.

the point of retreating. But Joan told the King to have no fear, for the town would be his next day. Then she picked up her standard, and a number of foot soldiers followed her, and these she ordered to cut faggots to fill the moat. They cut a great number, and the next day Joan cried, "Charge!" as a signal to throw the faggots into the moat. At the sight of this, the people of Troyes feared an assault and sent to the King to negotiate a surrender. And the King made terms with the townsmen and rode into Troyes with great ceremony, Joan carrying her standard beside him.

A little after this the King rode out of Troyes with his army and went to Châlons, and after that to Rheims. Joan said to him, "Have no fear. The people of Rheims will come out to meet you." And before they reached the city of Rheims, the citizens surrendered. The King was afraid that they might resist. For he had no artillery or engines with which to besiege them had they proved recalcitrant. But Joan bade the King ride boldly forward, for if he would but advance courageously he would recover his whole kingdom.

ONE OF THE KING'S COUNSELORS

François Garivel

(The King's counselor general in the Court of Aids—aged forty)

I remember the time of Joan the Maid's arrival. The King sent her to Poitiers, and she was lodged in the house of the late Master Jean Rabateau,[2] then royal advocate to the court of Parlement. And by the King's orders,

---

[2] Jean Rabateau, privy counselor, was advocate general to Parlement, which had been transferred from Paris, then under English occupation, to Poitiers in the "free zone" in 1427. He had died in 1444, after having been president

various solemn doctors and lawyers were called to Poitiers: to wit, Master Pierre de Versailles,[3] then abbot of Talmont and afterward Bishop of Meaux; Jean Lambert and Guillaume Aymeri of the Dominican order and Pierre Seguin of the Carmelite order, all learned in the Holy Scriptures; Matthieu Mesnage and Guillaume Lemarié, bachelors in theology; and several others of the King's counselors, licentiates in civil and canon law, who examined Joan on several occasions over a period of about three weeks....

... When they asked Joan why she called the King Dauphin and not King, she said that she would not call him King until he had been crowned and anointed at Rheims, the city to which she had resolved to lead him....

A PROFESSOR OF THEOLOGY

Seguin Seguin[4]

(Professor of theology, dean of the faculty of Poitiers, a Dominican friar—aged seventy)

The Chronicle of the Maid, which narrates the events of the time, says of him that he was "a very sour man". That is not the impression that he gives us. One cannot at any rate deny him a sense of humor, even when it is turned against himself....

---

of Parlement, which had been reinstated in Paris after the liberation of the capital.

[3] Pierre de Versailles, a former monk of Saint Denis and professor of theology, was destined to be Bishop first of Digne and then of Meaux. At the Council of Basel, he represented René d'Anjou and afterward the King of France himself. He was an ardent defender of Pope Eugenius IV, who entrusted him with a mission to Greece. He died in about 1446.

[4] Not the Seguin Seguin whose testimony we shall read after Garivel's.

Before I knew Joan, I had heard of her from Master Pierre de Versailles, professor of theology, who died Bishop of Meaux. He had heard about her from some soldiers who had gone to intercept her when she was on her way to find the King. They had laid an ambush to capture her and rob her and her company. But at the moment when they were about to do so, they had found themselves unable to stir from their positions; and so Joan had escaped without difficulty together with her company.

... I saw her for the first time at Poitiers. The King's Council had met there in the house of one La Macée, and with them was the lord Archbishop of Rheims, then chancellor of France.[5]

Besides myself there had been summoned Master Jean Lombard, professor of theology in the University of Paris, Guillaume Le Maire, canon of Poitiers and bachelor in theology, Guillaume Aymeri, professor of theology and a Dominican, Friar Pierre Turelure, Master Jacques Madelon, and several others whom I have forgotten. We were told that we had the King's orders to interrogate Joan and to report our opinion of her to the royal Council; and we were sent to the house of Master Jean Rabateau at Poitiers, where Joan was lodged, to examine her.

When we arrived, we put various questions to Joan, and, among other things, Master Jean Lombard asked her why she had come, saying that the King was most anxious to know what had impelled her to come to him. And she answered, boldly, that when she was watching the cattle her voice had spoken to her, saying that God had great pity for the people of France, and that Joan must go to France. On hearing this, she had begun to weep. Then the voice had told her to go to

---

[5] Regnault de Chartres. It was he who presided over the commission charged with examining her. As is well known, this dignitary was to join the party of Joan's enemies when events turned against her and she was taken prisoner.

Vaucouleurs, and that she would find a captain there who would lead her safely into France and into the King's presence, and that she must not fear. And so she had done and had come before the King without any hindrance. Master Guillaume Aymeri said to her, "You said the voice told you that God wishes to deliver the people of France from their present calamities. If He wishes to deliver them there is no need of soldiers." Joan replied, "In God's name, the soldiers will fight, and God will give them the victory." Master Guillaume was satisfied with her answer.

... I asked her what tongue her voice spoke, and she answered, "A better tongue than you do." And indeed I speak with a Limousin accent. And I asked her again whether she believed in God. She answered, "Yes, more than you do." And then I said to her, "God cannot wish us to believe in you unless he sends us a sign, to show that we should believe in you. We cannot advise the King to entrust you with soldiers, whom you would run into danger, merely on your bare assertion. Have you nothing more to say?" She answered, "In God's name, I have not come to Poitiers to make signs. But lead me to Orléans, and I will show you the signs I was sent to make." She went on to ask for as many soldiers as she should need and to be allowed to go to Orléans. And then she prophesied to me and those others present four things that were then still to come and that fell out as she foretold. First she said that the English would be defeated—that the siege they had laid to Orléans would be raised and that the town of Orléans would be freed of the English, but that she would send them a summons first. Then she said that the King would be anointed at Rheims. Thirdly, she said that the city of Paris would return to the King's rule, and then that the Duke of Orléans would come back from England. I have seen all this come true.

... We reported everything to the King's Council and concluded that, in view of our urgent need and the peril to the city of Orléans, the King might well make use of her help and send her to that city.

... We inquired—I and the other commissioners—about Joan's life and morals, and we found that she was a good Christian, that she lived the life of a Catholic, and that she had never been found neglectful of her duties. And to get further information as to her character, some women were sent to her, who reported to the Council on her actions and conduct. I believe that Joan was sent by God, because the King and the people under his rule had lost all hope and everyone thought that they should retreat. And I well remember how Joan was asked why she carried a standard. She replied that she did not wish to use her sword and did not wish to kill anyone.

Joan was very angry whenever she heard God's name taken in vain in an oath. She loathed men who swore. She told La Hire, whose habit and custom it was to swear frequently, to swear no more, and when he was tempted to swear by God to swear by his staff.

AN ADVOCATE TO THE COURT OF PARLEMENT

Jean Barbin

(Doctor in law—aged fifty)

He speaks about Joan and the clerks who examined her.

The clerks' final conclusions, after their interrogations and examinations, were that there was no harm in her, and nothing in her life contrary to the Catholic faith. Given the urgent state in which the King and his kingdom were, since both he and those who remained faithful to him were in despair and had no hope of help of any kind except from God, they reported that the King might well make use of her aid. And during their deliberations, a certain Master Jean Érault, professor of theology, related that he had heard, in addition, a prophecy by a certain Marie d'Avignon[6] who had come to the King years ago and told him that the kingdom of France would undergo great sufferings and would sustain many disasters. She spoke, too, of having had frequent visions concerning the desolation of France. In one of them Marie saw many pieces of armor that were brought before her, which frightened her. For she was afraid that she would be forced to put this armor on. But she was told to fear nothing, and that it was not she who would have to wear this armor, but that a Maid who would come after her would wear it and deliver the kingdom of France from its enemies. He firmly believed, he said, that Joan was this Maid of whom Marie d'Avignon had spoken.

The soldiers considered her a saint, for she behaved in such a godly way when with the army, both in her deeds and her words, that no one could have uttered a reproach against her.

I have heard Master Pierre de Versailles say that once, while this Master Pierre was at Loches in Joan's company, the people seized her horse by the legs and kissed her hands and feet. He told Joan that it was wrong of her to permit this, that it was not seemly, and that she must beware of this sort of thing, for it drove men to idolatry. Joan replied, "In truth, I should not know how to protect myself from such things of myself, if God did not protect me."

Joan was, in my opinion, a good Catholic, and all that she did was godly. What makes me say this is that she was reproachless in all things, in her conversation, her eating and drinking, and in everything else; and I have never heard anything unfavorable said about her, but have

---

[6] She was called "the Gascon woman of Avignon", and her prophecies aroused great interest at the beginning of the fifteenth century.

always heard her reputed and thought of as a good Catholic.

THE GRAND MASTER OF THE KING'S HOUSEHOLD

Raoul de Gaucourt

Another important figure in the kingdom, he was a knight who had fought as a crusader in the expedition to Nicopolis and had distinguished himself in 1415 at the defense of Harfleur, after which he was made prisoner by Henry V. He remained in England as a prisoner for thirteen years. On his return, Charles VII made him first chamberlain and captain of Chinon. Afterward he was entrusted with several confidential missions, among them an embassy to Eugenius IV, of which Simon Charles was also a member. He had been governor of Dauphiné, and then, in 1453, grand master of the King's household. Louis XI was afterward to dismiss him, regardless of his great age—he was then ninety—and his loyal services. He was present on the first occasion when Joan was received by the King in audience. He was a man of eighty-five at the time of testifying.

> I was present at Chinon, and in the castle, when Joan arrived, and I saw that poor shepherd girl when she appeared before His Royal Majesty in great humility and utter simplicity. I heard her speak the following words to the King: "Most noble Lord Dauphin, I have come and am sent by God to bring help to you and your kingdom." When the King had seen and heard her, he wanted more information about her. So he put her in the care of Guillaume Bellier, who was the master of his house, the captain of Troyes, and my lieutenant at Chinon. His wife was a most devout woman with a very

high reputation. The King further ordered that Joan should be examined by clerks, prelates, and doctors to discover whether what she said could or should be believed. This was done. For her deeds and words were examined by clerks for three whole weeks and more, both at Poitiers and at Chinon. Finally, when these clerks had duly examined her, they said that there was no harm either in her or in what she said; and then, after many interrogations, she was asked what signs she could show to prove that her words should be believed. She replied that the sign that she would show would be the raising of the siege of Orléans and the bringing of help to that city.

Joan was moderate in eating and drinking, and there issued from her lips no words that were not virtuous, edifying, and a good example to men. She was extremely chaste, and I have never heard that she ever had a man with her at night; but she always had another woman sleeping in her room at night. She often made confession; she devoted herself assiduously to prayers, heard the Mass every day, and frequently took the sacrament of the Eucharist; and she never allowed unfitting or blasphemous words to be uttered in her company. For that she detested.

ONE OF THE KING'S SQUIRES

Gobert Thibault

(Aged fifty)

I was at Chinon when Joan came to find the King, who was then residing at Chinon. But I had no great acquaintance with her there. I knew her better afterward. For when the King decided to go to Poitiers, Joan was taken there and lodged in the house of Master Jean Rabateau. I know that Joan was interrogated and examined at Poitiers by the late Master Pierre de Versailles, professor of theology, then abbot of Talmont, and at the time of his death Bishop of Meaux, also by Master Jean Érault, professor of theology; I accompanied them on the orders of the late Bishop of Castres. She was, as I have said, lodged in the house of one Rabateau, and it was in his house that Versailles and Érault spoke to Joan in my presence. When we arrived, Joan appeared before us, and she tapped me on the shoulder, saying that she would like to have a few men of my sort with her. Then Pierre de Versailles said to Joan that they had been sent to her by the King, and she replied, "Then I suppose that you have come to question me. But I do not know A from B." Then we asked her why she had come, and she answered, "I have come in the name of the King of Heaven to raise the siege of Orléans and to lead the King to Rheims for his coronation and his anointing." And she asked us if we had paper and ink, saying to Master Jean Érault, "Write what I tell you. 'You, Suffort, Classidas, and La Poule, I charge you, in the King of Heaven's name, to return to England.' " [7]

And on that occasion Versailles and Érault did nothing else that I remember; and Joan stayed at Poitiers as long as the King did.... I saw the men who brought Joan to the King, that is to say, Jean de Metz, Jean Coulon, and Bertrand Pollichon [*sic*], with whom she was most familiar and friendly. Once I was present when these men who had brought her told the late Bishop of Castres,[8] then the King's confessor, how they had crossed Burgundy and the districts occupied by the enemy. They had passed through without any hindrance, which astonished them greatly.

---

[7] The opening of her first letter of remonstrance, addressed to the English. See the next chapter; Suffolk, Glansdale, and John de la Pole were then besieging Orléans.

[8] Gérard Machet.

I have heard the late confessor say that he had seen it written that a Maid was to come who would help the King of France....

I was not present at the action before Orléans, but common fame had it that everything had been thanks to her, and that the outcome had been almost miraculous. I arrived at Beaugency on the day when Lord Talbot, who had been captured at Patay,[9] was brought there, and Joan was leaving the place with her soldiers for the town of Jargeau, which was stormed. The English were there put to flight, and Joan returned to Tours, where my lord the King was; and from Tours they took the road to Rheims, for the King's anointing and coronation. And Joan told the King and the soldiers to go boldly forward, that everything would turn out well, and that they must fear nothing. For they would find no one able to harm them and would not even meet with any resistance. She also said that she had no doubts about their having enough men, for many would follow them.

And Joan called the soldiers together between the towns of Troyes and Auxerre, and there were many of them, for everyone followed her. And the King and his people reached Rheims without hindrance. In fact, the King met with no resistance. The gates of all the cities and towns were opened to him.

Joan was a good Christian; she gladly heard the Mass every day and often received the Eucharist. She was greatly annoyed when she heard swearing, and that was a good sign, as the King's noble confessor said, and he gathered most careful information about her deeds and her life.

In the field, she was always with the soldiers, and I have heard many of Joan's intimates say that they never had any desire for her. That is to say, that sometimes

---

[9] See the details of the Loire campaign in the following chapter.

they had a carnal urge, but never dared to give way to it; and they believed that it was impossible to desire her. And often if they were talking among themselves about the sins of the flesh, and using words that might have aroused lecherous thoughts, when they saw her and drew near to her, they could not speak like this any more. Suddenly their sexual feelings were checked. I have questioned several of those who often slept at night close to Joan, and they answered me as I have said, adding that they never felt sensual desire when they saw her.

A COMPANION AT ARMS

Simon Beaucroix

(Squire, living at Paris, at the Hôtel Neuf—aged fifty)

Joan was a good and God-fearing Catholic. I well remember that when I was with her I never had a desire to sin.

Joan always slept in the company of young girls and did not like to lie with old women. She loathed oaths and blasphemies; she rebuked swearers and blasphemers. In the field, she would never let any of her company loot anything; and she was never willing to eat any provisions that she knew were looted. Once a Scotsman informed her that he had eaten some meat from a stolen calf; she was very annoyed and tried to slap the Scotsman for it.

She would never allow immoral women to come to the army and join the soldiers. That is why not one of them would ever have dared come near Joan. When she found any, she drove them away, unless the soldiers were willing to take them for their wives.

I think that she was a true Catholic who feared God and kept His commandments, and that she obeyed the precepts of the Church to the very best of her ability.

She showed pity not only to the French, but also to the enemy. I know that, for I was with her for a long time, and very often I helped her to put on her armor.

Joan was very upset and most displeased when some good women came to greet her and showed her signs of adoration. This annoyed her.

And lastly, here is a third companion at arms, who was particularly impressed with Joan's competence in the field of strategy.

ANOTHER COMPANION AT ARMS

Thibault d'Armagnac or de Termes

(A knight and captain of Chartres—aged fifty)

The battle of Patay
Joan had promised the French that none—or very few—of their men would be killed or wounded. Which proved correct. For only one of our men was killed: a nobleman of my company.... Except in matters of war, she was simple and innocent. But in the leading and drawing up of armies and in the conduct of war, in disposing an army for battle and haranguing the soldiers, she behaved like the most experienced captain in all the world, like one with a whole lifetime of experience.

In contrast to these soldiers, who were nearly all aristocrats, here is a man of the people, a simple tinker, a traveling merchant. He happened to be at Rheims at the time of the anointing, and, being a compatriot of theirs, made the acquaintance of Joan's father, Jacques d'Arc, and his son Pierre.

A TINKER

Husson Lemaître

(A native of Viville, near La Motte en Bassigny, some nine miles from Domremy, then living at Rouen—aged fifty)

I did not see Joan or have any acquaintance with her until the moment when she came to Rheims to have the King crowned. I was then staying in that town; and Joan's father and Pierre, her brother, were there too, and they became close friends of my wife and myself, for we were compatriots. They even called my wife, "Neighbor".

I was in my native country when Joan went to Vaucouleurs, to my lord Robert de Baudricourt, to ask him to take her, or to have her taken, to the King of France. And they said in those parts that this was a grace of God, and that Joan was led by the spirit of God....

Joan requested Robert de Baudricourt to give her men to lead her to my lord the Dauphin, or so I heard; Joan had the reputation thereabouts of being a good and modest young woman.... I have heard it said that while Joan was being taken from Vaucouleurs to the King, some of the soldiers of her escort pretended to be the enemy troops, and that those who were with her made a show of being about to take to their heels. But she said to them, "In the name of God, do not run away. They will do us no harm." And, to judge by what they said when she came to court, she recognized the King, although she had never seen him before. And finally, she led the King to Rheims without difficulty; that is where I saw her. From Rheims, the King went to Corbigny,[10] and then to Château Thierry, which surrendered to him.

---

[10] A priory to which the kings went after their anointing to touch sufferers from scrofula.

Here is the testimony of a woman who was really intimate with Joan after the anointing, for Joan lodged with her. She was a very intelligent woman and in a good position, since her husband, René de Bouligny, had been in his lifetime the King's adviser on financial matters.

JOAN OF ARC'S HOSTESS

Marguerite La Touroulde

(Widow of the late Master René de Bouligny—aged sixty-four)

When Joan came to the King at Chinon, I was at Bourges, where the Queen was. At that time, there was such misery and such shortage of money in this kingdom, and in the parts obeying the King, that things were in a pitiable state. And even those who were loyal to the King were all in despair. I know this because my husband was at the time receiver general, and he had not four crowns all told, of the King's money or his own. And the city of Orléans was besieged by the English, and there was no way of coming to its help. And it was in the midst of this misery that Joan arrived. And I firmly believe that she came from God and was sent to relieve the King and the people still obedient to him. For at that moment there was no hope except in God.

I only saw Joan, however, at the time of the King's return from Rheims, where he had been anointed. The King came to the city of Bourges, where the Queen was and I with her. When the King drew near, the Queen went out to meet him at the town of Selles in Berry, and I with her. And as the Queen went out to meet the King, Joan rode ahead and greeted the Queen. She was then led into Bourges and, by the command of the lord d'Albret, lodged with me, although my late husband had told me that she would be staying at the house of a certain Jeanne Duchesne. And she was in my house for three weeks, sleeping, eating, and drinking there. And almost every night I slept with Joan, and I never saw or noticed anything uncanny about her. But she behaved and continued to behave like an honest and Christian woman. She confessed very often, gladly heard the Mass, and often asked me to go to Matins; and at her request I did go and took her there several times.

Sometimes we talked, and someone said to Joan that of course she was not afraid of joining in an attack because she knew that she would not be killed. She answered that she had no more assurance of that than anyone else in the fight. And sometimes she told us how she had been examined by some clerks and had said in answer to them, "There is more in our Lord's books than in yours."

I afterward heard the men who led her to the King talking, and heard them say that at the outset they thought her presumptuous and that they meant to put her to the test. But once they were on the road, escorting her, they were ready to do anything that she wanted and were as anxious to bring her before the King as she was herself to get there. They could never have denied her anything that she asked. They said that at the outset they wanted to make sensual advances to her, but at the moment when they were about to speak they were so ashamed that they dared not tell her their intentions or utter so much as a word. I heard from Joan that the Duke of Lorraine asked to see her when he was ill; and Joan had gone to speak with him, and had told him that he was sinning and that unless he reformed his ways he would not be cured. She urged him to take back his good wife.[11]

Joan had a horror of the game of dice.

---

[11] Margaret of Bavaria, whom Charles of Lorraine had deserted for a girl called Alison Dumay.

Joan was very simple and ignorant and knew absolutely nothing, in my opinion, except the art of war. I remember that several women came to my house while Joan was there, bringing paternosters [rosaries] and other holy objects for her to touch. This made her laugh, and she said to me, "You touch them! They will be as good from your touch as from mine." She was very liberal in her almsgiving and gave most gladly to the poor and destitute, saying that she had been sent for the consolation of the poor and destitute.

And I saw her several times in the bath and in the hot-room, and so far as I could see I believe that she was a virgin. And from all that I know of her she was absolutely ignorant except in the matter of arms. For I have seen her ride a horse and wield a lance as well as the finest soldier, and the soldiers themselves were most astonished by this.

CHAPTER 5

Orléans

It had been decided that after the inquiry on Lorraine soil another should be held at Orléans. It was opened on February 22, 1456, and presided over by the Archbishop of Rheims, Jean Jouvenel des Ursins, in person. The two other apostolic commissioners, Guillaume Chartier and Richard Olivier, had not been able to join him, nor had Jean Bréhal, who had appointed Friar Jean Patin as his deputy. But Guillaume Bouillé was there.

If one attempts to assess the impression that the apostolic commission must now have had from the hearings of the case, which had begun slightly more than three months before, one must conclude that Joan would now have seemed to them a simple and pious girl who had been the victim of a political prosecution that had, in addition, been odiously faked—of one of those prosecutions, in fact, that are the almost inevitable product of foreign occupation.

At Orléans, everything changed. For the first time, the idea of a miracle must have dawned in the minds of the members of the bench. When they listened to the testimony gathered there between February 22 and March 16, they must have begun to think of Joan as sent by God, or rather have said to themselves that an intermediate belief was hardly possible: either her actions were the outcome of divine intervention, or they were of diabolical inspiration; in any case, they did not fit into the natural and normal framework of life and could not be explained by simple premonition, or even by auto-suggestion, as her deeds and behavior at Vaucouleurs and Chinon might be.

Here one must embark upon a parenthesis, for this rehabilitation case has given rise to controversies centered on just these statements about events at Orléans. We must repeat, therefore, that for a certain number of historians, according to whom the whole affair was really directed by Charles VII, this unanimous agreement of the witnesses in declaring that the circumstances of the relief of Orléans were beyond human understanding was merely a proof that the depositions were cunningly dictated and coordinated.

Now if the statements of all these people who played a direct or indirect part in the siege of Orléans are, in fact, unanimous, it must be observed that they emanate from the most diverse personalities. It would be credible, at a pinch, that Charles VII might have put pressure on Dunois, his cousin; that he might have had some influence on the depositions of such courtiers as Raoul de Gaucourt or Simon Charles would be still more plausible. But it is rather difficult to agree that his will could have been so powerful with the Duke of Alençon, who was then on bad terms with him and who, at the very moment of the rehabilitation trial, was plotting with surprising treachery to hand the Cotentin over to the English. And how could one suppose that the royal will alone could bring all the unimportant people of Orléans flocking to testify for Joan, as happened on March 16, the day on which Guillaume de la Salle, the notary whose duty it was to take these declarations, recorded thirty-six, all fervently in her favor, some from well-known citizens of the place, others from obscure inhabitants?

What is more, all these people had been far from waiting for the rehabilitation trial before considering Joan to be an envoy from Heaven and the delivery of their city a miracle. The procession that took place annually on May 8, the anniversary of the raising of the siege, is vouched for, as we have seen, as early as 1435. It is certain, besides, that from as early as 1440 Joan's mother lived at Orléans, received a pension from the people of the city, and was nursed at their expense when she was ill. None of this had been at the instance of Charles VII, but by the decision of the aldermen, or municipal councilors, who every month voted the sum of forty-eight Paris sous "for her nourishment".[1] These same inhabitants had accompanied Isabelle Romée, as we have seen, to the ceremony at Notre Dame that marked the opening of the case, and their enthusiasm had not failed to provoke some disorder there. There can be no doubt that if any royal intervention took place it was not necessary in their case. In fact, the evidence of these people who underwent the daily sufferings and privations of seven months of siege, who waited and struggled and made personal sacrifices, and then found themselves liberated when they had lost all hope, must be allowed a considerable value; for it is their own stories that they tell us.

Finally, one has Jean d'Aulon's evidence for the extraordinary character of this siege. Even if we suppose that the tribunal cleverly managed the depositions of the witnesses who filed before it, this could not have been true in his

---

[1] As a standard of comparison, a pint of good wine was then worth a sou.

case, for he testified before the ecclesiastical court at Lyons, and his evidence was sent from there in writing.²

What indubitably emerges from the account of the rehabilitation suit is that no one spoke of Orléans without emotion, that to a contemporary mind the supernatural had at that place interfered most violently with events, upsetting all the laws of probability or of the "humanly possible". And on this point it would be idle to seek for any other cause behind the unanimity of the witnesses except a unanimity of opinion. What is more, there is, as will be seen, a fervor about their stories that cannot be false. A historian is at liberty not to share this fervor or the convictions on which it is based, but in all good faith he is compelled to take note of it. When one reads the report, everything seems a great deal simpler than one had supposed. Right or wrong, the people of Orléans believed in miracles and had no need of urging to see the raising of the siege of Orléans as miraculous.

The apostolic commissioners were compelled by their office to distrust the hypothesis of a miracle. (The Church, after them, was to wait more than four hundred years before

---

² Let us deal with Hanotaux' singular error on this point. "At the beginning of the case," he writes, "in 1456, the Archbishop of Rheims ... begged one of the principal witnesses, Jean d'Aulon, to send his testimony." For him the fact that the Archbishop stated in his letter that the purpose of the English in accusing Joan of heresy was to strike at the King himself through her reveals a political "theme" that must have influenced the whole case (*Jeanne d'Arc*, p. 122). But it was *at the end of the case* that Jean Jouvenel des Ursins expressed himself in this way. His letter is dated April 20, 1456, and the hearings of the witnesses were to be complete on May 10. If we take no account of the preliminary inquiries, the hearings had begun on the previous December 15. By the time of his letter, the Archbishop of Rheims had every reason to have come to that conclusion, and what he said agrees well enough with the facts to excuse one from seeing in it any attempt to prejudge the case.

officially proclaiming Joan to be a saint.) Nevertheless, as happened to Guillaume d'Estouteville after the inquiry he conducted, they must have had, for the first time during the case, some feeling of supernatural happenings when they heard the testimony of the Orléans witnesses.

The circumstances of the siege of Orléans are too well known for it to be necessary to recall them here. We will confine ourselves, therefore—merely to facilitate the reading of the depositions that follow—to a brief enumeration of the chief episodes.

Orléans had been besieged since October 12, 1428, when after pillaging and destroying the sanctuary of Notre Dame de Cléry, Salisbury had come at the head of a strong English army to besiege the city of Prince [Duke] Charles, who had been a prisoner in England since Agincourt. Both these misdeeds had caused lively indignation in France, for it was against the customs of feudal honor to lay siege to a city whose lord was a prisoner. But the siege of Orléans, the key to the Loire, represented to the English the culmination of a fruitful series of expeditions that had enabled this same Salisbury, since the previous August, to take possession successively of the country between Dreux and Chartres, and of the fortresses of Toury, Le Puiset, Janville, Meung, and Beaugency. When he was killed on October 24, during an attack on the Bastille des Tourelles, which commanded the bridge of Orléans from the left bank, Salisbury was immediately replaced by Suffolk, Thomas Scales, and the famous Talbot.

Since this October 12, despite a passionate resistance—the people of Orléans had themselves gone to the extreme of demolishing their own suburbs, which were their pride, so that the English army should find no shelter there—the investment had only grown closer. An attempt led by Charles of Bourbon to intercept a convoy of provisions on its way

ORLÉANS

to the English camp had turned into a disaster and had then become ludicrous. This was the famous "Battle of the Herrings"—so called because the convoy's chief provisions were barrels of salt herring. It took place on February 12, 1429, the day before Joan left Vaucouleurs.

The English had decided to take their time and reduce the city by starvation; and they methodically constructed a whole series of works intended little by little to cut off its communications with the outside world. In addition to the Bastille des Tourelles, which they had stormed at the opening of the siege, the Bastille des Augustins, constructed on the ruins of a former convent of that name, the Bastille of Saint Loup, the redoubt or bulwark of La Croix Boissée, and the post of Saint Jean le Blanc were the chief of these works, which gradually enclosed the city.

After having convinced the King and dispatched letters of remonstrance to the captains of the besieging army, Joan made for Blois; and it was from there, on Wednesday, April 7, with banners flying and the clergy in the van, that the royal army[3] set out toward Orléans, loudly singing the *Veni Creator*.

---

[3] How great exactly were the forces present? The question has let loose floods of ink, and the estimates of historians vary on this point in the most disquieting fashion: from three thousand to twelve thousand fighting men on the English side and, in exact symmetry, though generally in inverse proportion, from twelve thousand to three thousand on the French. Each historian, moreover, supports his theory with absolutely definite and conclusive arguments.

The most recent works give six to seven thousand men both on the English side and the French, and this represents at least an honest mean.

Must one regret the lack of precise figures? Our age believes in figures, but one is invariably wrong when one tries to reduce history, at any rate medieval history, to numerical proportions. In the actual case of a siege, we must not forget that a number of elements would, anyhow, come in to falsify calculations. For instance, methods of defense were then much superior to methods of attack (the exact opposite of our modern situation). The Duke

The first question was how to get a convoy of provisions into the city, and this was done on the evenings of Thursday the twenty-eighth and Friday the twenty-ninth of April. Joan entered Orléans herself, went to the cathedral amid the joyful demonstrations of the people, and lodged at the house of the royal treasurer, Jacques Boucher. Then comes the epic that we know: a second convoy and the relief force got in beneath the eyes of the English besiegers on May 4; the English lost in succession the Saint Loup bastille (May 4) and the Bastilles des Augustins (May 6) and des Tourelles (May 7). On Sunday, May 8, Talbot ordered his troops to retire. Orléans was relieved.

We will not give any more accounts of the incredible enthusiasm of contemporaries. Throughout the whole kingdom and even abroad, notably in Italy, in Flanders, and in Germany, there were veritable paeans of rejoicing, expressed in the form of hymns and poems. It is most touching to find among these voices those of the two great poets of the time, Alain Chartier and Christine de Pisan. As for Charles of Orléans, the prince of poets, when he learned of the city's deliverance he ordered a robe "of fine Brussels

---

of Alençon, who took no part in the operations before Orléans but who afterward examined the siege-works, declared that with a few soldiers he would undertake to hold out in them for six or seven days against a contingent of any size.

The most reasonable solution still lies, it seems, in trusting the unanimity of contemporary accounts. It is improbable that a captain as brave as Dunois—who had, with La Hire, brilliantly raised the siege of Montargis two years previously (in 1427)—would not already have done everything in his power to relieve Orléans. When he, a captain used to heroic exploits, speaking of a situation in which his honor was involved—for he had been entrusted with the defense of the place—declares to us that the King's army was not sufficient to offer any further resistance to an attack by the besiegers, we must take his word for it.

scarlet" to be made for Joan, also a *"huque"* (a short blouse worn under a robe) of "deep green". Crimson and dark green were the colors of the Orléans livery, and it was the draper Jean Luillier, whose deposition we shall read, who provided the cloth for this, together with "white satin, samite, and other stuffs", for the sum of twelve gold crowns.[4]

No less famous and significant are the documents that prove the panic into which the English army was thrown by this unprecedented exploit. Some days after the raising of the siege, the regent Bedford, who had fallen back on Paris, was to address letters to the captains of the Norman ports forbidding them to let any deserter take a ship for England; and we know of the royal commands of May which were repeated in December 1430, ordering sanctions against soldiers who refused to cross over to France "for fear of the sorceries of the Maid".

THE BASTARD OF ORLÉANS

Jean, Count of Dunois and Longueville, is too famous a person for it to be necessary to dwell on him here. He was the bastard son of Louis of Orléans; and everyone knows how, after the assassination of Louis by Jean the Fearless, his widow, Valentina of Milan, reconciled the boy to her own children. "Jean is my son as you are", she said. "He has been stolen from me, but I have got him back, and I am sure that none of you will take better vengeance for his father than he." In fact, his whole life was devoted to the reconquest of the kingdom. It was he who was to give the signal for the recovery of Normandy by retaking Verneuil,

---

[4] It is well known that gifts of clothes in the colors of the prince who presented them were very usual in the Middle Ages.

which was occupied by Talbot, and he will be found also at the capitulation of Bordeaux.

From their first meeting, as we shall see, the Bastard took his place among those who had faith in Joan, and never in his life was he to go back on that faith. In contrast to so many others in the royal circle, he was one in whom neither jealousy of her successes nor doubts at her delays would produce any vacillations. In 1431, when Joan was a prisoner, he was to lead a vain campaign in the direction of Rouen; and that was the only serious attempt, except La Hire's attack on Louviers, that was made to free her.

He was fifty-one years old at the time of the rehabilitation.

Dunois

I believe that Joan was sent by God, and that her deeds in the war were the fruit of divine inspiration rather than of human agency.... And this is why: firstly, I was at Orléans, which was then besieged by the English, when certain rumors went round according to which a young woman called the Maid had passed the town of Gien,[5] in the assurance that she was going to the noble Dauphin to raise the siege of Orléans and to lead him to Rheims, there to be anointed. As I was in charge of the city, being lieutenant general in the field, I sent the lord de Villars, seneschal of Beaucaire, and Jamet du Thillay, who was afterward bailiff of Vermandois,[6] to the King for fuller information about this Maid. On their return from their mission to the King, they told me and said in public, before all the people of Orléans, who were most eager to know the truth about the coming of this Maid, that they had themselves

---

[5] Gien was the stage immediately before Sainte Catherine de Fierbois, where, as we know, Joan had a letter written to Charles VII to announce her coming.

[6] He was then captain of Blois.

ORLÉANS

seen her arrive at the King's court in the town of Chinon. They also said that the King had refused to receive her at first, but that she waited for the space of two days until she was permitted to come into the royal presence, although she said again and again that she had come to raise the siege of Orléans and to lead the noble Dauphin to Rheims to be anointed, and that she instantly required a company of soldiers, some horses, and some arms.

After the space of three weeks or a month, during which time the King ordered the Maid to be examined by clerks, prelates, and doctors in theology concerning her acts and sayings to find out if he could safely receive her, the King assembled a great number of soldiers to bring provisions into the city of Orléans. Then, after collecting the opinions of the prelates and doctors, which were that there was no wickedness in the Maid, he sent her in the company of my lord Archbishop of Rheims, then chancellor of France,[7] and of the lord de Gaucourt,[8] at present grand master of the King's household, to the city of Blois. Here there had arrived the men who were taking in the convoy of food, to wit the lord de Rais[9] and de Boussac,[10] the marshal of France, with whom were the lord de Culant,[11] the admiral of France, La Hire,[12] and the lord Ambroise de

---

[7] Regnault de Chartres, who died in 1443.

[8] We have read his deposition already (pp. 116–17). He was then bailiff of Orléans.

[9] Gilles de Laval, the famous "Bluebeard", who died at the stake in 1440.

[10] Jean de la Brosse; he was to take part in all Joan's campaigns.

[11] Louis de Culant. He was to take part in the Loire expedition, after Orléans, and to be left at Saint Denis as defender of the town after its return to the King of France.

[12] His death, which took place in 1443, deprives us of what would have been first-class testimony. La Hire, whose real name was Étienne de Vignolles, is known to have been a captain of mercenaries, and a terrible ravager. A contemporary chronicle (the *Chronicle of Metz*) tells us that he and the Duke of Alençon were the only captains to welcome Joan immediately; he took part in all her battles. His memory was celebrated with that of Dunois at the anniversary ceremonies for the liberation of Orléans.

Loré,[13] who has since become provost of Paris. They, together with the soldiers escorting the convoy of provisions and Joan the Maid, came from the direction of Sologne in regular array straight to the river Loire to the church called Saint Loup,[14] in which was a strong English force. And as the King's army and the soldiers who were bringing in the convoy did not seem to me, or to my lords the other captains, numerous enough to resist and to bring the convoy of provisions into the city, especially as they would require boats and rafts, which it would be difficult to obtain, to carry these provisions over—for it was necessary to go up river and the wind was exactly contrary—Joan spoke to me as follows: "Was it you who advised me to come here, on this side of the river, instead of going straight to where Talbot and the English are?" I answered that I and others, who were the wisest, had given that advice in the belief that it was the best and surest. Then Joan said to me, "In God's name, the counsel of the Lord God is wiser and surer than yours.[15] You thought you had deceived me, but it is you who have deceived yourselves, for I am bringing you better help than ever you got from any soldier or any city. It is the help of the King of Heaven. It does not come through love for me, but from God himself who, on the petition of Saint Louis and Saint Charlemagne, has had pity on the town of Orléans and has refused to suffer the enemy to have both the body of the lord of Orléans and his city."

---

[13] He took part in all Joan's campaigns and was made captain of Lagny. He died provost of Paris in 1446.

[14] We have seen that the English had turned this into a fortified bastille.

[15] Joan, in her impatience to fight, wanted to dash immediately on Orléans; the captains had preferred to take an indirect route, to cross the Loire as far up as Chécy and Jargeau, and to come to Orléans by following the river so as to avoid as many of the fortified bastilles as possible. But the adverse wind delayed this plan and threatened to immobilize the convoy.

ORLÉANS

Immediately, at that very moment, the wind, which had been adverse and had absolutely prevented the ships carrying the provisions for the city of Orléans from putting out, changed and became favorable. Sails were therefore raised, and I brought in the ships and rafts, and with me was Friar Nicolas de Geresme, now grand prior of France.[16] We passed the Church of Saint Loup, in spite of the English. From that moment, I had great hopes of her, greater than before, and I begged her to agree to cross the Loire and enter the city of Orléans, where they were most eager for her. But here she made difficulties, saying that she was unwilling to send her soldiers away since they were all well confessed and repentant and of good will; and therefore she was unwilling to come. I went to find the captains who were in charge of the soldiers, and begged and commanded them, for the King's sake, to agree to Joan's entering the city of Orléans while they, the captains, with their companies went back to Blois. Here they would cross the Loire to come to Orléans, since no nearer crossing could be found. These same captains agreed to my request and consented to cross at Blois.

Then Joan came with me, carrying her standard, which was white and on which was the figure of our Lord holding a fleur-de-lis in His hand. And she crossed the river Loire with La Hire and me, and we entered the town of Orléans together (on Friday, April 29, in the evening). That is the reason why I think that Joan, and all her deeds in war and in battle, were rather God's work than man's: the sudden changing of the wind, I mean, after she had spoken, which gave hope of aid, and the bringing in of the provisions in spite of the English, who were much stronger than the royal army, and the fact, furthermore, that this young girl swore that she had had a vision

---

[16] Of the Order of the Knights of Rhodes.

in which Saint Louis and Charlemagne prayed God for the safety of the King and of this city.

And I have another reason for believing that her deeds were of God. I wanted to go and fetch the soldiers who had crossed at Blois to come and help those in the city, but Joan would hardly wait, or agree to my going to them. On the other hand, she wanted to cite the English besiegers of the city before trying to raise the siege or attacking them; which she did. She cited the English in a letter written in her mother tongue, in very simple language. The substance of this letter was that they, these English, must agree to give up the siege and return to the kingdom of England, or else she would attack them so strongly that they would be forced to retire. This letter was sent to my lord Talbot,[17] and I swear that the English, two hundred of whom had previously been sufficient to rout eight hundred or a thousand of the royal army, from that moment became so powerless that four or five hundred soldiers and men at arms could fight against what seemed to be the whole force of England. And sometimes they so mastered the besieging English that they dared not leave their strongholds and bastilles.

And I have one more reason for believing that her deeds were of God. For on May 7, early in the morning, when the assault had begun on the enemy who were holding out beyond the bridge bulwark,[18] Joan was wounded by an arrow that penetrated her flesh between her neck and her shoulder for a depth of six inches. Despite this, she did not retire from the battle and took no remedy against the wound. The assault went on from morning till eight o'clock in the evening, so that there was hardly any hope of victory that day. Therefore I was

---

[17] He directed the siege after Salisbury's death, that is, from October 24, 1428, and commanded the Bastille of Saint Laurent, on the right bank.
[18] Or Les Tourelles.

going to break off and intended the army to retire into the city. Then the Maid came up to me and requested me to wait a little longer. Thereupon she mounted her horse and herself retired into a vineyard at some distance from the crowd of men; and in that vineyard she remained at prayer for the space of eight minutes. When she came back, she immediately picked up her standard and took up her position on the edge of the ditch. The moment she was there the English trembled with terror; and the King's men regained their courage and began to climb, delivering their assault against the bulwark and not meeting with the least resistance. Then that bulwark was taken, and the English who were in it fled. But they were all killed, among the rest Classidas[19] and the other principal English captains of this bastille, who intended to retire into the bridge tower but fell in the river and were drowned. This Classidas had been the man who had spoken most foully and in the basest and most infamous language against the Maid. So the bastille was taken, and I returned, together with the Maid and the rest of the French, to the city of Orléans, where we were received with great transports of joy and thanksgiving. And Joan was taken to her lodging so that her wound might be dressed. Once the surgeon had done his work, she had her supper, eating four or five toasts soaked in wine heavily watered, and she had taken no other food or drink all that day.

Next day,[20] in the early morning, the English left their tents and drew up in array for a battle. Whereupon Joan left her bed and put on only a light coat of mail, such as is known in French as a *jasseran*. However, she forbade anyone to go out against the English or to challenge them,

---

[19] William Glansdale, bailiff of Alençon for the King of England, who commanded the Bastille des Tourelles, or the bridge.

[20] Sunday, May 8.

but said that they must be allowed to retire; and they did retire unpursued, and from that hour the town was delivered from the enemy.

After the relief of Orléans, the Maid, with myself and the other captains of war, went off to find the King, who was at the castle of Loches, to ask him for armed bands with which to recover the castles and towns lying on the Loire river—that is to say, Meung, Beaugency, and Jargeau—so as to clear a safe and open road for him to go to Rheims for his coronation. She urged the King most earnestly and frequently to hasten and delay no longer. From that moment, the King made all possible haste and sent me, with Joan, the Duke of Alençon, and the other captains, to recover these same towns and castles. These towns and castles were in fact reduced to the King's obedience in a few days, thanks—as I believe—to the Maid.

After the liberation of Orléans from the English besiegers, these English gathered a large army to defend the towns and castles in question, and those others in their possession. While siege was being laid to the castle and bridge of Beaugency, the English army drew near to the castle of Meung on the Loire, which was still in their power. But they could not bring help to those of their number who were besieged at Beaugency. So when it came to their knowledge that this castle had been taken and restored to the royal allegiance, the English united all their forces. This made the French think that they were preparing to give battle. So they drew their own army up in battle array and made ready to receive the English attack. Then my lord the Duke of Alençon, in the presence of the lord constable,[21] of myself, and of several others, asked Joan what should be done. She

---

[21] Arthur de Richemont.

ORLÉANS

answered him loudly with the words, "See that you all have good spurs!" When those present heard this they asked her, "What did you say? Are we to turn our backs on them then?" "No," answered Joan, "it will be the English who will put up no defense. They will be beaten, and you will have to have good spurs to pursue them." And it was as she said. For they took to their heels, and they lost more than four thousand men in dead and prisoners.[22]

And I well remember going with the Maid to the castle of Loches, where the King was, after the relief of Orléans. The King was in his private room—what we call in French his "retreat"—and with him were my lord Christophe de Harcourt, and the Bishop of Castres[23]— then the King's confessor—and my lord of Trèves,[24] who had formerly been chancellor of France. Before entering this room, the Maid knocked on the door, and the moment she was inside, she fell on her knees and embraced the King's feet, pronouncing these words or others like them: "Noble Dauphin, do not take such long and copious counsel, but come as quickly as you can to receive a worthy coronation." Then my lord Christophe de Harcourt[25] engaged her in conversation and asked her whether it was her Counselor who said that. She answered Yes, and that she was receiving urgent promptings on this subject. Then Christophe said to Joan, "Will you not tell us here before the King what your Counselor does when he speaks to you?" She answered with a blush, "I understand well enough what you want to

---

[22] The battle of Patay, on June 18.

[23] Gérard Machet; he was not Bishop of Castres until after Joan's death. He died in 1448.

[24] Robert le Maçon, chancellor in 1418, then counselor to the King.

[25] A confidant of Charles VII, entrusted by him with a mission to the Duke of Burgundy.

know, and I will gladly tell you." Then the King said to her, "Joan, please tell him what he asks, in the presence of us all here." And she answered the King that she would and said these words or others like them: that when something was not going well because they would not leave it to her to follow the counsel that was sent to her from God, she would retire apart and pray God, complaining to Him that the men to whom she spoke would not readily believe her. And when she had prayed to God, she heard a voice which said to her, "Go, child of God, go, go! Go and I will help you." And when she heard this voice, she felt a great joy and wanted to be in that state always. And, what is more, when she thus repeated the words of her voices, she was seized with a marvelous rapture and raised her eyes to Heaven.

And I remember that after the victories of which I have spoken, the princes of the blood royal and the captains wanted the King to go into Normandy, and not to Rheims. But the Maid remained of the opinion that they should go to Rheims to anoint the King, and gave as reason for her advice that once the King was crowned and anointed the power of his enemies would decline continually until finally they would be powerless to harm either him or his kingdom. Everyone subscribed to her opinion, and the first place where the King halted with his army was before the city of Troyes. When he came there, he took counsel with the lords of his blood and the other military captains as to whether he should remain there and besiege and capture the city, or whether it would be better to pass on and, leaving this city of Troyes, go straight to Rheims. The King's Council was divided. There were various opinions on this subject, and they debated what was the best course. Then the Maid arrived and entered the council chamber, saying more or less these words: "Noble Dauphin, command your people to come and besiege the city of Troyes, and drag out your debates no longer. For in God's name, within three days I will lead you into the city of Troyes, by love, force, or courage, and that false Burgundy will be quite thunderstruck." Then the Maid immediately went over with the King's army, and pitched her camp alongside the moat. The positions that she took up were so admirable that even the two or three most famous and experienced captains would not have made as good a plan of battle. Indeed, the work that she did that night was so effective that the next day the bishop and citizens of the city offered their allegiance to the King,[26] in fear and trembling. And it was learned later that from the moment when she had given the King her advice not to go away from the city, the inhabitants had lost heart. They had done nothing but look for shelter and take refuge in the churches. When this city was brought back to the royal obedience, the King left for Rheims, where he met with perfect obedience; and there he was anointed and crowned.

... It was her habit every day, at Vesper time or at dusk, to retire into a church and have the bells rung for almost half an hour. Here she gathered the mendicant friars who followed the royal army, and at that hour she said her prayers and made these mendicant friars sing an anthem to the Blessed Virgin, the Mother of God.

And when the King came to La Ferté and to Crépy en Valois,[27] the people came out to meet him, rejoicing and crying, "Noel!" Then the Maid, who was riding between the Archbishop of Rheims and myself, said these words, "Here is a good people. I have never seen a people rejoice so much at the coming of so noble a king. May I be lucky enough, when I end my days, to be

---

[26] On July 10, 1429. The Bishop of Troyes, Jean Leguisé, was afterward ennobled by Charles VII in recognition of his services.

[27] On his return from Rheims in August 1429.

buried in this soil." When the Archbishop of Rheims[28] heard this, he said, "Joan, where do you expect to die?" And she answered, "Wherever God pleases. For myself, I do not know the time or the place, any more than you do. But please God my Creator that I may now retire, and lay down my arms, and go to serve my father and mother and keep their sheep, with my brothers and my sister, who will be glad to see me again."

As for her virtuous behavior among the soldiers, no living being was more sober than she, and I have very often heard my lord Jean d'Aulon[29] say—the knight, that is, who is now seneschal of Beaucaire, into whose care the King had put the Maid as the wisest of his captains and most approved for his honesty—that he did not believe any woman could be more chaste than the Maid. As for myself and the rest, when we were in her company we had no wish or desire to approach or have intercourse with women. That seems to me to be almost a miracle.

A fortnight after the Count of Chuffort[30] was imprisoned in the prison of Jargeau, a sheet of paper was passed to him containing four verses about a Maid who would come from Bois Chenu and ride against them on the backs of archers.

Finally, although Joan sometimes spoke gaily to hearten the soldiers about feats of arms or other warlike operations, which were perhaps never carried out, whenever she spoke seriously of the war she never affirmed anything except that she had been sent to raise the siege of Orléans and help the oppressed people in that city and the surrounding country, and to lead the King to Rheims to be anointed.

---

[28] Regnault de Chartres, who was soon to betray Joan.
[29] We shall read his deposition later.
[30] William de la Pole, Earl of Suffolk, who had been raised to the command of the English army after Salisbury's death.

SOME CITIZENS OF ORLÉANS

The other examinations at Orléans were of men like Raoul de Gaucourt or François Garivel whose depositions we have already reported. Then came March 16, the crowd's day. Thirty-six people appeared to give evidence on that day, and one can imagine that the clerk Guillaume de la Salle must have rejoiced when the session was over. The spokesman for the townsmen, the man who made the most detailed deposition, was Jean Luillier, noted on the town rolls as exercising the profession of mercer, that is to say, a wholesale merchant. This was no doubt the same man who, twenty-five years previously, had furnished the "fine Brussels scarlet" and the "deep green" cloth from which was made the livery offered to Joan by Charles of Orléans. He was about fifty-six.

Jean Luillier

He was asked about the Maid's entrance into Orléans.

Her entrance was greatly desired by all the town's inhabitants, because of her renown and of the rumors abroad. For it was said that she had told the King that she was sent by God to raise the siege of the town; and the citizens and inhabitants of the town were so hard pressed by the enemy who were besieging them that they did not know where to turn for help except to God.

He was asked whether he was in the town when she arrived.

Yes, she was received with as much joy and enthusiasm by all, men and women, small and great, as if she had been an angel of God. For they hoped that, by her agency, they would be delivered from their enemies—as afterward happened.

He was asked what she did in the town after her entrance.

She exhorted everyone to trust in God, for if we placed our hope and confidence in God we should be delivered from our enemies. She wanted to summon the English who were besieging the city before allowing the assault to be made on the enemy, to push them back; and this was done. For she summoned the English in a letter the substance of which was that they must agree to raise the siege and retire to the kingdom of England, or else they would be compelled to do so by violent means. And from that moment the English were terrified and had no longer the powers of resistance that they previously had. No more than a handful of our townsmen would often fight a great number of English, and each time they so overwhelmed their besiegers that the English no longer dared to come out of their forts.

He was asked about the raising of the siege.

It was in the month of May, on the seventh, in the year of our Lord 1429. I remember well how the attack was made on the enemy stationed on the other side of the bridge bulwark. They said that she had been wounded by an arrow during the attack; and it lasted from morning till evening, so that the townsmen wanted to retire into the town. Then the Maid came and ordered that there should be no retreat, and that they must not retire into the town yet. When she had said this, she picked up her standard and placed it on the edge of the ditch, and the moment she was there the English trembled and were afraid. The King's soldiers took fresh courage and began to climb, delivering an attack upon the bulwark, and they met with no resistance. Then the bulwark was taken, and the English in it took to their heels and were all killed. Classidas[31] and the other chief captains of this

---

[31] The English captain Glansdale.

English bastille intended to entrench themselves in the tower of the Orléans bridge, but they fell into the river and were drowned; and once the bastille was taken all those of the King's party returned to Orléans.

What happened next?

The next day [May 8] early in the morning, they left their tents and drew up in line of battle to fight, or so it seemed. When she learnt this, the Maid rose from her bed and put on her armor. But she did not wish the English to be attacked or any demands to be made of them, but ordered that they should be allowed to go. And in fact they departed unpursued; and at that hour the town was delivered from the enemy.

Was the siege raised and the city rescued from the enemy by means of the Maid and through her mediation rather than by force of arms?

I and all the people of the city believe that if the Maid had not come from God to help us, we the inhabitants and the city would shortly have been at the mercy and in the power of the enemy who were besieging us. I do not think that the inhabitants or the soldiers who were in the town would have been able to put up a long resistance against an enemy who was then so much superior to them.

Those who came forward after him[32] were not always satisfied with confirming his evidence; they tried hard to add their little personal recollections. The majority are described merely as citizens of Orléans, but some of them are known: Jacques de Thou, for instance, who was the grandfather of Christophe de Thou, future president of the Paris Parlement, whose descendants were to achieve fame. The name of one venerable old man stands out especially, who was eighty-seven when he gave his evidence but who was to

---

[32] A list will be found in Appendix D, p. 301.

live to the age of 118: Aignan de Saint Mesmin, head of one of the most important families of Orléans, whom Charles VII was shortly afterward to ennoble. Another name destined to become famous is that of Jean Beauharnais, the brother-in-law of Joan's page, Louis de Coutes, whose deposition we shall find further on. His younger brother, Guillaume Beauharnais, was to be the direct ancestor of Prince Eugène. With the townsmen came the priests. One sees canons of the Church of Saint Aignan and the prior of the Augustinians of Saint Magloire come to state what they know of Joan. One of them, Messire Pierre Compaing, remembers having seen her follow the Mass and shed tears at the moment of the Elevation. As a convincing proof of her saintliness, he adds that she persuaded the famous mercenary captain La Hire (a valiant soldier but a terrible pillager) to make confession. Finally, the women are no less eager; they are perhaps those same women whose marks of veneration somewhat annoyed Joan, but their eagerness is none the less very touching.

Jacques l'Esbahy

(Aged fifty)

I remember that two heralds were sent to Saint Laurent, one of whom was named Ambleville and the other Guyenne, to demand of the lord Talbot, Count Chuffort, and the lord of Scalles, on behalf of the Maid, that the English should depart in God's name or ill would befall them. The English kept back the one herald, Guyenne, and sent the other, Ambleville, with a message for Joan. Ambleville reported that the English had kept Guyenne to burn him. Then Joan replied to Ambleville, assuring him in God's name that they would do his companion no harm and bidding him go boldly back to the English, for no harm would befall him, either, and he would bring his companion back safe and sound—which proved true.

Moreover I noticed that when Joan entered Orléans for the first time she chose to go first of all to the cathedral to show her reverence for God her Creator.

All the people of Orléans agree that they never saw any signs that Joan attributed any of her achievements to her own glory. They say that she attributed all things to God and did everything that she could to prevent the people from honoring and glorifying her, and that she liked to be alone and solitary rather than in men's society, except when it was necessary for the conduct of the war for her to be so.

All maintain too that they never saw anything in Joan deserving of reproach, but that everything about her was humility, simplicity, chastity, and devotion to God and the Church. And they say, furthermore, that it was a great consolation to converse with her.

Réginalde

(Widow of Jean Huré)

One day a great lord was walking in the open street, cursing and blaspheming God in a most shameful fashion. When Joan heard and saw him, she was most troubled and immediately went up to him. Then, taking this blasphemous gentleman by the shoulder, she said to him, "Ah, sir, do you dare to blaspheme our Lord and Master? In God's name, you will withdraw your words before I go from here." And then, as I saw—I who speak to you here—that gentleman repented and at the Maid's exhortation begged for pardon.

CHAPTER 6

The Witnesses on Her Daily Life

The four testimonies that follow have been placed together because they come from persons who lived in close familiarity with Joan during the decisive year of her life, between Orléans and Compiègne.

Let us briefly go over her itinerary during this period. First, the Loire campaign. Far from intoxicated by her success at Orléans, Joan had only one idea in her head: to have the King anointed at Rheims. Although that plan of a progress right through occupied territory seemed folly to all the wise men in the royal circle, she undertook, with the help of the Duke of Alençon, to open the way from the Loire, and these are her famous victories: Jargeau on June 12, Meung on the fifteenth, Beaugency on the seventeenth, and finally, on the eighteenth the astounding victory of Patay, in which two thousand English were said to have fallen, while on the French side only three fighting men were killed.

On June 29 began the march on Rheims. Troyes opened its gates on July 10, Rheims on the sixteenth, and on the next day, Sunday, July 17, 1429, Charles VII was anointed at Rheims by the Archbishop, Regnault de Chartres.

Some French "collaborators" who were devoted to the English cause had left Rheims precipitately on the eve of Charles VII's arrival. Among them figured a citizen of Rheims, a counselor to the King of England, who had been made Bishop of Beauvais by the influence of the Duke of Burgundy—a certain Pierre Cauchon.

The sequel is well known: royal inaction, intrigues at court, led by La Trémoïlle and soon by the too impressionable Regnault de Chartres, the bishop of the anointing, in person. Instead of a pursuit, of a breathless advance on Paris, at the moment when every town was surrendering immediately upon the King's approach—Laon, Soissons, Château Thierry, Montmirail, Provins, La Ferté Milon, Compiègne, Senlis, Saint Denis, etc.—the opportunity was inexplicably allowed to pass.

Joan herself hesitated as to the course to pursue. She knew, however, that no impression could be made on the enemy except "at the lance's point", and that the truces they strove to conclude would only be trickery. She carried on the struggle. Wounded before Paris, beaten at La Charité sur Loire, she was finally captured at Compiègne on the evening of May 24, 1430. "I shall last for a year, hardly more", she had said on coming to Chinon.

THE "GENTLE DUKE"

Jean II, Duke of Alençon, prince of the blood royal. His father was killed at Agincourt; his great-great-grandfather, the grandson of Philip the Bold, King of France, had fallen at Crécy. He was Charles of Orléans' brother-in-law.

This man, whom Joan called her "pretty duke", must actually have been, at the time of Orléans and Patay, a handsome gentleman with all the ardor of his twenty-five years.

Like Dunois, he was immediately conquered by Joan and was to remain her supporter against the intrigues of the court.

There can be no doubt that there was a great warmth of feeling in the very pure friendship Joan felt for the "gentle duke", whom she had promised to bring back to his wife safe and sound, and whom she warned one day to move away from the place where he was "or that engine will kill you", as she said, pointing to a piece of artillery; and one moment later a ball fell on that spot, crushing the lord de Lude, who happened to be passing. As for the Duke, he seems to have lived beside Joan in a sort of bedazzlement, enslaved not only by her predictions and her exploits, but also by her personality, by her sporting accomplishments (astonished by the way in which she "tilted a lance", on the first day he made her the present of a horse), by her knowledge—in spite of her youth—of artillery, a weapon that defeated the hardened captain, by her handling of arms, and finally by the beauty of that young body, so close to him when in the course of their campaigns they slept "on the straw", and yet so well defended by the respect that she inspired. It is startling to think that less than a month after his deposition (on May 31, 1456), the Duke of Alençon was to be arrested for treason, and by Dunois himself.... Will one ever know what rancor, what ambition, or what wounded pride could have caused the "gentle duke" to correspond secretly with the enemy whom he had once fought? Whatever the cause, he was to be imprisoned at Aigues Mortes, then at Vendôme, and condemned by the judgment of his peers to be executed, a sentence that Charles VII was to commute to one of imprisonment. He remained a prisoner in the keep of Loches until the accession of Louis XI, who pardoned him. However, he seems at the moment when he gave his testimony to have recovered some of the ardent freshness and spontaneity of his youth. For his tale is quick and lively.

The Duke of Alençon

(Aged fifty)

When Joan came to find the King, he was at the town of Chinon, and I at Saint Florent.[1] I was riding out on a quail hunt when a message came that a Maid had come to the King who maintained that she was sent by God to drive away the English and to raise the siege which these English had laid to Orléans. That is why I went to the King next day, at Chinon, where he was, and I found Joan talking with the King. Just as I drew near, Joan asked who I was, and the King replied that I was the Duke of Alençon. Then Joan said, "You have come at a good time. The more of the blood royal there are together, the better it will be." And the next day Joan attended the King's Mass, and when she saw the King she bowed, and the King led Joan into a chamber; and I was with him and the lord de la Trémoïlle, whom the King held back, telling the others that they could retire.

Then Joan made the King several requests, among others that he should give his kingdom to the Lord of Heaven; and when he had made this gift, she said, the King of Heaven would do to him as he had done to his predecessors and restore him to his former state. And many other things, which I do not remember, were said right up to dinner time. After dinner the King went to walk in the fields, and there Joan ran at a tilt, and when I saw her do this—saw her wield a lance and run at a tilt—I gave her a horse. Then the King decided that the Maid should be examined by churchmen; and there were

[1] Saint Florent lès Saumur.

chosen the Bishop of Castres,[2] the King's confessor, the Bishop of Senlis,[3] and the Bishops of Maguelonne and of Poitiers,[4] also Master Pierre de Versailles, later Bishop of Meaux, and Master Jean(?) [Jourdain?] Morin, and several others whose names I do not remember. They questioned Joan in my presence, asking her why she had come, and who had made her come to the King. She replied that she had come from the King of Heaven, and that she heard voices and received counsel that told her what to do. But about that I do not remember. Afterward, when she was taking her meal with me, Joan told me that she had been very closely examined, but that she knew more and could do more than she had told her questioners.

Once he had heard the report of those whom he had deputed to examine her, the King wished Joan to go to the town of Poitiers; and there she was examined once more. But I was not present at that examination made at Poitiers. I know, however, that it was subsequently reported to the royal Council that those who had examined her said they found nothing in her contrary to the Catholic faith, and that, in view of his necessity, the King might well make use of her help. When he heard this, the King sent me to the Queen of Sicily[5] to collect the provisions to be taken to Orléans and organize troops to take them. And there I found the lord Ambroise de Loré,[6] and a lord Louis whose surname I forget, who had

---

[2] Gérard Machet.

[3] Not the bishop of 1429, who was an English supporter, but the one of 1456, Simon Bonnet.

[4] Hugues de Cambarel. In the Estates of 1426 he had only voted for the tax demanded by the King on condition that he would put an end to the soldiers' pillaging, and for that he narrowly escaped being thrown in the river by an accomplice of de la Trémoïlle, the lord of Giac.

[5] Yolanda of Aragon, Charles VII's mother-in-law, who had an excellent influence over him.

[6] See Dunois' deposition, above.

collected the provisions. But money was wanted, and to get money for those provisions, I returned to the King and informed him that they were ready. All that was necessary was to put down the money for the provisions and the soldiers. Then the King sent someone to discuss the sums needed to conclude the whole matter; both soldiers and provisions were ready to go to Orléans, to attempt to raise the siege, if that were possible.

Joan was sent with the soldiers, and the King had a suit of armor made for her.[7] So the royal army departed with Joan. About what they did on their way and what happened at the town of Orléans, I know nothing except by hearsay, for I was not present and did not accompany the army. But subsequently I saw the forts that stood before Orléans and examined their defenses. And I think that they were captured rather by a miracle than by force of arms, particularly the Bastille des Tourelles, at the end of the bridge, and the Bastille des Augustins. If I had been in either of them with a few soldiers, I would have undertaken to resist the whole power of the army, and I do not think that they would have taken me; and from what I have heard from the soldiers and the captains who were there, they all regarded almost everything that happened at Orléans as a miracle from God; they considered it to have been the work of no human hands but to have come from on high. I have heard this said several times by the lord Ambroise de Loré, formerly provost of Paris.

I did not see Joan again from the time that she left the King until the relief of Orléans. They succeeded in collecting together a band of the King's men to the number of six hundred lances, whose aim was to go to the town of Jargeau, which was in English occupation. That night they slept in a wood, and on the next came more of the

---

[7] The following entry is to be found in the accounts of Charles VII's treasurer Hémon Raguier, dated May 10, 1429: "To the Master Armorer, for a complete harness for the Maid, 100 livres *tournois*" (Quicherat, 5:258).

King's men, under the leadership of the lord Bastard of Orléans and the lord Florent d'Illiers,[8] and some other captains. Once they were all collected together, they found themselves to be about twelve hundred lances strong. Then there was a debate among the captains because some were of the opinion that they should attack the town and others held a contrary view, maintaining that the English were very powerful and were there in great numbers.

When Joan saw that there was discussion between them, she told them to fear no numbers and assured them that they would have no difficulty in attacking the English, for God was conducting their campaign. She said that if she were not sure that God was conducting their campaign, she would rather keep her sheep than expose herself to dangers like these. When they heard this, they made their way to the town of Jargeau, intending to take the suburbs and there spend the night. But on learning this, the English came out to meet them and at the outset drove the King's men back. But when Joan saw this, she picked up her standard and went to the attack, exhorting the soldiers to be of good courage. And they were so successful that that night the King's soldiers were lodged in the suburbs of Jargeau. I think that God was conducting that campaign, for that very night they posted no proper guards, and if the English had sallied from the town the King's soldiers would have been in great danger.

The King's men prepared their artillery and in the morning opened fire with their bombards and engines against the town; and several days later they held a council among them to discuss what they should do against the English who were in the town of Jargeau, so as to recover the place. While they were holding this council, news came to them that La Hire was holding parley with

---

[8] Captain of the town of Châteaudun.

the lord de Suffort.[9] Both I and the other leaders of that army were annoyed with La Hire; he was sent for and came. After his arrival, it was decided that there should be an attack on the town, and the heralds cried, "To the attack!" and Joan herself said to me, "Forward, gentle Duke, to the attack!" And as it seemed to me to be premature to start the attack so quickly, Joan said to me, "Do not have doubts. When God pleases, the hour is ripe. We must act when God wills it. Act, and God will act." And a little later she said to me, "O gentle Duke, can you be afraid? Do you know that I have promised your wife to bring you back safe and sound?" And indeed, when I left my wife[10] to come to the army with Joan, my wife said to Joan that she was very much afraid for me, that I had been taken prisoner before,[11] and that they had had to pay so much money for my ransom that she would have liked to beg me to stay. Then Joan answered her, "Have no fear. I will return him to you safe and sound, and in the state he is in now or in a better one."

During the attack on the town of Jargeau, Joan told me at one moment to retire from the place where I was standing, for if I did not "that engine"—and she pointed to a piece of artillery in the town—"will kill you." I fell back, and a little later on that very spot where I had been standing someone by the name of my lord de Lude was killed. That made me very much afraid, and I wondered greatly at Joan's sayings after all these events. After that, Joan went into the attack, and I with her. Just when

[9] William de la Pole, Earl of Suffolk.

[10] The sister of Charles of Orléans.

[11] At the battle of Verneuil in 1424. By the age of twenty-three, the Duke of Alençon had already spent five years as a prisoner. He had been imprisoned in the tower of Crotoy, where Joan was also to be imprisoned in the following year.

our soldiers were breaking in, the count de Suffort made his herald call to me that he wished to parley, but he was not heard and the attack was carried through. Joan was on a ladder, holding her standard in her hand; this standard was torn, and Joan herself was struck on the head by a stone, which broke on her steel cap. She was thrown to the ground, and as she picked herself up she cried to the soldiers, "Up, friends, up! Our Lord has doomed the English. At this very hour, they are ours. Be of good cheer!" And at that moment the town of Jargeau was taken,[12] and the English retired toward the bridges with the French in pursuit. And in the course of the pursuit more than eleven hundred of the English were killed.

Once the town was taken, I went with Joan and the army to the town of Orléans and from the town of Orléans to Meung, where the English were in the town, that is to say, the young Warwick[13] and Scales.[14] I spent that night with some soldiers in a church near Meung, where I ran into great danger; and the next day we took the Beaugency road, and in the fields we found more of the King's soldiers, and there an attack was made on the English who held Beaugency. After this attack, the English stripped the city and went into the castle. And guards were placed in front of the castle to prevent their coming out. We were in front of the castle when news came to us that the lord constable[15] was approaching with some soldiers. Joan, myself, and others in the army were much

---

[12] On June 12, 1429. Suffolk was here taken prisoner.

[13] The son of the Earl of Warwick (Richard Beauchamp), governor of the young King Henry VI, whose part in Joan's trial is well known (see later, the depositions of the Rouen witnesses). His son, who is mentioned here, was to be taken prisoner at Patay.

[14] Thomas Scales, who shared with Talbot and Suffolk the command of operations at the siege of Orléans.

[15] Arthur de Richemont. He was then in disgrace. Hence the remarks that follow.

THE WITNESSES ON HER DAILY LIFE

displeased by this and wanted to retire from the town. For we had orders not to receive the lord constable into our company. I said to Joan that if the constable came I should go. And the next day, before the arrival of the lord constable, news came that the English were approaching in great numbers, and with them the lord Talbot, and the soldiers cried, "To arms!" Then Joan said to me—for I was about to retire because of the lord constable's arrival—that we had to help one another. Finally, the English surrendered the castle on terms [on June 17] and retired with a safe-conduct, which I granted them, I being at that time the King's lieutenant with the army.

And while the English were retiring, someone came from La Hire's company and told me and the King's captain that the English were approaching, and that we should soon be face to face with them, and that there were more or less a thousand armed men. When she heard of this, Joan asked what this soldier had said, and when she was told she said to the lord constable, "Ah, noble Constable, you have not come through any act of mine, but since you have come, you shall be welcome." Many of the King's men were frightened and said that it would be a good thing to send for the horses. "In God's name," cried Joan, "we must fight them. If they were hanging in the clouds we should get them. For God has sent them to us for us to punish them." She maintained that she was certain of victory and said in French, "The gentle King shall have the greatest victory today that he has had for a long time. My Counsel tells me that they are all ours." And I very well know that the English were routed and killed without great difficulty; and among others, Talbot was made prisoner [on June 18]. There was a great slaughter of the English there, and afterward the King's men came to the town of Patay in the Blésois, in which town Talbot was brought before the constable and me, in the presence of Joan herself. I told Talbot that I had not believed in the morning that things would turn out so, and Talbot answered that it was the fortune of war. Then we went back to the King, who decided to go next to the town of Rheims for his coronation and his anointing.

I sometimes heard Joan say to the King that she herself would last a year and scarcely more, and that they must think during that year how to do their work well. For she said that she had four missions: to expel the English; to have the King crowned and anointed at Rheims; to free the Duke of Orléans from English hands; and to raise the siege the English had laid to Orléans town.

Joan was chaste, and she loathed those women who follow the soldiers. I once saw her at Saint Denis, on the way back from the King's coronation, chase a girl who was with the soldiers so hard, with her sword drawn, that she broke her sword. She was furious when she heard soldiers swearing and scolded them fiercely, myself in particular, since I swore from time to time. When I saw her, I restrained my language.

Sometimes, when we were in the field, I slept with Joan and the soldiers "on the straw", and sometimes I saw Joan get ready for the night, and sometimes I looked at her breasts, which were beautiful. Nevertheless I never had any carnal desire for her.

From all that I saw of her, I always considered her a good Catholic and a modest woman, and I have several times seen her take our Lord's Body; and when she saw the Host, she often wept copious tears. She took the Holy Eucharist twice a week and often made confession.

In everything that she did, apart from the conduct of the war, Joan was young and simple, but in the conduct of war she was most skillful, both in carrying a lance herself, in drawing up the army in battle order, and in placing the artillery. And everyone was astonished that she acted with such prudence and clear-sightedness in military matters, as cleverly as some great captain with twenty or thirty years' experience; and especially in the placing of artillery, for in that she acquitted herself magnificently.

JOAN'S SQUIRE

Jean d'Aulon

(Knight, royal councilor, and seneschal of Beaucaire)

He sent his deposition in writing. His duties kept him in the south, but as his testimony was of the greatest importance to the commissioners, the Archbishop of Rheims on April 20, 1456, asked him to go and say what he knew of Joan before the ecclesiastical court of Lyons. The vice-Inquisitor, Jean Desprès, before whom he appeared, sent his deposition in his original words, and it is in this form that it was incorporated in the report of the trial. His deposition turns out to be the last in date (May 20, 1456).

Jean d'Aulon was Joan's everyday companion, from Poitiers to Compiègne and even afterward, since he shared her fate as a prisoner, as did her brother Jean d'Arc. Dunois had told us how Charles VII chose him to keep personal watch over Joan because he was the wisest knight and the man of the most approved honesty at his court. His performance of this duty resulted in King Charles VII's afterward entrusting him with a number of confidential missions. On the solemn entry into Paris in 1437, it was he who walked beside the King, holding the bridle of his horse.

At the time of the rehabilitation trial, he was living in the castle of Pierre Scize at Lyons, which had been entrusted to him two years before, and it was there that the Archbishop of Rheims, Jouvenel des Ursins, wrote to him, begging him to set down in writing what he knew about Joan "since you have good and wide knowledge of her life, her conversation, and her behavior". It is valuable to us that his deposition was transcribed in French; it was dictated in attractive and direct language and is so graphic that we believe readers will not be impatient when they find certain episodes described by him that they have already heard about from Dunois or the Duke of Alençon, or be surprised that, in spite of its length, we have reproduced it almost in its entirety. His meeting with Joan was evidently the great adventure of his life, and there is not a detail, in the siege of Orléans for instance, that he did not conserve and communicate with all its living quality.

> It was about twenty-eight years ago, when the King our lord was at Poitiers, that I was told that the Maid, who came from the Lorraine country, had been brought to him by two gentlemen who said that they were in the service of Messire Robert de Baudricourt, knight. One was called Bertrand and the other Jean de Metz. And I went to the town of Poitiers to see her.
>
> After her presentation, the Maid talked with our lord the King in private and told him certain secrets that I do not know,[16] except that shortly afterward my lord sent for some members of his Council, among them myself.

[16] An allusion to the interview at court in which Joan succeeded in convincing the King of his legitimacy. The editor of the abridged reports of the two cases, which was made in the reign of Louis XII, describes the scene as Charles VII must have related it to his intimates toward the end of his life. Joan had spoken to the King of three requests he had made to God, when at prayer, on All Saints' Day 1428, in the chapel of the castle of Loches. These concerned his own doubts concerning his legitimacy. This revelation of Joan's must both have encouraged him to think of himself as the "true King" of France and reassured him as to Joan's mission.

He told us that the Maid had said that she was sent from God to help him to recover his kingdom, which at that time was largely occupied by the English, his ancient enemies.

After this declaration of the King's to the gentlemen of his Council, it was decided to interrogate the Maid, who was then about sixteen years old, or thereabouts, on certain points touching her faith.

For this purpose, the King sent for certain masters of theology, jurists, and other experts, who examined and interrogated her on these points well and diligently.[17]

I was present at the Council when these scholars made their report of what they had found in the Maid; and it was publicly stated by one of them that they had neither seen, learned of, nor become acquainted with anything in the Maid that should not be present in a good Christian and a true Catholic, which they considered her to be; and it was their opinion that she was a very good person.

When the King had received the scholars' report, this Maid was put into the care of the Queen of Sicily, mother of the Queen our sovereign lady, and of certain ladies who were with her. These ladies saw and visited the Maid, and spied upon her and examined the privy parts of her body. But after they had seen and examined all that was necessary for their purpose, the Queen said and told the King that she and her ladies had found her beyond any doubt to be a true and intact virgin, with no signs of corruption or violation. I was present when the Queen made her report.

Once he had heard this, because of the great virtue that there was in that Maid, and because she had said that she had been sent by God, the King concluded in his Council that henceforth he should avail himself of

---

[17] We have already had an account of this examination.

her aid in his wars, seeing that she had been sent to him for that purpose.

It was then decided that she should be sent to the town of Orléans, which was then besieged by the English. Therefore men were given her as personal attendants, and others for her escort.[18]

I was appointed as her guard and escort by our lord the King.

To protect her body, my lord the King had armor made exactly to fit her, and when that was done he picked out a certain number of soldiers to lead and escort her carefully, with those of her company, to the town of Orléans.

Immediately after that she started out with her men along the Orléans road.

When it came to the knowledge of my lord Dunois, who was then known as my lord the Bastard of Orléans, and who was in the city to protect and guard it from the enemy, that the Maid was coming that way, he immediately collected a great number of soldiers, including La Hire and others, to go out and meet her. For this purpose, and in order to be sure of bringing her safely into the city, this lord and his men got into a boat and went up the river Loire for about three quarters of a mile in search of her, and there they found her....

The Maid immediately boarded the boat, and I with her, and the rest of her men turned back toward Blois. And we entered the city safe and sound with my lord Dunois and his people.[19] And my lord Dunois had her well and decently lodged in the house of one of the important citizens of the town,[20] who had married one of its most important ladies.

---

[18] An allusion to her personal bodyguard, of whom d'Aulon was one. He acted in the capacity of squire and bodyguard, as he will say in a moment.

[19] On Friday, April 29. (See Dunois' deposition above.)

[20] Jacques Boucher, the treasurer.

THE WITNESSES ON HER DAILY LIFE 165

After my lord Dunois, La Hire, and certain other captains of our lord the King's party had conferred with the Maid concerning the best measures for the protection, guarding, and defense of the city, and also to decide on the best means of beating the enemy, it was considered and concluded between them that they would have to summon a force of our party's soldiers who were then at Blois, and that someone must go and fetch them. For this office and to bring them into the city, my lord Dunois, myself, and certain other captains were chosen; and we went with our men into the Blois district to summon them and bring them in.

When we were ready to go and summon this army from Blois, the fact came to the Maid's knowledge and she immediately mounted her horse. Then with La Hire and a certain number of her men, she went out into the fields to guard us from any attack by the enemy. And to do this, the Maid placed herself and her men between the enemy's army and the city of Orléans. So successful was she that notwithstanding the great power and numbers of the English army, thanks be to God, my lord Dunois and I got through with all our men and safely went our way. And the Maid and her men regained the city in equal safety.

As soon as she learned that we were returning and bringing the reinforcements we had gone to fetch, the Maid immediately mounted her horse and rode out with some of her men to meet us and help us, and if it had been necessary she would have rescued us.

Then before the enemy's eyes, the Maid, Marshal Dunois, La Hire, and I who speak to you now entered that city with our men, without meeting with any opposition.

That same day, after dinner, my lord Dunois came to the Maid's lodging, where she and I had dined together. During his speech with her, my lord Dunois told her that he had heard for certain on good authority that one Ffastolf,[21] an enemy captain, was soon to join the besieging army, both to bring them aid and reinforcements and also to revictual them, and that even now he was at Yinville.[22]

The Maid was highly delighted with this news, so it seemed, and said to my lord Dunois these words or others like them: "Bastard, Bastard, in the name of God, I command you to let me know as soon as you hear of Ffastolf's coming. For if he gets through without my knowing it, I swear to you that I will have your head cut off." To which my lord Dunois answered that he did not doubt that, and that he would certainly let her know.

After this conversation, I lay on a couch that was in the Maid's room to take a little rest, for I was tired and weary; and Joan lay down with her hostess on a bed also, to sleep and get some rest. But when I was beginning to doze, the Maid suddenly sprang out of bed and woke me with the great noise she made. And when I asked her what was the matter, she replied, "In God's name, my Counsel has told me that I must attack the English. But I do not know if I should go to their bastille or against Ffastolf, who is to revictual them." Thereupon I got up quickly and armed the Maid as quickly as I could.

While I was arming her, we heard a great noise and loud cries from those in the city, who shouted that the enemy were doing great harm to the French. Then I too had myself armed; and as I was doing so, the Maid left the room without my knowledge and went out into the street, where she found a page on a horse. Immediately she made him dismount and quickly mounted the beast herself. Then as straight and as fast as she could,

---

[21] An English captain of mercenaries.
[22] Janville.

she made her way right to the Burgundy gate[23] where the greatest noise came from.

I immediately followed the Maid, but I could not ride so fast that she was not at the gate already.

When we came there, we saw them bringing in one of the townsmen, who was severely wounded. The Maid asked the men who were carrying him who he was, and they replied that he was a Frenchman. And then she said that she never saw French blood without her hair standing on end.

Then the Maid and I and several other soldiers in our company went out of the city to help the French and fight the enemy with all our might. And when we were out of the gate, I thought I had never seen so many men at arms of our party as I saw then.[24]

From there we made our way to a very strong enemy bastille called the Saint Loup bastille, which was immediately attacked by the French and carried by assault with very few losses. All the enemy in it were killed or made prisoner, and the bastille remained in French hands.[25]

After this, the Maid and the men of her company retired into the city of Orléans, where they refreshed themselves and rested all that day.

Next day, when the Maid and her people saw how great a victory they had won over their enemies on the day before, they came out of the city in fair order to attack a certain other bastille in front of the place, called

---

[23] One of the gates in the walls of Orléans that gave on to the Gien or Burgundy road.

[24] This may refer to the army assembled by Charles VII, whom the Maid's coming roused from their apathy, or to the fact that the men of Orléans, cheered by her presence, ran to arms more eagerly than they had ever done before.

[25] The events of May 4, 1429.

the Bastille of Saint Jean le Blanc.[26] However, when they saw that they could not go straight overland to attack it, since the enemy had built another very strong fort at the end of the city bridge, they decided that they must cross to a certain island that lay in the Loire, where they would assemble for the assault on this Bastille of Saint Jean le Blanc. And in order to cross the other arm of the Loire, they brought up two boats, with which they made a bridge to bring them to the bastille.

This done, they approached the bastille, which they found entirely deserted. For when they saw the Frenchmen coming, the English in it departed and took refuge in another stronger and larger fort, called the Bastille des Augustins.

When the French saw that they were not strong enough to take this bastille, it was decided that they must therefore retire without doing anything.

In order to be sure of getting back safely, the most famous and bravest of the French soldiers were ordered to stay behind to prevent the enemy from attacking them while they were passing into the city; and for this deed the lords de Gaucourt and de Villars—who was then seneschal of Beaucaire—and myself were chosen.

While the French were retiring from Saint Jean le Blanc to reach the island, the Maid and La Hire crossed in a boat, each with a horse, from the further side of the island. And once on land, they mounted their horses, both of them with lance in hand.

And when they saw the enemy coming out of their bastille to attack our men, La Hire and the Maid, who were always in the van to protect the rest, swiftly couched their lances and were the first to strike out at the enemy.

---

[26] This was really a simple lookout post, lying on the right bank of the Loire, but protected by the Bastille des Tourelles, which was near and commanded the bridge. Jean d'Aulon explains as much in the lines that follow.

> Then everyone followed them and began to strike out at the enemy so effectively that they drove them back into the Bastille des Augustins.

The passage that follows takes us a little away from the story of the siege. But it is curious and rather revealing of the mentality of the time.

> While this was happening, and while I was guarding their passage with the others picked and ordered to do so, among whom was a most valiant soldier from Spain by the name of Alfonso de Partada, I saw a certain man of their company pass in front of me, a handsome man, tall and well armed. As he passed, I asked him to stay a little with the rest of us to put up a defense against the enemy in case of need. But he replied, out of hand, that he would do nothing of the sort. Then Alfonso told him that he might remain behind just as well as the others, for there were men quite as brave as he in the rearguard. He answered Alfonso with a blank refusal. Upon which there passed certain haughty words between them, and they agreed to ride together, and simultaneously, upon the enemy to prove which of them was the braver and which of them performed his duty best; and hand in hand they rushed against the enemy bastille at top speed and came to the foot of the fence.
>
> When they came up to the fence of this bastille, I saw inside it a big, strong, powerful Englishman, well equipped and armed, who was putting up such a resistance that they could not break through the fence. I then pointed this Englishman out to one Master Jean, the artilleryman, and asked him to fire at him since he was dealing so much damage and destruction to all who tried to approach the bastille. This Master Jean immediately did. The moment he had picked him out he aimed his weapon at him, to such effect that he laid him dead on the ground.

Then the two men at arms gained an entry, through which all the rest of their company passed and burst into the bastille. They then attacked it sharply and most thoroughly from all directions, with such success that in a short time they had stormed and taken it. And the majority of the enemy in it were either killed or captured, and those who were able to escape retired into the Bastille des Tourelles, at the end of the bridge. So the Maid and those with her were victorious over the enemy for that day, and the great bastille was captured,[27] and the lords with their men and the Maid remained beside it all that night.

The next morning the Maid sent to fetch all the lords and captains who were outside the captured bastille, to discuss what was next to be done; and on their advice it was decided after due deliberation to attack that day a great bulwark that the English had built in front of the Bastille des Tourelles. They concluded that it would be necessary to capture and hold that before doing anything else. To carry this plan into effect, the Maid, the captains, and the soldiers scattered in various directions, early that morning, in front of the bulwark, which they then attacked from every side. They made every endeavor to capture it, and in fact pressed their attack upon it from early morning until sunset. But they were unable to take it or even to gain a foothold; and at sunset the lords and captains who were with Joan concluded that it was time to sound the retreat, since the hour was already very late and they certainly would not be able to capture it that day. Moreover, they were all very weary and exhausted. So the retreat was sounded, and at the trumpet's call each man retired for that day.

---

[27] The Bastille des Augustins, taken on May 6. Jean d'Aulon reports only the capture of one section at which he was personally present.

As they were retreating, the man who had carried the Maid's standard and was still holding it, being tired and weary, handed it to one called the Basque, who was one of the lord de Villars' company. Now because I knew this Basque to be a brave man, and because I was certain that nothing but harm would result from this retirement and that the bastille and bulwark would remain in enemy hands, it occurred to me that if the standard were advanced, the soldiers' courage being as great as I knew it to be, those who were with us might still carry the bulwark that night. Then I asked the Basque whether, if I were to turn and run toward the foot of the bulwark, he would follow me; and he promised to do so. Then I leaped into the ditch and came under the bulwark wall, covering myself with my buckler for fear of stones and leaving my companion on the other side in the certainty that he would follow close after me. But when the Maid saw her standard in the Basque's hands she was afraid that she had lost it. For he was by now in the ditch. She then seized her standard by the pole so firmly that he could not hold it, crying, "Oh, my standard, my standard!" And she shook the standard so vigorously that I imagined the others might suppose that she was making a sign to them. So I shouted, "Oh, Basque, is this what you promised me?" Then the Basque tugged at the standard so hard that he tore it from the Maid's hands, and then he came on to me, carrying the standard. Thereupon all the Maid's army rushed together and immediately rallied, and they attacked the bulwark so sharply that within a short time they had taken both it and the bastille, from which the enemy retired. Then the French entered the city of Orléans over the bridge.[28]

---

[28] On May 7. It will be remembered that the Bastille des Tourelles defended the approach to the bridge, which was the means of communication between the city of Orléans and the left bank of the Loire.

That same day I had heard the Maid say, "In God's name, tonight we shall enter the city over the bridge." And when they had done so, the Maid and her men retired into the city of Orléans, where I had her wounds tended, for she had been struck by an arrow during the assault.

Next day all the English who still remained inside the town in parts other than the Bastille des Tourelles raised the siege and departed, discomfited and in confusion. And so, thanks to the help of our Lord and the Maid, the city was delivered from the hands of the enemy.

Some time after the return from the King's anointing, it was decided by his Council, which was then at Mehun sur Yèvre, that it was very necessary to recover the town of La Charité, which was held by the enemy, but that the town of Saint Pierre le Moûtier, which they also held, must be captured first.

To collect the soldiers for this expedition, Joan went to the town of Bourges, which she made her assembly point, and from there, with a considerable number of men, of whom my lord d'Albret was the captain, she went to besiege Saint Pierre le Moûtier.

After the Maid and her men had been investing the place for some time, orders were given for an attack. The attack took place, and those who were there did their very best to capture it. But because of the great number of soldiers in the town and its great strength, and also because of the resistance that the garrison put up, the French were forcibly compelled to retire. At that moment, I came up. But I had been so severely wounded in the heel by an arrow that I could neither stand nor walk without crutches. I saw that the Maid had been left with a very small company of her own men and others and had no doubt that harm would ensue. So I mounted a horse and rushed toward her. I asked her what she was doing there alone like that, and why she did not retire with the rest. After taking her helmet from her head, she answered that she was not alone, that she still had fifty thousand men in her company, and that she would not leave that spot until she had taken the town.

At that moment, whatever she might say, she had not more than four or five men with her, which I know for certain, as do several others who also saw her. Therefore I told her out of hand to go away and retire like the rest. She told me, however, to send for faggots and withies to form a bridge over the moat so that it might be possible to get near. And when she had said this she shouted out loudly, "Faggots and withies, everybody, so that we can make a bridge!" And they were immediately brought and put in position. The whole thing utterly astonished me, for the town was immediately carried by assault, and at that time there was no great resistance.[29]

All the Maid's exploits seemed to me rather divine and miraculous than otherwise. It would have been impossible for anyone as young as the Maid to perform such deeds except at the will and guidance of our Lord.

For the space of a whole year, at the orders of our lord the King, I remained in the Maid's company, and during that time I neither saw nor learned anything about her that was not consonant with a good Christian; I saw the excellence of her life and the honesty of her behavior in each and all of her deeds.

I knew that Maid to be a very devout creature; she stood most devoutly when attending our Lord's divine services, which she continually wanted to hear; that is to say, High Mass in whatever place she was, and also the subsequent Hours on solemn festivals, and the Low Mass on other days. She was in the habit of hearing Mass every day, if that was possible.

---

[29] The siege took place in November 1429.

Several times I have seen and known her to confess and receive the sacrament, and she did everything that a good Christian man or woman should do. Never, during the time that I was with her, did I hear her swear, blaspheme, or take our Lord's name or that of His saints in vain, for any cause or on any occasion whatever.

Although she was a young girl, beautiful and shapely, and when helping to arm her or otherwise I have often seen her breasts, and although sometimes when I was dressing her wounds I have seen her legs quite bare, and I have gone close to her many times—and I was strong, young, and vigorous in those days—never, despite any sight or contact I had with the Maid, was my body moved to any carnal desire for her, nor were any of her soldiers or squires moved in this way, as I have heard them say and tell many times.

JOAN'S PAGE

Louis de Coutes

Louis de Coutes, whom her men used to call *Mugot* or *Imerguet*, was not more than fourteen or fifteen and was learning the profession of arms under Raoul de Gaucourt when Joan arrived at Chinon. He was, says the *Chronicle of the Maid*, "a very courtly man". Chosen to be Joan's page, together with a certain Raymond (the same, no doubt, who was killed beneath the walls of Paris), he did not leave her thereafter until the operations before the capital. His deposition is full of lifelike details. He tells how, like the urchin he was, he ran off in a fright when he saw people of high rank coming to visit Joan; and again, how on the day when Joan was warned by her "Counsel" that a skirmish had started up beside the Saint Loup bastille and had herself hastily armed, he passed her standard out to her through a first-floor window because he had forgotten to give it to her; and how one day he saw her comforting a wounded Englishman, and how he too was present at the coronation in his capacity of page.

> In the year when Joan came to the King from Chinon, I was fourteen or fifteen years old and served and lived with my lord de Gaucourt, who was captain of the town of Chinon. At that time, Joan arrived in the place with two men, and she was taken to the King. I often saw Joan go to the King and return; a lodging was provided for her in a tower of the castle of Couldray. And I lived in that tower with Joan; and all the time that she was there I was with her continuously, all day long. At night, she had women with her, and I well remember that during the time that she was in that tower of Couldray many of high rank came on several occasions to talk with Joan. What they said or did I do not know, for I always ran off when I saw them coming; and I do not know who they were.
>
> During the time that I was with Joan in the tower, I often saw her on her knees and praying, as I supposed. However, I was never able to hear what she said, although sometimes she wept. Then Joan was taken to Poitiers, and afterward she came back to Tours, to the house of a person called Lapau. It was there that my lord the Duke of Alençon gave Joan a horse; and it was there at Tours that I and a certain Raymond were told that we must be Joan's pages. From that time, I was always with Joan and went everywhere with her, serving her in my office as page both at Blois and at Orléans until we came before Paris.
>
> While she was at Tours, a suit of armor was given to her, and then Joan received her rank from the King. And from Tours she went to Blois and stayed there for some time—I do not remember for how long; and then it was

decided to retire from Blois and go to Orléans through the Sologne country, and Joan retired with her company of soldiers, exhorting them to put all their trust in God and to confess their sins. And I often accompanied Joan when she took the Blessed Sacrament.

When we arrived before Orléans from the Sologne direction, Joan, I, and several others were conveyed across the water to the city side, and from there, we entered Orléans. Joan was most exhausted when she arrived, for she had not taken off her armor to sleep the night before she left Blois. At Orléans she was lodged in the treasurer's house[30] beside the Bannier gate, and in that house she received the Eucharist.

The next day, the one on which we made our entry into Orléans, Joan went to see the Bastard of Orléans and spoke with him; and she came back very angry because, as she told me, it had been decided that there should be no attack that day. However, Joan went to the bulwark that the King's men held facing the English bulwark, and from there she addressed the English opposite, requesting them in God's name to retire, otherwise she would drive them away. And one called the Bastard of Granville answered Joan most abusively, asking whether she expected them to surrender to a woman, and calling the French who were with Joan "unbelieving pimps".

After that, Joan returned to her lodging and went up to her room, and I thought that she had gone there to sleep. But a little later she came down again and said to me, "Oh, wicked boy, why did you not tell me that French blood is being spilled?" and she urged me to go and fetch her horse. In the meantime, she had herself armed by her hostess and her hostess' daughter, and when I had harnessed her horse I found her ready in her armor. She told me to fetch her standard,

---

[30] Jacques Boucher. See the depositions of Dunois and the Duke of Alençon above.

THE WITNESSES ON HER DAILY LIFE

which was upstairs, and I handed it to her through the window.

When she had her standard, Joan galloped off in the direction of the Burgundy gate;[31] and her hostess bade me run after her, which I did. There was an attack or a skirmish going on the Saint Loup side, in the later course of which the bulwark was taken, and Joan met several wounded Frenchmen on the road, which made her angry. The English were preparing their defense when Joan hurried up; and as soon as the French saw her they gave a shout, and the fort and Bastille of Saint Loup was taken. And I have heard that some churchmen resumed their vestments and came out to meet Joan; and she received them and did not allow them to be harmed. She had them brought to her at her lodging. But the rest of the English were killed by the Orléans men.

And that evening Joan came to dine at her lodging. She was very abstemious and very often ate no more than a hunk of bread all day. I was astonished that she ate so little. When she stayed at home, she ate only twice a day.

The next day, toward the hour of Terce,[32] our lord the King's soldiers crossed the river in boats to attack the Bastille or fortress of Saint Jean le Blanc. And the French took it, also the Bastille des Célestins (Augustins), and Joan crossed the river with her men, and I with her. We reentered Orléans, where Joan went to bed in her lodging with the women, as was her habit. For she always had a woman sleeping with her at night if she could find one. If she could not, at such times as we were fighting or in the field, she slept in her clothes.

Next day, against the will of several lords who thought that she would be exposing the King's men to great peril,

---

[31] Jean d'Aulon also describes this incident, which was to end with the taking of the Saint Loup bastille (May 4).
[32] Nine o'clock in the morning.

Joan threw open the Burgundy gate and a small gate that was beside the great tower, and she crossed the water with some soldiers to break in to the bastille or fort of the bridge,[33] which the English still held. Here the King's men hung on from the hour of Prime[34] till night before delivering their final attack. And there Joan was wounded and took off her armor so that her wounds could be dressed; and after they had been tended, she resumed her armor and went with the rest to take part in the attack, which had lasted continuously from the hour of Prime until night. Finally the bulwark was taken. And Joan had stayed all the time with the attacking soldiers, inciting them to be of good courage and not to retire, for soon the fort would be theirs.

She told them that when they saw the wind blowing her standard in the direction of the fortress, then they would capture it. But toward evening, when the King's men saw that they were achieving nothing and that night was already near, they despaired of taking the fort. Joan, however, continued to persist and promised them that they would capture the place without fail that day. The King's men got ready to attack again; and when the English saw this they put up no defense. They were terrified, and practically all of them were drowned. In that last attack, there was no defense put up by the English side.

Next day [May 8, 1429], all the English retired from around the town to Beaugency and Meung. The King's army, and with it Joan, followed them; and there the English debated whether to give up the town of Beaugency or to fight. But when the day for fighting came they retired from that town of Beaugency, pursued by the King's men, with whom was Joan. La Hire led the

---

[33] Or Les Tourelles. This took place on May 7.
[34] Six o'clock in the morning.

advance guard, which greatly annoyed Joan, who liked to command the advance guard herself. The King's men, however, behaved so valiantly that La Hire with his forward troops fell on the English and won a victory. Almost all the English were killed.[35]

Joan was very pious and was greatly distressed by such slaughter. Once when a Frenchman was bringing in some English prisoners, he knocked one of them on the head and left him for dead. When Joan saw this, she dismounted and received the Englishman's confession, raising his head and comforting him as much as she could. Then, together with the King's army, Joan went to the town of Jargeau, which was taken by assault; and there many English prisoners were taken, among them Suffort and La Poule.[36]

Then, after the relief of Orléans, Joan went with the army to the King, who was at Tours, and it was decided that the King should go to Rheims to be crowned. And the King set out with his army, and Joan with them, toward Troyes, which surrendered to him, and from there to Châlons, which also opened its gates to him, and then to Rheims, where our lord the King was crowned and anointed, and there I was present. For I was, as I have said, Joan's page and was always with her. And I remained with her until the moment when she came to the walls of Paris.

From everything that I knew of her, Joan appeared to me a good and modest woman who lived a Christian life. She heard the Mass very gladly and never missed a possible opportunity of doing so. She was angry when

---

[35] Louis de Coutes is here describing in brief the whole Loire campaign, including Patay. (See the Duke of Alençon's deposition.) Further on, he dwells on the capture of Jargeau, which actually took place on June 12, before the capitulation of Beaugency on June 17.

[36] Suffolk and his brother, John de la Pole, the captain of Avranches.

she heard anyone blaspheming God's name or anyone swearing. I heard her reprimand my lord Duke of Alençon several times for swearing or uttering some blasphemy. On the whole, nobody in the army would have dared to swear or blaspheme in front of her for fear of a reprimand from her.

She would not allow women with the army. Indeed, once, near the town of Château Thierry, when she saw the mistress of one of the soldiers, who was a knight, she chased her with a naked sword. But she did not strike the woman. She warned her gently and kindly that she must never appear in soldiers' company again, or she, Joan, would do something to her that she would dislike.

JOAN'S CONFESSOR

Jean Pasquerel

Jean Pasquerel was a mendicant friar, an Augustinian hermit of the convent of Bayeux. He had been on the same pilgrimage with Isabelle Romée, who, as we know, at the time when her daughter left Vaucouleurs to find the King, was making the pilgrimage to Notre Dame du Puy at Velay, which was to that age what Lourdes is to ours. The group of pilgrims from Lorraine were impressed by his saintliness and persuaded him to go in search of Joan. He found her on getting back to Tours, where he was at that time lector in the convent. He became Joan's confessor and did not leave her side until her capture at Compiègne.

To him we owe the text of the last summons that Joan addressed to the English; perhaps it was to him that she dictated it. And it is he too who gives details of the standard that was painted for her, that standard which she declared, during her interrogation, to be forty times dearer to her than her sword. They reproached her then for having had the names of Jesus and Mary painted on it, which names also appear on her letters. At this distance of time, it seems incomprehensible that such a reproach should have been uttered by churchmen. The explanation is that just in those years the cult of the Sacred Name of Jesus was being propagated by Saint Bernardine of Siena, and the device "Jesus Maria" was used by the mendicant friars of all orders. For the Rouen judges, creatures of the University, this was a heinous crime. And one can imagine that in 1456, at the precise moment when the great quarrel between the orders and the Sorbonne was coming to a climax, Pasquerel must have felt singularly moved at thus testifying to Joan's predilection for the mendicants, a subject to which he reverted several times during the course of his deposition.

> The first time that I heard Joan speak and tell how she had come to the King, I was at Puy; and in that town were Joan's mother and some of those who had brought Joan to the King.[37] And as they knew me a little they told me that I must come with them to see Joan, and that they would not let me go until they had brought me to Joan. And I went with them to the town of Chinon, and from there to Tours, to the convent of which I was lector.
>
> There at Tours, Joan was lodged in the house of Jean Dupuy, a citizen of the town. I found Joan at his house, and the men who had brought me spoke to her like this: "Joan, we have brought you this good Father. If you knew him well, you would like him exceedingly." Joan answered that she was very pleased to see me, that she had already heard of me, and that on the following day she would

[37] Perhaps Colet de Vienne and Richard Larcher, the servants of Jean de Metz and Bertrand de Poulengy.

confess to me. The next day I heard her confession and sang the Mass before her, and from that hour I followed her always and remained with her up to the town of Compiègne, where she was captured.

I have heard that when Joan came to the King she was twice examined by women to discover what she was, man or woman, wanton or virgin. She was found to be a woman, and a virgin maid. The women who examined her were, as I have heard, Lady de Gaucourt and Lady de Trêves.[38] She was then taken to Poitiers to be examined by the clerks in the University there, to discover what should be done about her. Her examiners were Master Jourdain Morin, Master Pierre de Versailles, who died Bishop of Meaux, and several others. When they had examined her, they concluded that, considering the danger that then threatened the whole kingdom, the King might well avail himself of her help, and that they had found nothing in her contrary to the Catholic faith.

After this she came to Chinon and expected to speak with the King. But this time she could not. However, after a session of the Council, she did speak with him. But as she was going into the royal lodgings that day, a man sitting on his horse near the entrance said, "Is not that the Maid there?" swearing to God that if he had her for a night she would be no maid next morning. Then Joan said to the man, "Oh, in God's name, do you take His name in vain when you are so near your death?" And an hour later that man fell into the river and was drowned. And I tell you this as I heard it from Joan and from several others who said they had been present.

The Count of Vendôme brought Joan to the King and introduced her into the audience chamber. When the

---

[38] Jeanne de Preuilly and Jeanne de Mortemer. Both were at the court of Yolanda of Sicily, the King's mother-in-law.

King saw her, he asked Joan her name, and she answered, "Gentle Dauphin, I am called Joan the Maid, and the King of Heaven has sent me to see that you are anointed and crowned in the city of Rheims, and you shall be lieutenant of the King of Heaven, who is King of France." And after the King had put her some other questions, Joan repeated, "I tell you on behalf of the Lord that you are the true heir of France and the King's son. He has sent me to you to lead you to Rheims, there to receive your coronation and your anointing, if you will." After he heard this, the King said to those who were present that Joan had told him a certain secret that nobody knew or could know but God.[39] That is why he had great confidence in her. I have heard all this from Joan's own mouth, for I was not present myself.

I have also heard her say that she was displeased by all these interrogations, and that they stopped her doing the work for which she had been sent. She said that now was the time when action was necessary, also that she had asked the messengers of her Lord—that is to say, of God—who appeared to her, what she ought to do. And they had told her to take up the standard of her Lord. And therefore Joan had her standard made, with the image of our Savior painted on it, sitting in judgment among the clouds of Heaven, and with Him a painted angel holding a fleur-de-lis in his hand, which Our Lord was blessing. I was at Tours, where the standard was painted.[40]

---

[39] This refers to the prayer made by the King in the secrecy of his oratory at Loches, on All Saints' Eve 1428, of which Joan knew the time, the place, and the tenor.

[40] There is to be found in the accounts of Hémon Raguier, the royal treasurer, the following entry: "And to Hauves Poulnoir, painter, living at Tours, for painting and furnishing stuff for a great and a small standard for the Maid, 25 livres *tournois*" (Quicherat, 5:258).

A little afterward Joan went with the rest of the army to raise the siege that was then being laid to Orléans. I was in her company and did not leave her until she was taken prisoner before Compiègne. I served her as chaplain and heard her confession and sang her the Mass.

Joan was most devoted to God and the Blessed Virgin, and she confessed almost every day, and often took Communion. She asked me also when we were at a place where there was a convent of mendicant friars to remind her on what days the children brought up by the mendicants received the Eucharist, so that she could receive it with them, which she often did.... When she was making confession, she wept.

When Joan left Tours to go to Orléans, she asked me not to leave her but still to stay with her as her confessor; and I promised to do so. We were at Blois for about two or three days, waiting for the provisions that were being loaded on to boats there; and it was there that she told me to have a standard made to assemble the priests, what is called in French a *banner*,[41] and on that standard to have painted the image of our Lord crucified; and this I did. When the standard was made, Joan bade me assemble all the priests twice a day, in the morning and the evening; and when they came together, they sang anthems and hymns to Saint Mary, and Joan joined them. And she would not let the soldiers mix with the priests unless they had confessed, and she exhorted all the soldiers to confess in order to come to this gathering; and at the gathering itself all the priests were prepared to hear anyone who wanted to confess.

When Joan departed from Blois to go to Orléans, she had all the priests assembled round this standard, and the

---

[41] This banner, which differed from the standard and the pennon already mentioned, was intended to be carried in procession by the priests and monks accompanying the army.

priests marched in front of the army. When they had assembled, they left in the Sologne direction, singing the *Veni Creator Spiritus* and many other anthems, and they camped that night in the fields and did the same on the night following. And on the third day, they approached Orléans, where the English had mounted their siege works along the Loire bank, and the French came so close to the English that the French and English were within view of one another, and the King's soldiers brought in the provisions. Now the river was so low that the ships could not ride up or touch the bank where the English were; and suddenly the water rose, so that the ships could touch land on the French side; and Joan boarded them with some soldiers and crossed to Orléans.[42]

On Joan's orders, I returned to Blois with the priests and the standard. Then, some days later, I returned with some soldiers to Orléans from the Blésois side, with the priests and the standard. We met with no hindrance. When Joan heard of our coming, she came out to meet us, and together we entered Orléans without hindrance and brought in the provisions under the Englishmen's noses. And the astonishing thing is that the English with their great deployment of forces, armed and ready for battle, saw the King's men, so small a company compared with them; they saw them, they heard the priests singing—I was in the middle of them carrying the standard—and nevertheless not an Englishman stirred, and they made no attack on the soldiers and priests.

Once arrived at Orléans, the soldiers went out again at Joan's urgent plea and went over to the attack against the English, who were in the fort or Bastille of Saint

---

[42] Jean Pasquerel was the only one to give this version of the sudden change that allowed the ships to reach Orléans. For Dunois and the other witnesses it was a change in the wind that made the operation possible. He has just been describing the days from April 27–29. Cf. Dunois' deposition.

Loup. After taking a meal, I went with the rest of the priests to Joan's lodging, and the moment we arrived Joan cried out, "Where are the men who should be arming me? The blood of our men is flowing on the ground." And once armed, she immediately sallied from the city and went to the fortified point of Saint Loup where the assault was going on. On the road she found many wounded, which distressed her greatly, and she joined the rest in the attack with such success that by strength and violence the fort was taken and the English in it made prisoners. I remember that it was on the eve of our Lord's Ascension,[43] and many English were killed there. For this Joan was very sorry, saying that they had died without confessing, and she wept bitterly for them and immediately made confession to me. And she told me publicly to exhort all the soldiers to confess their sins and give thanks to God for the victory they had won. For if they did not, she said that she would stay with them no longer. She also said on that vigil of our Lord's Ascension that in five days the siege of Orléans would be completely lifted and that there would be no English left in front of the city. Which was the case. For, as I have said, that Wednesday the fort or Bastille of Saint Loup was taken—the place where the monks are now—and in that fort were more than a hundred picked men, well-armed, of whom not one remained that was not captured or killed. That evening when she returned to her lodging she told me that on the morrow, which was the feast of our Lord's Ascension, she would not fight and would not arm, out of respect for the feast; and that same evening she asked to confess and to receive the Eucharist, which she did. And on that same evening she gave orders that no one was to

---

[43] On Wednesday, May 4, therefore. (See the accounts of Louis de Coutes and Jean d'Aulon.)

go out of the city next day, nor to make an assault or attack, unless he had previously come to make confession; and that precautions must be taken that dissolute women should not follow the army. For it was on account of such sins that God was allowing the war to be lost. And what Joan had ordered was carried out.

On that day of our Lord's Ascension [Thursday, May 5], Joan wrote to the English who were in the forts or bastilles in the following manner:

"You Englishmen, who have no right in this realm of France, the King of Heaven commands and bids you by me, Joan the Maid, to leave your forts and return into your own country. Otherwise, I will give you such a harrying that no one will ever forget it. This I write to you for the third and last time, and I shall not write again. Signed: Jesus Maria, Joan the Maid." And after this: "I should have sent you my letter politely, but you keep back my messengers [in the original French, my heralds]. For you have detained my herald named Guyenne.[44] Please send him back to me, and I will send you some of your men who were captured in the Bastille of Saint Loup. For they were not all killed."

Then she took an arrow, tied the letter with a thread to the tip, and told an archer to fire this arrow at the English. "Read; here is news!" she cried.

The English received the letter with the arrow and read it. When they had done so, they began to shout: "Here's news from the Armagnacs' whore!" When she heard this, Joan began to sigh and weep copious tears, invoking the King of Heaven to her aid. Then she was comforted, as she said, for she had had news of her Lord. And that evening after dinner she ordered me to get up

---

[44] Two heralds had been assigned to her at the same time as her two pages; their names were Guyenne and Ambleville. See p. 148 (Jacques l'Esbahy's deposition).

next day earlier than I had done on Ascension day, for she would confess to me very early; and this she did.

And that day, Friday, the day after the feast of the Ascension, I got up early and heard Joan's confession, and sang the Mass to her and her men at Orléans. Then they went out to the attack, which lasted from morning till evening. And that day the Bastille des Augustins[45] was taken by storm, and Joan, who generally fasted on Fridays, could not fast that day. For she was too exhausted and therefore dined. After dinner, a valiant and famous knight came to visit her, whose name I do not remember. But he told Joan that the King's captains and soldiers had held counsel together, that they saw how inferior they were in numbers to the English, and that they knew it had been by God's especial grace that they had won the successes that they had. "Seeing that the town is well-stocked with provisions, we shall be very likely to hold it until the King sends aid," he added, "and the council do not think it needful for the soldiers to sally forth tomorrow." Joan replied, "You have been to your council, and I to mine. And believe me, the counsel of my Lord will be put into effect, and will endure, while your counsel will perish." Then, turning to me, who was beside her, she said, "Get up early tomorrow, earlier than you did today, and do your very best. Keep close to me all the time. For tomorrow I shall have much to do, more than I ever had, and tomorrow the blood will spurt from my body above my breast."

The next day, Saturday, I got up very early and sang the Mass; and Joan went out to attack the fort on the bridge, where the Englishman Clasdas[46] was; and the

---

[45] See the account of the taking of the Bastille des Augustins, on May 6, in Jean d'Aulon's deposition.

[46] William Glansdale, the defender of Les Tourelles, which was captured on May 12.

attack there lasted from morning to sunset without a pause. In that attack, Joan was struck after the midday meal, as she had predicted, by an arrow above the breast, and when she felt the wound she was afraid and wept; and she was comforted, as she said. And when some soldiers saw her thus wounded, they wanted to lay a charm on her, but she refused it, saying, "I would rather die than do what I know to be a sin, or to be against God's law." She said that she knew she must die one day, but did not know when, where, how, or at what hour; but that if a salve could be put on her wound without sin, she would willingly be cured. And they put olive oil and pig's grease on it, and afterward she confessed to me, with tears and lamentations. Then she returned to the attack, shouting, "Clasdas, Clasdas, give in, give in to the King of Heaven! You have called me a whore, but I have great pity for your soul and your men's souls." Then Clasdas, armed from head to foot, fell into the Loire and was drowned; and Joan, moved to pity, began to weep bitterly for the soul of this Clasdas and of the rest, who were drowned there in great numbers. That day all the English who were on the far side of the bridge were captured or killed.

Then on the Sunday [May 8], before sunrise, all the English who had remained on the battlefield collected together and passed by the moat of the city and went to the town of Meung sur Loire, where they remained for some days. And that Sunday there was a solemn procession in Orléans and a sermon, and it was decided that we should go to the King. Joan went to him, and the English gathered together and went to the town of Jargeau, which was taken by storm. Then the English were fought and conquered near the town of Patay.[47] Then Joan, wishing to push on further, as she had said, for the King's

---

[47] The Loire campaign up to the battle of Patay (on June 18) is here reduced to a few words.

coronation, led him to Troyes in Champagne, and from Troyes to Châlons, and from Châlons to Rheims, where the King was miraculously crowned and anointed [on July 17, 1429], as Joan had predicted on her very first arrival. And several times I heard Joan say that there was a mystery about her achievement, and when men said to her, "Never have such things been seen as have been seen in your actions. Such actions are not to be read of in any books",[48] she would reply, "My Lord has a book in which no clerk has ever read, so perfect is it in its instruction."

---

[48] Already they were saying, "This girl from Lorraine has no equal...."

CHAPTER 7

The First Imprisonment

On the evening of May 24, 1430, while she was leading a sortie in the defense of Compiègne, which was being besieged by the Anglo-Burgundians, Joan was caught outside the city when the portcullises that closed the gate had been lifted. For a long time Guillaume de Flavy, the captain of Compiègne, was suspected of treason; today he does not appear to have been guilty. Only an unlucky chance seems to have been responsible for this undue haste. However that may be, Joan fell, dismounted, into the hands of the Bastard of Vendôme, a vassal of Jean de Luxembourg, Count de Ligny, who was commander of the Burgundian contingent that was besieging Compiègne. When he heard this news, the Duke of Burgundy, Philip the Good, hurried to the spot "more delighted than if a king had fallen into his hands", in the words of the chronicler Georges Chastellain. He had Joan imprisoned first in the castle of Beaulieu en Vermandois, and then in the castle of Beaurevoir, which belonged to Jean de Luxembourg himself. It was there that the famous attempt to escape took place; and it was there also that Cauchon came on to the scene, arriving to negotiate for the purchase of the prisoner on behalf of the King of England, who was finally to have her for the sum of ten thousand gold crowns.[1] An English escort led her by way of Arras, Le Crotoy, Saint Valery, Eu, and Dieppe, to Rouen, which was to be her final destination. The Earl of Warwick also brought to Rouen at the same time the young King Henry VI—he was only nine, and was crowned King of France in Paris on December 16, 1431, the year of Joan's burning. One may wonder whether the eyes of the Maid and of the child-king ever met, whether Joan ever saw the person to whom she was being sacrificed.

For this whole period, we possess only one testimony before the court of rehabilitation, which we here give. Some historians have been surprised at this; some have even chosen to see in it something more than an omission, to construe it as a deliberate abstention, and to use the fact as evidence for their theory of a "directed" trial.

It is strange that it has not occurred to them that a prisoner has, automatically, hardly any witnesses to speak for him. Who could have appeared of those who saw Joan in prison or during her unhappy journey, in the course of which good care must have been taken that she was seen by nobody? One piece of evidence would have been infinitely valuable, the testimony of "the Lady of Luxembourg", for instance, the aunt of Jean de Luxembourg, who hesitated for five months before giving Joan up. She had frequent—and friendly—conversations with the prisoner in the castle of Beaurevoir. But we know that she died even before Joan, on November 13, 1430. Obviously neither her jailers nor the soldiers of her Anglo-Burgundian escort could have been

---

[1] The author computed this as equal to some $225,000 by mid-twentieth-century standards.—TRANS.

summoned to France for the trial, even if they could have been found. Certainly the Duke of Burgundy himself, Philip the Good, who had come to see his vassal's prisoner, would have provided a curious testimony. But there was no question of calling to the witness-bar the great Duke of the West; and, besides, at that time Burgundy was once more no part of France.

Moreover, it would be an error derived from an entirely modern viewpoint to forget the purpose of the rehabilitation trial. The witnesses were certainly not called in order that the commissioners might reconstruct Joan's history, but to allow them to judge whether she was or was not a heretic. Her story was only of interest to them in so far as it helped them to find Joan either a guilty person or an innocent victim. If the facts, therefore, which public opinion proclaimed miraculous, and first among them the relief of Orléans, had a particular importance in their eyes, as had the circumstances of her condemnation, and also the heroine's origins (since here a guarantee of her piety and her beliefs was to be found), one cannot see what could have interested them in the empty period between Compiègne—or even Rheims—and Rouen.

One must reckon it a lucky chance, therefore, that at the time of the rehabilitation one French knight was found who had been in Jean de Luxembourg's service and who had had an opportunity of seeing Joan in her prison at the castle of Beaurevoir while she was waiting for her fate to be decided. He seems to have taken a sympathetic interest in her and never to have missed a chance of seeing her, for after one visit, this time in her prison at Rouen, he went with the crowd to the cemetery of Saint Ouen on the day of her famous public "abjuration".

THE MAN WHO SAW JOAN AT BEAUREVOIR
Haimond de Macy
(Knight)

I saw Joan for the first time when she was held in the castle of Beaurevoir on behalf of my lord the Count de Ligny [Jean de Luxembourg]. I saw her in prison several times, and I spoke with her on several occasions. I tried several times playfully to touch her breasts. I tried to slip my hand in, but Joan would not let me. She pushed me off with all her might. She was indeed a modest woman, both in her language and her behavior.

Joan was taken to the castle of Le Crotoy, where a very important man was kept prisoner. This was Master Nicolas de Queuville, chancellor of Amiens cathedral, and a doctor in both civil and canon law. He often sang a Mass in the prison, which Joan attended as often as she could. I heard from this Master Nicolas later that Joan had confessed to him and that she was a good Christian and most devout. He spoke very well of Joan.

Joan was then taken to the castle at Rouen[2] and imprisoned in a cell that looked out on the countryside. As soon as she was here, the Count de Ligny came to see her, and I with him. One day when the Count de Ligny went to see Joan he was accompanied by the Earls of Warwick and of Stauffort,[3] also by the present chancellor of England, the Count de Ligny's brother, who was then Bishop of Thérouanne,[4] also by myself. The Count de Ligny then addressed Joan in these words: "Joan, I have come here to offer you ransom on

---

[2] Consigned to an English escort at Le Crotoy on November 21, she arrived at Rouen a little before Christmas and was there imprisoned in the castle of Bouvreuil.

[3] Humphrey, Earl of Stafford, constable of France for the English king.

[4] Louis de Luxembourg.

condition that you promise never again to take up arms against us." She answered, "In God's name, you are mocking me. For I know very well that you neither have the wish nor the power to do so." And this she repeated several times, for he persisted in this statement. Then she said, "I know very well that the English will have me killed, because they believe they will gain the kingdom of France after my death. But even if they bring a hundred thousand more of the Goddams than are here at present, they will never have the kingdom." The Earl of Stauffort was incensed by this speech and half drew his dagger to strike her, but the Earl of Warwick prevented him.

A little later, while I was still at Rouen, Joan was led into an open space in front of Saint Ouen, where a sermon was read to her by Master Nicolas Midy,[5] who said to her, among other things, in my hearing, "Joan, we feel great pity for you. You must retract what you have said, or we shall hand you over to the secular arm." But she answered that she had done no wrong, and that she believed in the twelve articles of the faith and the ten precepts of the Decalogue. She then said that she referred to the court of Rome and was willing to accept everything that the Holy Church believed. Nevertheless she was pressed very hard to retract. But she said to them, "You take great pains to pervert me." Then, to escape from her danger, she said that she was quite willing to do all that they wanted. So one of the King of England's secretaries who was there, Laurent Calot by name, took a little written schedule from his sleeve and handed it to Joan for her to sign; and she replied that she could neither read nor write. All the same, this secretary, Laurent Calot, held the schedule out to her, and with it a pen

---

[5] An error of memory. It was Guillaume Érard who read the sermon at Saint Ouen; Nicolas Midy was to "preach" in the Vieux Marché.

for her to sign. And mockingly Joan drew a circle on the document. Then Laurent Calot took Joan's hand with the pen and forced her to make some mark, which I have forgotten.[6]

I believe that Joan is in Paradise.

---

[6] See later testimonies concerning the scene of the "abjuration". Joan could sign her name. However, after the circle that she "mockingly" traced she only signed with a cross that day—as the verbatim account of the scene, included in the records of the condemnation suit, testifies.

CHAPTER 8

The Rouen Witnesses

A certain number of witnesses had been heard by the inquirers in Paris between April 2 and May 12 (notably the Duke of Alençon, whose testimony we have seen). Hearings were also resumed at Rouen on May 10, and between the tenth and the fourteenth the witnesses appeared before the apostolic commissioners or their substitutes, generally to confirm their previous statements. The majority of these Rouen witnesses had been heard already, either in December 1455 or in the course of the ecclesiastical inquiry of 1452. The inquiry was, therefore, complete at the end of May 1456, when Jean d'Aulon sent his written testimony.

We shall find, therefore, in the following pages depositions relative to Joan's condemnatory trial. We have already noted, as the reader will remember, what was said by the scribes who recorded this trial. But their evidence there only concerned the falsifications introduced by Cauchon and his accomplices, which the commissioners had not been able to detect until they had the original documents in their hands. Here we shall be concerned with "Joan's Passion"; and here we shall be faithfully following the sequence of the rehabilitation trial. In their sessions in December 1455, the apostolic commissioners examined the original documents, which enabled them to see to what extent the procedure had been perverted in 1431, while in their final inquiry, in May 1456, the depositions concerning Joan's conduct before her judges and in her last days were gathered together or confirmed.

So for the members of the tribunal charged with the rehabilitation, events developed in a curious manner, leading them from a merely legal task—the examination of a trial that everyone supposed to have been correct but that proved to have been falsified—to the heart of a shattering drama. They knew everything already in rough outline, but certainly never suspected the details that were going to transfigure Joan before their eyes and to give her the features that she was to wear to all eternity. Guillaume Bouillé and, to a greater extent, Jean Bréhal, the Inquisitor, the men who conducted the preliminary inquiry, were the only two to discern at that moment what had really taken place at Rouen twenty-five years before.

Joan, as will be remembered, had been brought to Rouen under an English escort a little before December 25, 1430. She was imprisoned in a tower of the castle of Bouvreuil, constructed in ancient days by Philip Augustus to defend Rouen against the English. In this same castle, the little English king Henry VI had been living since July 29, under the guardianship of his tutor the Earl of Warwick (father of the King-Maker). The town had been under English occupation for the last ten years, and another personage was living there who was to be the real manager of Joan's trial. This was the so-called "Cardinal of England", Henry Beaufort, Bishop of Winchester.[1]

---

[1] Cardinal since 1427, in which year he had been charged by Pope Martin V to lead a crusade against the Hussites. But the money and men collected on this excuse had been employed in besieging Compiègne.

The condemnation case opened on February 21, 1431. We know how public sessions were replaced on March 10 by interrogations behind closed doors in this same castle. The examination was concluded on the seventeenth of that month. The indictment was read in the course of the sessions of March 27 and 28. Next they proceeded to the prosecution and "admonitions"; and it was then that Joan was threatened with torture. The scene of the "abjuration" took place at the cemetery of Saint Ouen on May 24, 1431. After that there was the very short "trial for relapse" on Tuesday, May 29. Finally, on Wednesday, May 30, Joan was burned in the square of the Vieux Marché.

Who desired Joan's death, and why was it desired? This was the first question the inquirers might rightfully ask themselves. On this point, as will be seen, the answers of the Rouen witnesses were very clear.

A BENEDICTINE MONK

Thomas Marie[2]

As Joan had done wonders in the war, and as the English are commonly superstitious, they reckoned that there was something supernatural about her. That, in my opinion, is why in all their counsels and in other places they desired her death.

How do you know that the English are superstitious? Everybody knows it. Why, it is quite proverbial.

---

[2] This Benedictine was prior of the convent of Saint Michel, near Rouen. He had taken no personal part in the case, but, living at Rouen as he did, he followed the whole business from afar.

A FORMER ASSESSOR

Pierre Miget[3]

If she had not been harmful to the English she would never have been treated and condemned as she was. But they were more afraid of her than of a large army....

... I heard an English knight say that the English feared her more than a hundred men at arms. They said that she used spells and feared her on account of the victories she had won....

She was so utterly simple that she believed the English would release her for money and did not believe that they desired her death.

ANOTHER ASSESSOR

Jean Fabri (or Lefevre)[4]

I believe that the English were not very fond of Joan. If she had been of the English party, I do not think they would have been so active against her or have been so rigorous in their treatment of her.

I believe that they prosecuted her because they were afraid of her.

---

[3] Prior of Longueville le Giffard: as a character rather more than suspect. He had been assessor in the condemnatory trial and had always given his judgments in the sense required by Cauchon. In the remainder of his deposition, he offers the excuse that he was afraid.

[4] Another dubious character. Jean Fabri, hermit of the order of Saint Augustine and Bishop of Demetriada, had also been an assessor in the condemnatory trial. He was clearly most embarrassed when making his deposition. He had the merit, however, of once having taken Joan's part against her interrogators, for which he was soundly put in his place.

As for fear and pressure,[5] I know nothing of that. But I do know about the other part of that article, and I believe that the case was started on English initiative and with English money.

Others are more positive and more explicit.

A DOMINICAN

Friar Isambart de la Pierre[6]

Judging from the case and all that was done in connection with it, it is my belief and judgment that the English acted against her out of hatred and malice, and that they had no other purpose than her death.

ANOTHER DOMINICAN

Friar Jean Toutmouillé[7]

Common fame had it that the English prosecuted Joan out of a perverse desire for vengeance, and that they gave visible signs of their malice. For before her death the

---

[5] Pressure exercised on the judges. The second part of his answer refers to Article 3 of the interrogatory in twenty-seven articles that was drawn up for the inquiry.

[6] We shall often have occasion to mention his name, and later on we shall give his first deposition (p. 232) made at the time of the royal inquiry in 1450. He was a Dominican of the convent of Saint Jacques in Rouen, and he was an assessor in Joan's condemnatory trial. But he was one of the very few who dared to offer her counsel and guidance, at his own risk and peril, as will be seen. He was also one of the three persons who were with Joan right up to the stake—the other two were Friar Martin Ladvenu and the sheriff's officer Jean Massieu.

[7] Another Dominican of the same convent. He played no part in the first trial, but accompanied Friar Martin Ladvenu when he went on the last day to tell Joan in prison by what pains she would die. He had described the

English proposed to lay siege to Louviers, but they quickly changed their minds and said that they would not besiege the town until the Maid had been examined. And the sequel offers patent proof of this. For immediately after her burning, they went and besieged Louviers. They reckoned that while she was alive they would have no glory or success in the field of war.

A PRIEST

Jean Riquier[8]

It was commonly said that the English dared not besiege Louviers until she was dead.[9]

... Joan was taken to Rouen and a case opened against her on the charge of heresy. I was then a chorister in Rouen cathedral, and sometimes I heard the church dignitaries[10] talking about this case. I heard Master Pierre Maurice and Master Nicolas Loiseleur, among others whose names I do not now remember, say that the English feared her so much they dared not besiege Louviers while she was alive, that it was necessary to please them, that a case must quickly be framed against her and that an excuse would be found for putting her to death.

---

scene at the time of the royal inquiry, to which he was called. It is only an abstract from his deposition that we give here. For the rest, see p. 244.

[8] As he explains further on, he took no part in the case, for at the time he was no more than a youth of fifteen. At the moment of the deposition, he was priest of the parish of Heudicourt (Eure).

[9] There exists an order signed by Laurent Calot, the royal secretary, commanding Thomas Blount, treasurer, to furnish the sums necessary for the siege of Louviers. This order is dated June 2, 1431, three days after Joan's death.

[10] He is speaking of the canons of Rouen cathedral.

It was not merely a case of threats. Certain Englishmen translated the matter into deeds. Numerous examples will be found later on. But here is one reported by Guillaume Manchon, the principal scribe in the case.

Guillaume Manchon

> One day someone whose name I do not remember said something about Joan that displeased the lord de Stauffort.[11] This lord de Stauffort pursued him with drawn sword to a place of sanctuary with such venom that if that lord had not been told that the place where this man had run was a holy spot, and gave a right of refuge, the lord de Stauffort would have stabbed the fellow.

And Thomas Marie concludes to this effect:

> I certainly believe that if the English had had such a woman they would have honored her highly and not treated her in that way.

Once Joan was delivered into their hands, the English could purely and simply have executed her. But that would straightway have made her a martyr, and the regent Bedford[12] was too careful to rush things like that. Besides, being a man of his day, he understood that by holding Joan he now possessed the best means of discrediting the French king forever. To the sight and knowledge of the whole world, Charles VII owed his anointing and coronation at Rheims to Joan alone. In the oil and the crown lay the office of king, and if it were possible to prove that

---

[11] Humphrey, Earl of Stafford, who has been mentioned in Haimond de Macy's testimony.

[12] He, of course, died in 1435 in the same castle of Bouvreuil in which Joan had been imprisoned.

this extraordinary girl was no more than a miserable heretic, and that her vaunted mission was no more than an imposture, the French royal line would be destroyed forever. By repercussion, the dual monarchy of England and France, then in the hands of Bedford's nephew Henry VI, would be established. What was more, the idea was in the air. In 1429 an anonymous clerk, replying to the panegyric that Jean Gerson had written in person in praise of the Maid, had maintained that Joan might possibly be nothing but a heretic. Early in her imprisonment, the University of Paris had claimed that she should be submitted to them for judgment. It is true that the University was filled with creatures of the English king and made itself the deliberate champion of the "dual monarchy".

But from the military point of view, Paris was not safe. At Rouen, on the other hand, the English felt masters of the situation. Moreover, they had a ready-made instrument to conduct the case in the person of the Bishop of Beauvais, who had been driven from his diocese by Joan's victories. He would be all the easier to manipulate because he coveted the see of Rouen, then vacant. It was true that he was not qualified to act as a judge outside his diocese and, furthermore, according to the rules of canon law, Joan should only have been judged by the bishop of the diocese from which she came, or of the place where she was alleged to have committed heresy. But that proviso was overridden; on December 28, 1430, Bedford made the chapter of Rouen confer on Cauchon a "territorial concession" authorizing him to proceed to judgment. Then on January 3, he ordered that Joan should be handed over to him.

For the rest, let us hear the witnesses. Firstly:

Guillaume Manchon

I had no knowledge of Joan before she was brought to Rouen. From what was said, she had been captured in the diocese of Beauvais. For that reason my lord Pierre Cauchon, then Bishop of Beauvais, claimed the right to judge her and exercised all his powers to have her handed over to him. He wrote to the King of England and to the Duke of Burgundy, from whom he finally obtained her, at the cost, however, of a sum amounting to a thousand livres or crowns. He had also to pay an annual revenue of three hundred crowns to a soldier of the Duke of Burgundy's, the man who had actually captured her and to whom the English king had granted this reward. Finally a case was begun against Joan on grounds of faith, and I was chosen to make the record together with one Guillaume Boisguillaume.

Then, reverting to the subject in the course of another deposition:

Whether the judges proceeded out of hatred or other causes I leave to their consciences. I know, however, and firmly believe that if she had been of the English party they would not have treated her so, or have started such a case against her. She was brought to Rouen rather than to Paris, in my opinion, because the King of England and the chief men of his Council were in the town of Rouen. And she was imprisoned in the castle of Rouen. I was compelled to act as scribe in this case, and I did so, though reluctantly, because I should not have dared to disobey the lords of the King's Council. The English instituted the prosecution, and it was at their expense that it was conducted. I do not think, however, that the Bishop of Beauvais was compelled to prosecute Joan, nor was the promoter Jean d'Estivet. They did what they did voluntarily. As for the assessors and other counselors, I do not think that they would have dared to refuse. There was no one who was not afraid.

Boisguillaume[13]

(The second scribe in the case)

I know very well the lord Bishop of Beauvais instituted the case against her, because, as he said, she had been taken prisoner within the limits of the diocese of Beauvais.[14] Whether it was out of hatred or for what other cause I leave to his own conscience. I know, however, that all the costs were borne by the English king; and I know very well that the Bishop himself and the others who took a hand in the case received letters of safeguard[15] from the King of England, for I saw them.

Thomas Marie[16]

In this case some acted out of fear, and some out of zeal (for the English party).

---

[13] See page 52.

[14] Historians have often discussed the question whether Compiègne was at that time part of the see of Beauvais; it seems now to be established that it was. But even so, this was not a sufficient reason for Cauchon to arrogate to himself the right to try Joan.

[15] See Jean de Mailly's answers, for mention of these letters of safeguard, which the authors of the case obtained from the English king to guarantee them should an appeal be made to the Pope (p. 265).

[16] See p. 199.

... I do not believe what is contained in that article,[17] especially on the subject of fear and threats. I believe rather that it was a question of favor (i.e., that the judges were bought), especially since some of them, as I believe and have heard, received presents.

Richard de Grouchet

(Canon of the Collegiate Church of La Saussaye, in the diocese of Évreux; he was an assessor in the condemnatory trial)

In my opinion, one section of those who took part in the trial did so voluntarily and in a partisan spirit. Others were forced against their wills and showed great fear, among them Master Nicolas de Houppeville, who was in great danger. So were Jean Pigache and Pierre Minier, as they told me, also myself who was with them. We only gave our opinions and took part in the trial out of fear, threats, and terror, and it was in our minds to run away. I have often heard from the lips of Master Pierre Maurice that the English were most displeased with him for warning her, at the time of the first sermon, to stick to her good resolutions. He was in great danger of a beating, as he told me.

He returns to this point in a further deposition, on the subject of the article dealing with the judges' freedom of opinion.

This article is true in point of law. As for the facts, the aforesaid Pigache and Minier and I, too, gave our opinions in writing, according to our consciences. This did

[17] This refers to Article 5 of the interrogatory, which deals with the alleged pressure exerted on the judges.

not suit the Bishop and his assessors, who said to us, "So this is what you have done, is it?"

Isambart de la Pierre[18]

He deals with the question thus:

> Some of those who took part in the trial of the case were, like the Bishop of Beauvais, motivated by their partiality; some, like certain of the English, by a desire for vengeance; and others, like the Paris doctors, by greed for gain. Still others were moved by fear, like the sub-Inquisitor and others whom I do not remember. And the whole thing was done on the initiative of the King of England, the Cardinal of Winchester, the Earl of Warwick, and other Englishmen, who paid the expenses incurred in the staging of the trial.

THE PRISON

After the responsible parties, the prisoner: how was Joan treated in the Rouen prison where she was kept for five months?

We have seen from the preceding testimonies that it was only by a perversion of the rules of procedure that Cauchon could be chosen to judge Joan. But another "irregularity" is laid bare.

Here, to begin with, are two witnesses who took no part in the trial but who interpret for us the feeling of curiosity that Joan aroused. Both were able to see her in prison, the

[18] See p. 201.

first because he was a lawyer and had connections, the second because he was an official of the city judiciary.

Laurent Guesdon

(Citizen of Rouen and advocate in the lay court; a married clerk)

I saw Joan only at the moment when she was brought to Rouen. As many people were curious to see her, I went also to the castle of Rouen, and it was there that I saw her for the first time.

Pierre Daron

(Lieutenant to the bailiff of Rouen)

I had no acquaintance with Joan until the time when she was brought to Rouen. I was then city procurator and, being most curious to see her, looked for a suitable excuse to satisfy my curiosity. I met Pierre Manuel, advocate to the English king, who was also most anxious to see her, and we went together. We found her in a tower of the castle, with fetters on her legs, which were attached to a great wooden block. She had several English guards. This man Manuel spoke to her in my presence and told her mockingly that she would not have been there if she had not been led there; and he asked her whether she knew before her capture that she would be taken. She answered that she had had a strong suspicion. He then asked her why she had not taken special precautions on the day when she was captured, since she had suspected that this would happen. She replied that she had known neither the day nor the hour in which she would be captured, nor when this would occur. And that was all that we said to her.

I saw her once more during her trial, when she was being led from her prison into the great court of the castle.

Isambart de la Pierre

I saw her in the prison of Rouen castle in a very dark room fettered and chained.

Jean Massieu

Joan was kept a prisoner and remained in that place under the guard of five Englishmen, of whom three stayed in her room at night and two remained outside the door. And I know for certain that at night she lay chained by the legs with two pairs of irons, and tightly secured by another chain which passed through the legs of her bed and was attached to a great block of wood five or six foot long, by means of a lock. In this way she was unable to stir from her place.

And elsewhere, in the course of another deposition:

As for her prison, Joan was in a room in the center of Rouen castle, approached by eight stairs. There was a great bed in it on which she slept; and there was a great block of wood on which was a chain, to which Joan was attached by means of fetters on her legs. These were secured to the log with a lock that was let into it. And there were five English guards of the lowest sort, whom we should describe in French as common torturers, to watch her. And they were most eager for Joan's death, and often mocked her; and she reproached them for it.

THE IRON CAGE

> And I have heard from Étienne Castille, the blacksmith, that he made an iron cage for her, in which she was held in a standing position, secured by the neck, the hands, and the feet, and that she was kept in it from the moment when she was brought to Rouen until the opening of her trial. However, I never saw her in it. For when I led her out or in she was always unchained.

One might suppose that this iron cage was an invention of Jean Massieu, whose evidence is slightly suspect and who had a tendency to exaggerate in order to whitewash himself. But here is other testimony on this point, the impartiality of which is not open to suspicion.

Pierre Cusquel

He is a simple citizen of Rouen, probably a master mason.

> Joan was brought to this city of Rouen by the English and imprisoned in the castle of Rouen in a room beneath a staircase on the side looking out to the open country. There I saw her incarcerated. And I think that the assessors in the case acted out of partiality for the English, and that they would not have dared oppose them. As to the pressure exercised, I know nothing of that.
> ... This is what I saw. For by permission of Master Jean son (Johnson), then overseer of the castle masonry, I went into Joan's prison two or three times and spoke with her. I advised her to be prudent in her speech, since they desired her death. I know that an iron cage was made for her in which she would have been kept in a standing position. I saw it being weighed at my house. But I did not see Joan in that cage.

Thomas Marie

I was told by the ironsmith that he had made a cage in which Joan was to have been kept in a standing position.
Was she put into it?
I think so. As for her guards, I know nothing of them.

Pierre Boucher

(Vicar of the parish of Bourgeauville in the diocese of Lisieux; he was present two or three times at hearings of the trial, but took no part in it)

I know quite well that she was imprisoned in Rouen castle, but I do not know whether she was fettered. No one spoke with her except by permission of certain Englishmen who were her guards. I never saw her leave the prison except accompanied by these Englishmen, who must, I think, have lived with her in a single room of which there were three keys. One was kept by the lord Cardinal (Winchester), or his clerk (the keeper of his privy seal), the second by the Inquisitor, and the third by the promoter Master Jean Benedicite (d'Estivet). The English were desperately afraid that she might escape.

JOAN IN PRIVATE

Isambart de la Pierre

The Bishop of Beauvais belonged to the English party, and this same Bishop when he opened the case ordered that she should be kept in chains. It was he who sent Englishmen to guard her, and this same Bishop forbade anyone to speak with her except by his permission or that of the promoter, who was known as Benedicite.

Guillaume Manchon

The Bishop of Beauvais belonged to the English party. And, as I saw, even before the Bishop began to investigate the case, Joan was already in chains. Then, when he had gathered some information, she was handed over to the guardianship of four Englishmen, who were ordered by the Bishop and the Catholic Inquisitor to guard her faithfully. She was cruelly treated, and at the end of the case, instruments of torture were displayed before her. She was then dressed in male clothing and complained that she could not give it up for fear that her guards would violate her in the night. Once or twice she complained to the Bishop of Beauvais, to the sub-Inquisitor, and to Master Nicolas Loiseleur that one of her guards had tried to rape her. For that reason, these Englishmen were sternly warned by the Earl of Warwick, following the reports of the Bishop, the Inquisitor, and Loiseleur, not to make another attempt on her; and two new guards were chosen.

Thomas Marie

After the first sermon, when she was returned to her prison in the castle, she was subjected to such torments and vexations that she declared she would rather die than stay any longer in the company of these Englishmen.

JOAN'S ILLNESS

Jean Tiphaine

(The Duchess of Bedford's physician and assessor in the case)

He claimed to have given no judgment during the deliberations. This was untrue; the minutes of the trial vouch for the contrary.

When Joan was ill, the judges sent me to visit her, and I was brought to her by the man d'Estivet. In the presence of d'Estivet, of Master Guillaume de la Chambre, doctor of medicine, and of several others, I felt her pulse in order to discover the cause of her complaint. I asked her what was wrong and where she felt pain. She answered that a carp had been sent to her by the Bishop of Beauvais, of which she had eaten, and that she thought that to have been the cause of her illness. Then d'Estivet upbraided her, saying that this was false, and he called her a wanton. "It is you, you wanton," he said, "who have taken aloes and other things that have made you ill." This she denied, and there was a liberal exchange of abuse between Joan and d'Estivet. Later I tried to find out more about Joan's illness, and the man with her said that she had vomited a great deal.

I know no more, and I do not remember having given any opinion during the case except in this matter of her illness.

Guillaume de la Chambre

(Another physician, also summoned to the trial)

As for her illness, the Cardinal of England and the Earl of Warwick sent for me. I visited them with Master Guillaume Desjardins, doctor of medicine, and other physicians. Then the Earl of Warwick told us that Joan had been ill, as he had been informed, and that he had sent for us to take care of her. For the King would not have her on any account die a natural death. The King, in fact, valued her highly and had paid dearly for her, and he did not want her to die except at the hands of justice. He wanted to have her burned, and by frequent visits we saw to it that she recovered. I went to see her with Master Guillaume

Desjardins and the others. We felt her on the right side and found her feverish. So we decided to bleed her. When we reported this to the Earl of Warwick, he said to us, "Take care with your bleeding. For she is a cunning woman and might kill herself." Nevertheless she was bled, and this immediately improved her condition. Once she was cured, a certain Master Jean d'Estivet came on the scene and exchanged some abusive language with Joan. He called her a wanton and a whore, which so greatly annoyed Joan that she had a relapse and became feverish again. This came to the Earl's knowledge, and he forbade d'Estivet to abuse Joan any more.

Now this imprisonment in a lay prison was illegal; since she was being tried on a religious charge by an ecclesiastical court, Joan should have been kept in an ecclesiastical prison and guarded by women. This she never ceased to demand right through the trial, and we shall see what weight there was behind this "irregularity", notably after the "abjuration" scene.

Pierre Miget[19]

As for her imprisonment, the English put her in a lay prison and put her in chains. Nobody was allowed to speak to her, and she was guarded by Englishmen who prevented anyone from speaking to her. But I did not know that she was in irons.

Jean Fabri[20]

Joan was imprisoned in the castle of Rouen. But how that happened I do not know. It greatly displeased some

---

[19] See p. 200.
[20] See p. 200.

of the assessors, however, that Joan was not put in an ecclesiastical prison. I complained about that myself. For it did not seem to me proper procedure to put her in the hands of laymen, and particularly of Englishmen, since she had been handed over to the Church.[21] Several agreed with me, but no one dared to raise the subject.

THE INTERROGATIONS

Here, for a start, is a little incident that shows the sinister zeal with which Cauchon's friend, Jean d'Estivet, the promoter of Beauvais and his companion in his flight from Rheims, performed his duties. This took place as Joan was passing from her prison to the place of interrogation.

Jean Massieu

As, in leading Joan from her prison to her place of trial, I several times passed the castle chapel, I let her, at her request, stop there and say her prayers. For this I was several times reprimanded by the said Benedicite, the promoter of the case. "What makes you so bold, wretch," he said to me, "as to let that excommunicated whore come near here without permission? I will have you put in a place where you will never see sun nor moon for a month if you do it again." And when the promoter saw that I did not obey him, he took up his stand several times before the chapel door; and Joan expressly asked, "Is the Body of Jesus Christ here?"

---

[21] By Bedford himself, as we have seen. But even while he was having her tried by a Church court, he continued, against all the regulations, to keep her in a lay prison. And Cauchon was his accomplice in this. (See Guillaume Manchon's testimony later, about the abjuration scene, p. 241.)

In another deposition he gives the following details:

> I was at Joan's trial each time she came up for judgment before the judges and clerks; and because of my office I was deputed clerk to Master Jean Benedicite, promoter of the case, to call Joan and all the others who were cited in that case. And from what I saw I believe that they were acting out of hatred, by favor, and for the purpose of dishonoring the King of France, whom she served. They were acting out of vengeance, and for her death, not reasonably or for the honor of God and the Catholic faith. I am moved to say this because when my lord of Beauvais, who was judge in the case together with six churchmen—to wit, Beaupère, Midy, Maurice, Touraine, Courcelles, and Feuillet or some other in his place—when they interrogated her, I say, before she had answered one, another member of the court would throw in another question, for which reason she was often hurried and confused in her replies.

He returned several times to this point in the course of his depositions.

> When Joan was interrogated, there were six assessors with the judges, who put questions to her. And sometimes just when one of them was asking a question or she was replying to it, another would interrupt her; so much so that several times she said to her interrogators, "My dear lords, please take your turns!"
>
> I well remember that they often asked Joan questions in several parts, and several of them asked her difficult questions at the same time. Then, before she could reply to one, another put another question. She disliked this, and said, "Please take your turns." And I was surprised to see how well she could reply to the subtle and tricky questions that were asked her, questions that an educated

man would have found it difficult to answer well. The examination generally went on for from eight to eleven hours.

Other witnesses describe the proceedings.

Guillaume de la Chambre

As for the interrogations, I once saw the abbot of Fécamp examining Joan; and Master Jean Beaupère intervened with a number of different questions, which Joan did not wish to answer all together. So she told them that they were greatly prejudicing her by harassing her like this and that she had replied to those questions already.

And here is the man in the best position to judge the interrogations because he wrote them down:

Guillaume Manchon

The ones who seemed to me, as I remember, most zealous for the English cause were Beaupère, Midy, and Touraine.... During the trial, Joan was harassed by numerous and diverse questions. Nearly every day, there were interrogations in the morning that lasted for about three or four hours. And sometimes they extracted difficult and subtle questions from what Joan had said and faced her with them after lunch in a second interrogation that lasted for two or three hours. And sometimes they switched from one interrogatory to another, changing their manner of asking questions as well: and despite this change she answered wisely. She had a very good memory. For very often she would say, "I answered you on that point in another place", or, indicating me, "I refer to the clerk...."

Nicolas Taquel

(The third scribe in the case)

I was present when certain judges put very difficult questions to her, to which she replied that she was in no position to answer and referred the questions back to them. And several of the doctors and members of the court said to her at times, "You are quite right, Joan."

Guillaume Manchon

She was quite a simple girl, so it seemed to me, although sometimes she answered very wisely, and sometimes very simply, as can be seen from the record of the trial. I do not think that she would have been capable of defending herself alone in so difficult a case against such learned men, if she had not been inspired.

Jean Fabri

A skeptic. Even at the moment when he testifies for the rehabilitation, he refuses to believe in Joan's revelations. Nevertheless, on his own confession, he believed her to be "inspired".

In certain particulars, they asked very searching questions. But she extricated herself very well. Sometimes they abandoned the interrogatories and moved from one subject to another to see if she would shift her ground.

They made long examinations, which lasted from two to three hours and which greatly exhausted the doctors who took part in them. Whether this was by deliberate design I do not know.

... I was present at the trial up to the first sermon preached to her at Saint Ouen, but not again after that. Joan appeared to me to be about twenty. She was most saintly and answered wisely, so wisely indeed, that for three weeks I thought her inspired, although she insisted a great deal—too much in my opinion—on her revelations.

AN EXAMPLE OF HER REPLIES

Boisguillaume

(Second scribe)

During the trial, Joan very often complained that they put subtle questions to her that had no connection with the case. I remember that she was asked more than once whether she was in a state of grace. She replied that it was a very big thing to answer a question like that. But finally she replied, "If I am, may God keep me in it, and if I am not, may God make me so, for I had rather die than not be in the love of God." Her interrogators were dumbfounded by this answer, and they stopped at this point, asking her no more questions for the moment.

Thomas Marie

She might have been eighteen years old, in my opinion. As for her simplicity and ignorance, I have heard someone who was present at the trial say that she answered the questions as wisely as the most learned clerk could have done.

Jean Riquier

I have heard it said that she answered so wisely that if certain of the doctors had been interrogated as she was, they would hardly have replied as well.

Martin Ladvenu

In my opinion she might have been eighteen or nineteen; in her bearing, she was very simple, but in her answers full of wisdom and discernment.[22]

HER MEMORY DURING THE HEARINGS

At the service of her astounding wisdom was a most uncommon memory:

Martin Ladvenu

I well remember that Joan answered very wisely. For sometimes, when she was interrogated on a subject upon which she had been interrogated before, she would answer that she had replied to that question already and say nothing more. Then she had her previous answer read back by the clerks.

Jean Marcel

A simple Rouen citizen. He only speaks from hearsay, but reports the words of one of the judges.

I heard Master Jean Le Sauvage of the Dominican order, who often spoke to me about Joan, say that he had followed the case against her. But he would only speak of it with great repugnance. However, he told me one thing:

---

[22] One wonders where Anatole France got the strange idea that there was a conspiracy at the rehabilitation trial to present Joan as "almost an idiot" in order to throw the miracle into higher relief. *All* the witnesses insist, on the contrary, on the wisdom of her answers.

that he had never seen a girl of that age work such havoc with her examiners. He was most astonished by Joan's answers and her memory. For she remembered everything that she had said.

Jean Fabri

They greatly exhausted her by long interrogations, which lasted for two or three hours.... Sometimes her interrogators cut their questions so short that she could hardly answer them; the cleverest man in the world would have had difficulty in answering them. I remember one moment during the case when she was being examined about her visions. They read her a schedule containing her own answers, which seemed to me to have been badly transcribed, for she had not answered like that. I told Joan to be careful. She asked the scribes who had written this schedule to read it to her again; and then she told them that what she had said had been the exact opposite, and that they had not written it down correctly. Her reply was put right in the script. Then Master Guillaume Manchon told Joan that he would be careful in future.

Pierre Daron

I heard some people say during the trial that Joan was miraculous in her answers and that she had a remarkable memory. For once when they were interrogating her on a point on which she had already been interrogated a week before, she answered, "I have been asked that before, on such a day", or "I was interrogated about that a week ago, and I answered like this." Even though Boisguillaume, one of the scribes, told her that she had not answered that question, some of those in court protested that Joan was right. Then they read the answers for that particular day and found that Joan was speaking the truth. She was greatly elated and told Boisguillaume that if he made another mistake she would pull his ears.

Jean Tiphaine

I did not know Joan until she was brought to Rouen for her trial. The first time I was asked to attend I refused to go. But when I was asked a second time, I went and watched, and listened to the questions and to her replies. She made very fine replies. On the occasion when I attended the trial, the judges and assessors were in a small court behind the great court of the castle. She answered very prudently and wisely, and with great boldness.

The first time that I was called for this case I refused to go; and the second time I went because I was afraid of the English, and so that they should not see that I was unwilling to go, and so that I should not thereby incur their anger. What their intentions were in proceeding against her I do not know.... On the day when I was present Master Beaupère was the principal interrogator, and he put the questions. However, Jacques de Touraine of the Order of Minorites interrogated her at times. I remember this Master Jacques asking her once whether she had been at a certain spot where some Englishmen had been killed; and Joan answered, "Yes, in God's name, I was. Don't be so soft, but speak out! Why did they not leave France and go home to their own country?" There was a great English lord present—I have forgotten his name—and he said when he heard that, "She really is a good creature. Why is she not English!" He said that to Master Guillaume Desjardins and me. There is no great learned doctor who would not have been quite puzzled and confused if he had been questioned by such lords and before such a great assembly as Joan was.

METHODS OF INTIMIDATION

Everything was done, however, to confuse her. The wicked part played by Nicolas Loiseleur will be remembered (see pp. 50–51). He tried to drive Joan to her own ruin.

Pierre Miget

I only know what people have told me, that a man went to talk to her in the night, pretending to be a prisoner of the French king's party. He tried to persuade Joan to persist in her assertions, and that the English would not dare to hurt her. From what Guillaume Manchon, one of the scribes, told me, it was a certain Master Jean [sic] Loiseleur who pretended to be a prisoner.

Many of those who were present at the trial were most indignant and considered her execution most cruel and wrong. The general opinion was that the judgment had been unjust.

What is more, there had been the torture scene. Here is the torturer's testimony.

Maugier Leparmentier

(Unmarried clerk, summoner to the episcopal court of Rouen—aged fifty-six)

I first knew Joan when she was brought to Rouen, and I saw her in the castle of Rouen, where my colleague and I were ordered to put her to the torture. She was then interrogated a little. And she replied with so much wisdom that everyone present was astonished. In the end, my colleague and I retired without touching her.

JOAN HAD NO ADVOCATE

In defending herself against all these powers in league, Joan was alone.

And here is another argument for the nullity of the condemnatory trial: the absence of a defending counsel, which is testified to by the witnesses.

Pierre Boucher

All that I know is that she was alone, sitting on a high chair; and I heard her answer without any counsel.

Martin Ladvenu

I know quite well that Joan had no director or counselor or defender right up to the end of the trial, and that no one would have dared to have anything to do with directing, counseling, or defending her, out of fear of the English. I have heard that several who went to the castle at the judges' orders to counsel and direct Joan were harshly turned back and threatened.

Jean Fabri

All I know is that at the moment when they asked Joan whether she was in a state of grace, I said that it was no question to put to such a woman. Then the Bishop of Beauvais said to me, "It would have been better for you if you had kept your mouth shut."

... I was not in court right through the case. But when I was there, I never saw Joan with a counsel or heard her ask for one.

His evidence on this point is confirmed by other witnesses:

Jean Massieu

Jean Fabri, of the Order of the Hermits of Saint Augustine, at present Bishop of Demetriada, often saw Joan riddled with questions about her being in a state of grace; and although the answers she gave were in his opinion satisfactory, they persisted in constantly questioning her on this subject. He protested that this was harassing her too much. But her interrogators told him to be quiet. I do not know who said this to him. I have forgotten. But I do remember that the abbot of Fécamp seemed to me to be pressing this point rather out of hatred for Joan and zeal for the English than out of any desire for justice. Furthermore, when Master Jean de Châtillon, then archdeacon of Évreux, told the Bishop and the assessors that the case as they were trying it seemed to him invalid—I do not remember for what reason—I, whose task it was to summon the assessors and counselors, was forbidden ever to call Châtillon to the case again; and from that hour Châtillon had no further part in it.

Master Jean de la Fontaine was entrusted with her interrogation for some days. But after having played this part in the trial, he stayed away. For he had mentioned certain things that he thought should not have been done in this case. Master Jean Lemaître, the Inquisitor assigned to this case, tried several times to excuse himself and did his best to take no part in it. But he was told by certain persons known to him that if he did not take part, he would himself be in danger of his life. He acted under English pressure, and I heard him say several times, "There is a good risk of death, as I can see, if one does not act as the English wish in this case."

... There was an occasion during Joan's interrogation when Jean de Châtillon spoke somewhat in Joan's favor, saying that she was not bound to answer on this point or something of the sort—I do not remember exactly what. This displeased my lord Bishop of Beauvais and certain of his supporters, and there was a great uproar at these words. The Bishop then told Châtillon to be quiet and let the judges speak.

Friar Guillaume Duval

(A Dominican of the convent of Saint Jacques at Rouen—aged forty-five)

When they were trying Joan, I took part in one session with Isambart de la Pierre. Finding no proper place to sit in the court, we went and sat close to the Maid; and when she was being interrogated and examined, Friar Isambart advised her what to say by touching her or making her some sign. When the session was over, I was deputed, with Friar Isambart and Master Jean de la Fontaine, to visit her and counsel her that day after dinner. We went to the castle of Rouen together, to visit and admonish her; and there we found the Earl of Warwick, who attacked Friar Isambart most spitefully and indignantly, with biting abuse and scornful invective. "Why did you keep touching that wicked woman this morning? Why did you go on making signs to her? 'Sdeath, villain, if I catch you again trying to get her off or helping her with warnings, I will have you thrown in the Seine." Isambart's two companions then hid themselves in their convent out of fear. All these things I saw and heard, but no more. For I was not present at the trial.

For the dangers incurred by Martin Ladvenu, Isambart de la Pierre, and Jean de la Fontaine on account of the counsel they gave Joan we have the evidence of:

Guillaume Manchon

Master Jean de la Fontaine was lieutenant (substitute) for my lord of Beauvais from the beginning of the trial until the week after Easter, 1431, and had to interrogate Joan in his absence. Nevertheless he was also present with the Bishop at all the other sessions of the trial. And the Maid was strongly urged to submit herself to the Church by this same La Fontaine, by Friar Isambart de la Pierre, and by Martin Ladvenu. They informed her that she must understand and believe the Church to mean our Holy Father the Pope and those presiding over the Church Militant. They said that she need have no doubts about submitting herself to our Holy Father the Pope and to the holy Council. For there were as many notable clerics of her party there as of the opposition, and that if she did not do so she would put herself in great danger. And the next day after this warning she said that she was willing to submit to our Holy Father the Pope and to the holy Council.

When my lord of Beauvais heard her say this, he asked who had been to speak to her on the previous day. The guard answered that it had been the said La Fontaine and the two friars. In their absence, the Bishop stormed most angrily against Jean Lemaître, the Inquisitor's vicar, and threatened to do them a violent mischief. And when it came to La Fontaine's ears that he was threatened for his action, he left the city of Rouen and did not return. As for the two friars, if Lemaître had not made excuses for them and begged for their pardon, saying that if any mischief were done to them he would not take part in the trial, they would have been in danger of their lives. And after that the Earl of Warwick ordered that no one except the Bishop of Beauvais or someone deputed by him should enter the Maid's prison, and that the Bishop should go in whenever he wished. But the vicar had no right of entry without him.

WAS JOAN IN REBELLION AGAINST THE CHURCH?

As for the substance of the interrogatories, here is the testimony of her judges:

Guillaume de la Chambre

I only knew Joan during her trial, in the course of which I was often called with other doctors and lawyers. As I see it, she was a good girl. For I heard afterward from Master Pierre Maurice that he had taken her confession, and that he had never heard such a confession, either from a doctor or from anyone else. On the basis of that confession, he considered that she was walking in God's ways, in a just and holy manner.

As for the zeal that animated the judges, I refer that to their own consciences. I know, however, that I would rather not have given my opinion of the case. I signed it, all the same, because I was forced to by the Bishop of Beauvais. Several times I offered the Bishop excuses, saying that it was not my profession to offer opinions on such a subject. But finally I was told that if I did not sign as the others had done I should be sorry that I had ever been at Rouen. That is why I signed. Threats were made to Master Jean Louhier [Lohier] and Master Nicolas de Houppeville also. They were threatened with drowning because they were reluctant to take part in the trial.

Pierre Miget

He too is skeptical about Joan's revelations, and yet she did not strike him as a heretic.

> I did not see Joan ... until she was brought to Rouen, and there I saw her several times during her trial. I think that she replied both wisely and as a good Catholic on the matter of faith, having regard to her age and her station, although it seemed to me that she insisted too much on the visions that she claimed to have had. She seemed to me a simple girl, and if she had been free, she would have been as good a Catholic, I think, as any other.

He underlines this in the course of another deposition.

> From Joan's replies I could see nothing about her that was not good and Christian, except these revelations, which she said she had had from the saints, and her belief in them. But I heard her say that her heart was for God, and that she wished to obey God and the Church.

THE APPEAL TO THE POPE

And here is the principal point: Joan declared that she put herself in the Pope's hands. She even expressly appealed to the Pope. But, in violation of all the rules of the Inquisition courts, this appeal was not registered. And here are two more reasons why the trial was invalid: Joan refused to accept her judges and appealed to the Pope, but nothing was done about it.

Guillaume de la Chambre

I well remember that once when she was being interrogated by the Bishop and some of the assessors, she said that this Bishop and the others were not her judges.

I have heard Joan say that she put herself in the hands of our lord the Pope.

Pierre Miget

I well remember Joan's saying several times that for what she had said and done she would answer to our lord the Pope.

Richard du Grouchet

At the time of the judgment, I both saw and heard Joan asked whether she was willing to submit to the Bishop of Beauvais and certain others there present, who were named. Joan replied that she was not, but that she submitted to the Pope and the Catholic Church. She asked to be taken before the Pope. When she was told that the records of her case would be sent to the Pope to judge, she answered that she did not wish it to be dealt with in that way, for she did not know what they would put in those records. She demanded to be taken to him, so that she could be interrogated by the Pope himself.

I do not know whether it was put or written in the records that she did not submit herself to the Church, and I saw no signs of this insertion being prevented. But I do know that when I was present Joan always submitted to the judgment of the Pope and the Church.

It was on Cauchon's formal instructions that the appeal to the Pope was neither implemented nor registered.

Isambart de la Pierre

> When Joan was asked whether she wished to submit herself to our father the Pope, she said that she did, provided that she could be led and taken to him, but that she did not wish to submit herself to those there present—that is to say, to the Bishop of Beauvais—since they were her mortal enemies. And when I pleaded with her to submit to the General Council then assembled,[23] at which were many prelates and doctors of the French king's party, Joan said, on hearing this, that she submitted to the Council. Then the Bishop of Beauvais interrupted me violently, saying, "Be quiet, in the devil's name!"
>
> On hearing this, Master Guillaume Manchon, who was writing the proceedings, asked the Bishop whether he should record her submission. The Bishop answered no, that it was not necessary. And Joan said to him, "Oh, you write down everything that is against me all right, but you will not record anything in my favor." And I do not believe that remark was written down, either, though it aroused a great uproar in the court.

THE EXAMINATION AS TO VIRGINITY

The Poitiers judges had had Joan examined to see whether she was a virgin, and we have stressed the importance of this examination already. Since she took the name of the

---

[23] The Council of Basel.

Maid, Joan would have been convicted of imposture if she had been found not to be a virgin. It was, furthermore, a guarantee of her mission, as we have seen, that she belonged to God alone, whose envoy she claimed to be. And as the English never stopped casting doubts on her purity—an extraordinary virtue, indeed, in a girl who lived among soldiers and slept beside them "on the straw"—this examination was of decisive importance at Rouen; of such decisive importance that when the result was brought to Cauchon he took good care to make no mention of it.

Jean Fabri

> I do not know whether she was examined or not. But I do know that once when they asked her why she was called the Maid, and if she was one, she answered, "I can assure you that I am, and if you do not believe me, get some women to examine me." And she proclaimed herself ready to submit to the examination, provided it were conducted by decent women, as was the custom.

Guillaume de la Chambre

He gives his opinion as a physician.

> I have heard that Joan was examined to discover whether she was a virgin or not, and that she was found to be one. And I know, in so far as one can know by the art of medicine, that she was a virgin and intact. For I saw her almost naked when I examined her at a time when she was ill. I felt her loins, and her flesh was very firm, so far as I could see by the look of it.

Jean Marcel

I have heard that the Duchess of Bedford[24] had Joan examined to see whether she was a virgin or not, and that she was found to be a virgin. And I heard also from Jeannotin Simon, a tailor, that the Duchess of Bedford ordered him to make a woman's tunic for Joan, and that when he tried it on her, he softly put his hand on her breast. She was annoyed and slapped Jeannotin's face.

Further details on this matter are provided by one of the scribes. They testify to the importance the English attached to this examination.

Boisguillaume

I heard several people whose names I have forgotten say that Joan was examined by certain matrons and found to be a virgin, and that the examination took place on the orders of the Duchess of Bedford, also that the Duke of Bedford concealed himself in a place from which he could watch Joan's examination.

Jean Massieu

I know very well that she was examined to see whether she was a virgin or not by some matrons and midwives at the Duchess of Bedford's orders, and that chief among them was Anna Bavon and another matron whose name I do not remember. After that examination, they declared that Joan was a virgin and intact, and this I heard from

---

[24] Anne of Burgundy, daughter of Charles the Bold and wife of the Duke of Bedford, regent of France during Henry VI's minority.

Anna herself. As a result of this, the Duchess of Bedford had the guards and others forbidden to do her violence.

THE COMEDY OF THE ABJURATION

Cauchon plainly wanted to obtain from Joan the disavowal of her mission, and a disavowal in public. This idea was to obsess him up to Joan's death and afterward. When he conceived the scene in the cemetery of Saint Ouen, he certainly imagined that he would achieve his ends. Joan was placed on a platform facing that on which were the judges and the assessors. It was the first time that the crowd was allowed to see her, and many were the witnesses who said, with Jean Marcel, "I saw her for the first time when the sermon was read to her at Saint Ouen."

One of the best-known University doctors, Master Guillaume Érard, an intimate friend of Cauchon's, who was to die in England in about 1439, was chosen to read her the hortatory sermon. What was necessary was to persuade her to abjure her alleged errors of faith and to decide her to wear her woman's clothes again. Let us quote, on Érard's behalf, this passage from the deposition of his former servant:

Jean de Lenozolles

> When I returned to Rouen about Whitsun, I found my master, who told me that he had been ordered to preach Joan a sermon, and that he greatly disliked this. He told me that he wished he were in Flanders.

However, on that morning of May 24, Érard, the old Sorbonne doctor, had rediscovered all his eloquence:

Isambart de la Pierre

I was present at the first sermon read to her by Master Guillaume Érard, who chose for his theme: "The branch can produce no fruit unless it remain on the vine." He said that there had never been such a monster in France as Joan, who was a witch, a heretic, and a schismatic, and that the King who favored her was like her, and that it had been with the help of such a heretic that he had tried to recover his kingdom. This last saying makes me believe that one of their motives was the wish to defame His Royal Majesty.

This is also the opinion of ...

Martin Ladvenu

I was present at the time of the first sentence and of the sermon preached at Saint Ouen by Master Guillaume Érard. And I firmly believe that the thing was done out of hatred for the King of France, and in order to discredit him. For in one passage of his sermon, Master Guillaume Érard burst out with, "Oh, royal house of France, you have never known monsters till now. But now you are dishonored for giving your faith to this woman, this witch, heretic, and child of superstition." To which Joan replied, "Do not speak of my king. He is a good Christian."

The details of the scene are given us by ...

Jean Massieu

When she was led to Saint Ouen to be preached to by Master Guillaume Érard, in the course of the sermon and about halfway through, after the preacher had cast obloquy on Joan, he began to cry out very loudly, "Oh, France, you are greatly abused. You have always been a most Christian country. Yet Charles, who calls himself your king and your governor, has subscribed, like a heretic and a schismatic, to the words and deeds of a good-for-nothing woman, an infamous woman abounding in all dishonor. And not the King only, but all the clergy of his obedience and in his realm by whom she has been examined and not rebuked, as she has said." Then, turning to Joan, he spoke to her with raised finger, "I am speaking to you, Joan, and I tell you that your king is a heretic and a schismatic." To which she replied, "By my faith, my lord, saving your reverence, let me tell you, and swear it on my life, that he is the noblest Christian of all Christians and loves the Faith and the Church better than any. He is not as you say." Then the preacher said to me, "Make her be quiet."

Massieu was standing, in fact, beside Joan on the rostrum, for it was his duty to read the famous schedule of abjuration to her.[25]

> When Joan was required to sign this schedule, there was so great a murmur among those present that I heard the Bishop say to someone, "You will pay for this." He insisted that he had been insulted, and that he would not proceed until he received an apology. In the meantime, I warned Joan of the danger that she was in, in the matter of this signature to the schedule. I saw very well that Joan did not understand the schedule, or the danger that she was in. Then, when she was pressed to sign it, Joan said, "Let this schedule be seen by the clerks and by the Church in whose hands I ought to be placed. If they advise me that I should sign it and do what I am told, I

---

[25] See above: "The Examination of the Trial," pp. 64–65.

will do it gladly." Then Master Guillaume Érard said to her, "Do it now, or else you will end your life today in the fire." Then Joan said that she would rather sign it than be burned. And at that moment, there was a great uproar in the crowd that was present, and stones were thrown. By whom I do not know.

The former clerk (secretary) to Jean Beaupère adds two very significant details when he shows Cauchon receiving orders from Henry Beaufort, Cardinal of Winchester, and adds that a pyre had already been prepared in the square.

Jean Monnet

(Canon of Paris and professor in theology—aged fifty)

I was at the sermon preached at Saint Ouen and was myself on the platform, sitting at the feet of Master Jean Beaupère. When the sermon was finished and they were beginning to read the sentence, Joan said that if these priests were advising her according to their consciences, it seemed to her that she ought gladly to do as she was counseled. On hearing this, the Bishop of Beauvais asked the Cardinal of England what he should do, in view of Joan's submission. The Cardinal then replied to the Bishop that he should receive Joan as a penitent. Then they put away the sentence that they had begun to read, and Joan was received as a penitent. At that time, I saw the schedule of abjuration that they had read, and I think that it was a little schedule of about six or seven lines; and I well remember that she left it to the judges' consciences to decide whether she ought to retract or not. The day that this took place, they say that the executioner was in attendance waiting for her to be handed over to the secular arm.

The pyre had been prepared, and the executioner was there. However, in principle, the pains of fire were only applicable to a relapsed heretic. Had Cauchon set his snare solely for the purpose of subsequently making a relapsed heretic of Joan? It is not impossible.

Guillaume du Désert[26]

> I was present at the first sermon preached at Saint Ouen. I there saw and heard Joan make her abjuration, submitting herself to the decision, judgment, and commands of the Church. There was an English doctor present listening to the sermon, and he was most displeased when her abjuration was accepted; and when she laughed as she pronounced certain words of the abjuration, he said to the Bishop of Beauvais that he was wrong in accepting this abjuration and that she was making a mock of them. The Bishop answered in a fury that he was a liar and that, since she was being tried for heresy, it was his duty to work for her salvation rather than her death.

The English, in fact, had not understood this maneuver at all.

Jean Favé

(Master of Arts and licentiate in law, master of the King's Requests)

> It was said that a case had been instituted against her on a matter of faith and that the English took the initiative and paid the fees of the doctors and others who were called to the case. As for the fear and pressure exercised,

---

[26] Assessor in the condemnatory trial.

after the first sermon, when Joan was being taken back to her prison in Rouen castle, the pages mocked at her, and their English masters let them do so; and from what I heard, the principal Englishmen were most indignant with the Bishop of Beauvais, the doctors, and the other assessors in the case, because she was not found guilty, sentenced, and handed over for execution. I have even heard it said that certain Englishmen, in their indignation, raised their swords against the Bishop and the doctors as they walked back from the castle, saying that the King had certainly wasted his money on them. But they did not strike them. I have heard it said too that the Earl of Warwick complained to the Bishop and the doctors after this second sermon, saying that things were going badly for the King, since Joan was slipping out of their hands. But one of them answered, "Do not worry, my lord. We shall catch her all right...."

After this alleged abjuration Joan was sentenced to perpetual imprisonment, a conclusion that must certainly have astounded the commissioners of the rehabilitation. "What impelled the judges to condemn her to imprisonment for life when they had promised her that she would not be punished?" They put this question to Guillaume Manchon in one of the interrogatories. "I think the reason was", said he, "the division of power[27] and their fear that she might escape." However that may be, the real sentence of condemnation was read that day by Cauchon, when, despite Joan's pleading, he ordered her to be taken back to a secular prison. It is Manchon, once more, who describes the scene:

---

[27] That is to say, because France was divided between the powers of England and her own king.

Guillaume Manchon

As they were leaving Saint Ouen, after the sermon and the Maid's abjuration, Loiseleur said to her, "Joan, please God you have done a good day's work and saved your soul." "Now," said she, "will you churchmen take me to one of your own prisons, so that I shall not be in the hands of the English any longer." But my lord of Beauvais answered, "Take her where you brought her from." She was led back to the castle therefore, whence she had come.

THE MALE CLOTHING

One of the few precise points in the famous schedule of abjuration was that Joan henceforth renounced the wearing of male clothing. In this way, it was left ludicrously easy to compel her in one way or another to resume those clothes, and then to have her declared a relapsed heretic.

Jean Massieu

After dinner that day, she put off her male clothes in front of the council of churchmen, and put on women's clothes, as she had been ordered to. It was then the Thursday or Friday after Whitsun, and her male clothes were put in a sack in her prison room. On the following Sunday morning, which was Trinity Sunday, when it was time for her to get up she said to her English guards, as she told me, "Take off my chains. I am going to get up." Then one of the Englishmen pulled off the woman's clothing that covered her, and they emptied the sack in which were her male clothes. These they flung to her, saying, "Get up", and stowed her woman's clothes in the bag. Then, as she told me, she put on the male clothing that they had given her. But first she said, "Sirs, you know very well that this is forbidden me. I will not wear them." Nevertheless they refused to give her any other clothes, and the argument went on till noon. Finally, she was compelled to go out—in order to fulfill a physical need—and to wear those clothes. When she came back, they still refused to give her any others, notwithstanding all her demands and supplications.

Others have given a slightly different account of this incident.

Martin Ladvenu

As for the question whether anyone came to her in the night and in secret, I heard from Joan's own lips that a great English lord entered her prison and tried to rape her. That was the reason, she said, why she had resumed male clothes.

Pierre Cusquel

People said that the sole cause of her condemnation was that she had resumed male clothes, and that she would not have done so and did not do so except to prevent the advances of the soldiers with whom she lived. I asked her why she wore these male clothes, and that was her answer.

THE SECULAR ARM

The case for her relapse was heard, at Cauchon's urgent request, on May 29. Let us recall the fact that, out of forty judges, thirty-six supported the abbot of Fécamp in his demand that the schedule of abjuration should be read to Joan a second time, to make certain that she had thoroughly understood it. Cauchon passed this over, and next day he was to commit a final irregularity. Once "handed over to the secular arm", the prisoner should properly have received her sentence from the secular court. In Joan's case, there was no sentence. She was immediately handed over to the executioner. Also, contrary to all the rules of procedure, the churchmen—or Cauchon at least—were present at her execution. He still hoped to hear her retract.

Martin Ladvenu

It was evident to the judges that she had submitted to the will of the Church and that she was a faithful and repentant Christian; and it was by their permission and with their orders that I administered the sacrament to her. She was handed over as relapsed[28] to the secular judges. But I do not think she would have been proceeded against in this way if she had belonged to the English party. I am certain that she was taken up by the English soldiers, who were there in great numbers, as soon as she was abandoned by the Church, and this without any sentence from the secular judge, although the bailiff of Rouen and the council of the lay court were there. I know this because I was with Joan continuously from the castle to the moment when she gave up the ghost; and it was I who, on the judges' orders, administered to her the sacraments of penitence and the Eucharist.

---

[28] Because she had again worn male clothing.

Laurent Guesdon

I was present when the last sermon was preached to her in the Vieux Marché at Rouen. I was there with the bailiff, because at that time I was the bailiff's lieutenant. The sentence was pronounced by which Joan was handed over to the secular arm. Immediately after that sentence, and without a moment's delay, she was placed in the bailiff's hands. Then without the bailiff or myself, whose duty it was to pronounce sentence, pronouncing any sentence, the executioner took Joan, without more ado, to the place where the wood was prepared; and she was burned. I do not think that this procedure was right, because shortly afterward a malefactor called Georges Folenfant was also sentenced to be handed over by the ecclesiastical court to the secular arm; and after the sentence this man Georges was taken into "the hurly-burly" (the bailiff's court), and there condemned by the secular judges. He was not led straight to the stake.

JOAN APPEALS TO GOD

One witness tells us of Joan's plaints and her solemn protestation when they came to tell her by what death she was to die.

Friar Jean Toutmouillé

(Dominican of the convent of Saint Jacques at Rouen)

On the day when Joan was handed over to the secular arm and delivered to be burned, I visited her prison in the morning with Friar Martin Ladvenu, who had been sent by the Bishop of Beauvais to tell her that she was to die, to induce her to true contrition and penitence, and to hear her confession; all of which the said Ladvenu did with great solicitude and charity. And when he told the poor woman by what death she was to die that day, by order and decree of her judges, and when she had heard the hard and cruel death that was so near to her, she began to cry out most sadly and pull and tear at her hair. "Alas," she cried, "am I to be so cruelly and horribly treated that my pure and unblemished body, which has never been corrupted, must today be consumed and burned to ashes! Oh, I had rather be seven times beheaded than be burned like this. Alas, if only I had been in the prisons of the Church to which I have submitted, if I had been guarded by churchmen and not by my enemies and foes, I should not have come to this miserable end. Oh, I call upon God, the great Judge, to see the great wrongs and griefs that are done me." And she complained exceedingly of the oppressions and violences that had been done to her in prison by her jailers and by others who had been let in to harm her.

After these lamentations, the aforementioned Bishop entered, and she said to him immediately, "Bishop, my death is your doing." And he began to remonstrate with her, saying, "Be patient, Joan. You are to die because you did not keep your promise to us, and because you returned to your former sin." And the poor Maid answered him, "Oh, if you had only put me in the Church court's prisons and entrusted me to decent and proper ecclesiastical warders, this would never have happened. Therefore I appeal against you to God."

After this I went out, and I heard no more.

HER LAST COMMUNION AND HER DEATH

By an extraordinary paradox, though she was declared an excommunicated heretic, Joan was nevertheless allowed to receive the last sacraments.

Jean Massieu

On the Wednesday morning, the day on which Joan died, Friar Martin Ladvenu heard her confession; and when he had heard it he sent me to the Bishop of Beauvais to notify him that he had heard her confession and that she asked to receive the sacrament of the Eucharist. The Bishop collected a few men together, and after some discussion between them, I was told to tell Friar Martin to give her the Eucharist and anything else she might ask for.

HER LAST MOMENTS

In the course of another deposition, the same Jean Massieu recounted the whole scene at the stake, in which he took part.

On the Wednesday, the day on which she was condemned, before she left the castle, the Body of Jesus Christ was brought to her without due reverence, without stole or lights, which greatly displeased Friar Martin, who had heard her confession. So I was sent to fetch a stole and lights, and then Friar Martin gave her the sacrament. And then she was led to the Vieux Marché, and beside her walked Friar Martin and myself, with an escort of eight hundred soldiers armed with axes and swords.[29] And when she came to the Vieux Marché, she listened to the sermon with great fortitude and most calmly, showing signs and evidence and clear proof of her contrition, penitence, and fervent faith. She uttered pious and devout lamentations and called on the Blessed Trinity, and on

---

[29] See note 33 below, p. 254.

the blessed and glorious Virgin Mary, and on all the
blessed saints in Paradise, naming many of them in her
devotions, her lamentations, and her true confession of
faith. Also she most humbly begged all manner of people, of whatever condition or rank they might be, and
whether of her party or of the other, for their pardon
and asked them kindly to pray for her, at the same time
pardoning them any harm they had done her. This she
continued to do for a very long time, perhaps for half an
hour, and until the end. The judges who were present,
and even several of the English, were moved by this to
great tears and weeping, and indeed they wept most bitterly. Some, and several of these same English, recognized God's hand and made professions of faith when
they saw her make so remarkable an end. They were
glad to have witnessed her end and said that she had
been a good woman. When she was handed over by the
Church, I remained with her, and she asked most fervently to be given a cross. And when an Englishman
who was present heard this he made her a little one out
of wood from the end of a stick, and handed it to her.
She received it and kissed it most devotedly, uttering pious
lamentations and acknowledging God our Redeemer, who
suffered for our redemption on the Cross, of which she
had there the symbol and representation. Then she put
that cross on her breast between her body and her clothes
and humbly asked me to let her have the crucifix from
the church so that she could gaze on it continuously
until her death. And I saw to it that the clerk of the
parish church of Saint Sauveur brought it to her. When
it was brought, she embraced it closely and long and
clung to it until she was tied to the stake. And while
she was saying her prayers and piously lamenting, I was
urgently pressed by the English, and by one of their
captains in particular, to hand her over to them, as they

were in a hurry for her death. While I was doing my best to comfort her on the scaffold, this man said to me, "What, priest, are you going to keep us here till dinnertime?" Then without any formality or any reading of the sentence, they dispatched her straight to the fire, saying to the executioner, "Do your duty." And so while she was still uttering devoted praise and lamentations to God and the saints, she was led off and tied to the stake. And her last word, as she died, was a loud cry of "Jesus".

This deposition is completed by that of Martin Ladvenu, who also sustained Joan up to her last moments.

Martin Ladvenu

On the morning of Joan's death, by permission and order of the judges and before her sentence was brought to her, I heard Joan's confession and administered our Lord's Body to her, which she received with such humility, devotion, and copious tears as I could not describe. And from that moment, I did not leave her until she gave up the ghost. Almost everyone who was there wept for pity, in particular the Bishop of Thérouanne, Louis de Luxembourg. And I have no doubts about her having died a true Catholic; indeed, I should like my soul to be where I believe Joan's to be now.

After the sentence, she got down from the platform from which she had heard the sermon and was led by the executioner, without further sentence from the lay judge, to the place where the wood was prepared for her burning. This wood was piled on a scaffold, beneath which the executioner lit his fire. And when Joan saw the fire, she told me to get down and to raise our Lord's Cross very high so that she could see it; and this I did.

Right up to the end of her life she maintained and asseverated that the voices she heard were of God, and that all that she had done she had done at God's command, and that she did not believe that she had been deceived by her voices, and that the revelations she had received were from God. And that is all I know.

Jean Fabri

I was present at the sermon preached by Master Nicolas Midy in the Vieux Marché, and in my opinion she ended her days as a Catholic. She cried, "Jesus, Jesus", and she wept so, uttering such pious lamentations that I do not believe there could be any man so hard of heart that he would not have been moved to tears if he had been there. The lord Bishop of Thérouanne and all those present wept from extreme pity. And I remember well how at that last sermon in the Vieux Marché Joan prayed all the priests there present each to say her a Mass. I did not stay till the end, but went away, for I should not have been able to go on looking.

Pierre Boucher

At the moment when they were tying her up, she implored and specially invoked Saint Michael. I saw her die like a good Christian, and the majority of those present—there were perhaps ten thousand of them—wept and lamented and said that it was most pitiful.

Guillaume de la Chambre

I was present at the last sermon preached in the Vieux Marché at Rouen by Master Nicolas Midy. After that sermon was over, Joan was burned. The wood was already prepared for her burning, and she uttered such pious lamentations and prayers that many wept. But some of the English laughed. I heard her say these words, or something like them: "Oh, Rouen, I am much afraid that you may suffer for my death." Then she began to cry, "Jesus!" and to invoke Saint Michael, and finally she was choked by the fire.

Pierre Miget

On the day when she was handed over to the secular arm she began to cry and lament, invoking the name of the Lord Jesus ... and I could not bear to see it and went away, moved to tears of pity. And many did the same, in particular the Bishop of Thérouanne, who died Cardinal of Thérouanne.[30]

Jean Riquier

Master Pierre Maurice visited her that morning, before she was led to the sermon in the Vieux Marché; and Joan said to him, "Master Pierre, where shall I be tonight?" And Master Pierre answered her, "Do you not trust in God?" She said that she did and that, with God's aid, she would be in Paradise. This I have from Master Pierre himself. When Joan saw the fire set to the wood, she began to cry aloud, "Jesus, Jesus!" and right up to her death she went on crying, "Jesus!" And when she was dead, being afraid that it might be said that she had escaped, the English told the executioner to push the

---

[30] Louis de Luxembourg, the brother of the man who handed the Maid over to the English.

fire back a little so that the spectators could see her dead, and no one could say that she had escaped....

... I heard Master Jean Alépée, then canon of Rouen, who was present at Joan's death and wept abundantly, say in my presence and in the presence of those around me, "I wish that my soul were where I believe the soul of that woman to be."

Pierre Cusquel

I was not present at the last sermon and at Joan's condemnation and execution because my heart would have been too pitiful to bear and suffer the spectacle. But I certainly heard that she received our Lord's Body before she was condemned....

I have heard that Master Jean Tressard, the King of England's secretary, wept and groaned with sorrow on his way back from Joan's execution. He shed tears of grief for what he had seen there, and said, "We are all lost, for it is a good and saintly person that has been burned." He thought that her soul had been accepted into God's hands, and that when the flames were all round her she went on crying the name of the Lord Jesus....

It was common report and almost all the people protested that a great wrong and injustice had been done to Joan.... After Joan's death, the English had her ashes collected and thrown into the Seine because they feared that she might escape, or that certain people might believe that she had done so.

As a final precaution, it was necessary that Joan should be seen and known to be dead by everyone, and that no relics should be made of her ashes.

Maugier Leparmentier

On the day of Joan's burning, the wood was prepared for the fire before the sermon was finished or the sentence pronounced. The moment the sentence had been read by the Bishop, she was led to the fire without any delay, and I saw no sentence pronounced by the lay judge. She was immediately led to the fire, and once in the fire she cried out six times and more, "Jesus!" and even with her last breath she called so loudly on Jesus that all those present could hear her; almost everyone wept for pity. And I heard that after her burning, her ashes were collected and thrown into the Seine.

But they could not prevent the voice of the people from proclaiming her a martyr and recounting her miraculous deeds.

Jean Massieu

I heard from Jean Fleury, the bailiff's clerk and scribe, how the executioner had told him that when the body was burned in the flames and reduced to ashes her heart remained intact and full of blood. And he was told to collect her ashes and all that remained of her and throw them into the Seine, which he did.

Thomas Marie

Many men told me that the name of Jesus had been seen written in the flames of the fire in which she was burned.

Isambart de la Pierre

One of the English, a soldier who particularly loathed Joan and who had sworn to carry a faggot to her pyre with his own hand, was struck with a stupor or a kind of ecstasy when he was doing so and heard her crying on the name of Jesus in her last moments. He was taken to a tavern near the Vieux Marché to be restored to his senses with the aid of strong drink. And when he had eaten with a friar of the Dominican order, this Englishman confessed to the friar, who was an Englishman, that he had committed a grievous sin, and that he repented of what he had done against Joan, whom he considered a saint. For it seemed to this Englishman that he had seen a white dove flying from the direction of France at the moment when she was giving up the ghost. And the executioner,[31] after his midday meal on that same day, came to the Dominican convent and said to me that he greatly feared he was damned, for he had burned a saint.

Cauchon had not heard the recantation he had hoped for. He reflected for some days and, on June 7, 1431, collected seven witnesses, whom he compelled to declare that before her death she had denied her voices. He wanted to make Guillaume Manchon register these declarations so that they might be included in the records of the case. But Manchon refused to do so. We will conclude with his testimony.

Guillaume Manchon

I attended the continuation of the trial up to the end, except for some examinations by persons who spoke to her apart, as private persons. Nevertheless my lord of

---

[31] His name was Geoffroy Therage.

Beauvais wanted to force me to sign those too, which I refused to do.[32]

I saw Joan led to the scaffold. There were seven or eight hundred soldiers around her,[33] carrying sticks and swords; so many indeed that there was no one bold enough to speak to her except Friar Ladvenu and Master Jean Massieu. She listened patiently right through the sermon and afterward uttered her plea for God's grace, her prayers, and her lamentations, with such remarkable devotion that the judges, prelates, and all those present were moved to great weeping and tears when they saw her utter her pitiable griefs and sad plaints. I never wept as much for anything that befell me and could not finally stop weeping for a whole month afterward.

With a part of the money that I was paid for the case, I bought a little missal, which I still possess, to remind me to pray for her. I never saw such signs of penitence at any Christian's end.

---

[32] An allusion to those posthumous testimonies that Manchon refused to register.

[33] The number is certainly exaggerated. Ladvenu says a hundred and twenty. [Jean Massieu also says eight hundred, but Nicolas de Houppeville also says one hundred and twenty.]

CHAPTER 9

The Trial of the Judges

In the preceding pages, we have quoted numerous passages from depositions of persons who were, if not judges in the condemnatory trial, at least assessors: Richard de Grouchet, Guillaume du Désert, Jean Fabri, Pierre Miget, Jean Tiphaine, Guillaume de la Chambre—pretty poor creatures, all of them, who had been dragged along by the current of events and who trembled for their safety. Their evidence is chiefly valuable for the interesting facts that they record.

In addition, certain depositions deserve printing in their entirety; for it is most valuable to discover from a few examples drawn from the life the attitude of these judges when confronted with the terrible responsibility they had incurred twenty-five years earlier. The least one can say of them is that they cut a pretty poor figure; they refused to plead guilty, but all their answers betrayed embarrassment and a bad conscience.

Nothing is more striking than to compare their answers to those that Joan made to them at the time when they were her judges. There was nothing she said during the trial that found her guilty that did not express courage, pride, and sometimes a magnificent insolence. ("Take care, you who call yourselves my judges.") Here, by contrast, we shall only witness pitiable evasions: they do not know; they did nothing; they no longer remember. There is an eloquence in this last confrontation between Joan and her judges.

André Marguerie

(Canon of Rouen, archdeacon of Petit Caux,
ex-counselor to the King of England—aged seventy-six)

He is not, by the way, the most guilty of the former judges. He disapproved of her secular imprisonment and received rough treatment from Cauchon. But he lied when he said that "he did not take much part in the case." The records mention his presence at almost all the sessions.

We will give in parentheses before each of his answers the gist of the article to which it refers. The details of these articles will be found in the Appendix.

(*On the hatred of the English for Joan and on their pressure*)

The English soldiers loathed Joan and desired her death, as I believe. I believe that there were several of them who sought her death, so that she could do them no more harm.

I heard that Joan was captured near Compiègne in the diocese of Beauvais. She was brought to this city of Rouen and imprisoned in the castle of Rouen, where a case was brought against her by the Bishop of Beauvais and the vice-Inquisitor at the expense of the English, but whether it was under English pressure I do not know.

I have heard that some incurred reproaches for not saying the right thing from the English standpoint. But I do not know that anyone was in great danger on that account, although I did hear that Master Nicolas de Houppeville did not give any opinion.

(*On the pressure exercised on the notaries*)

I could not make any statement under this head, or under the next, for I was seldom in court.

(*On Joan's having no advocate*)

I know nothing.

(*On her imprisonment*)

I did not see her in prison, but I believe that she had English guards. For they had the wardenship of the castle in which she was imprisoned.

In the course of a second examination he adds, however:

In that respect it has always seemed to me faulty procedure that she should have been kept in a lay prison on a religious charge, and especially after her first sentence, when she was condemned to life imprisonment.

(*On Joan's attitude*)

In my opinion, Joan showed wisdom in certain of her replies.

(*On Loiseleur's visit in disguise*)

I know nothing.

(*On the stiffness of the interrogatories*)

There is probably truth in that article.

(*On the examination as to virginity*)

I believe that she was examined to see whether she was a virgin or not. But really I could not swear to it. I do know, however, that during the case she was considered to be a virgin.

(*On Joan's faith*)

I know nothing.

(*On her submission to the Church*)

I rather believe the contrary. For I sometimes heard Joan say that on certain matters she would believe neither priest nor Pope nor anyone else, because she had that from God. And I believe that to have been one of the reasons why she was prosecuted.

(*On the editing of the report*)

I know nothing.

(*On the sentence*)

I know nothing.

(*On her condemnation*)

I know nothing about what was done, nor whether she was unjustly condemned, nor whether any injustice was committed in the course of the trial.

(*On the details of her execution*)

Although I was present at the last sermon, I was too deeply moved by compassion to stay for her execution. For the rest, all that I know is that several of those present, in particular the Cardinal de Luxembourg, then Bishop of Thérouanne, wept.

(*On Joan's last moments*)

I know nothing about her prayers, but she seemed in some distress, for she said: "Rouen, Rouen, shall I die here?"

(*On the actions of the English*)

I think that several unimportant Englishmen acted out of hatred and fear. But as for the princes of the Church, I do not believe it. A certain chaplain of the Cardinal of England who was present at the first sermon said to the Bishop of Beauvais that he was too favorable to Joan; and the Bishop replied, "You are a liar. I would not show favor to anyone in any cause." And this chaplain was then reprimanded by the Cardinal of England, who told him to keep silent....

I believe that after Joan's death her ashes were collected, by the order of the Cardinal of England, and thrown into the Seine. I know nothing more.

Nicolas Caval

(Canon of Rouen—aged sixty)

A personal friend of Cauchon, to whose will he was executor. He pretended only to have been at one hearing, although he was present as assessor at the majority of the sessions of the condemnatory trial.

(*On the English hatred for Joan*)

I do not think that the English had any great love for her.

(*On their pressure*)

I certainly accept the substance of that article.

(*On the beginning of the case*)

The current rumor was that Joan was imprisoned in the castle of Rouen, and that a case was being brought against her for heresy. As for the rest, I do not know what to say.

(*On the degree of liberty of the judges*)

I do not know.

(*On the pressure exercised on the notaries*)

I could not give evidence on that. I believe that the notaries wrote accurate reports and were free from all fear.

(*On Joan's having no advocate*)

I know nothing.

(*On her prison*)

Joan was imprisoned in Rouen castle. I know nothing more.

(*On Joan's attitude*)

In my opinion, she was very young. As for her answers, I only heard her once in court, and she spoke with considerable wisdom.

In the course of a second examination he returned to this subject.

I saw Joan during the case, at which I was present on several days. I was not summoned to it, however. I only took part in one hearing, and she replied with considerable wisdom. And she had a very good memory. For when they asked her a question she would say, "I have already answered that, and in these words ..."; and she would make the notary turn up the day on which she had given her answer. And they found it all to be exactly as she had said. Considering how young she was, people were astonished.

(*On Loiseleur's visit in disguise*)

I know nothing and have never heard the subject mentioned.

(*On the interrogatories*)

I know nothing. I refer you to the records.

(*On the sentence*)

I know of course that she was burned. As to whether that was just or unjust, I refer to the records of the case.

(*On her condemnation*)

I know nothing.

(*On her execution*)

I was present neither at her condemnation nor at her execution. I did not see the crowd of Englishmen. I did however hear from several people that she called out and invoked the name of Jesus in her last moments, and that many were moved to tears.

(*On the English hatred for her*)

I believe that the English feared her before she came into their hands. But whether it was for the reasons contained in the article that they brought a case against her, I do not know.

(*On public opinion*)

I have already set down all that I know.

Jean Beaupère

(Canon of Rouen and Master of Theology—aged seventy)

The "famous professor" of Paris University, he was delegated by that body as its representative at Joan's trial, together with Nicolas Midy, Pierre Maurice, Gérard Feuillet, Jacques de Touraine, and Thomas de Courcelles, whom we shall meet again later. He was a personal friend of Cauchon's and, like him, made a career under the aegis of Bedford. He gathered numerous canonries, which represented an equal number of fruitful revenues. At Rouen, at Besançon, at Sens, at Paris, at Beauvais, at Laon, at Autun, at Lisieux, everywhere he occupied offices that brought him in profits, although he could not fulfill his duties, having a maimed right hand. He was one of the most influential and vocal priests at the Council of Basel, the right-hand man of the anti-pope Felix V, and the University of Paris' representative at his court.

He was entrusted with Joan's interrogation several times during her trial, and he was clearly still bitter against her for her proud answers.

The deposition that we give is drawn from the royal inquiry of 1450. Its text has come down to us in French.

> As for the visions mentioned in Joan's trial, it was and still is my theory that they were due to natural rather than supernatural causes and were the product of the human mind. However, especially on this matter, I refer to the records.

Before she was brought to Saint Ouen to hear the sermon, I went to her prison during the morning, with permission, and warned her that she was shortly to be brought to the scaffold to hear the sermon. I told her that if she were a good Christian she would say on the scaffold that she submitted all her deeds and words to the ordinances of our mother the Holy Church, and to the ecclesiastical judges in particular. And this she said on the scaffold, upon the request of Master Nicolas Midy. In view and consideration of that, she was sent back to prison after her abjuration, although certain Englishmen reproached the Bishop of Beauvais and the Paris doctors for favoring Joan in her errors.

After her abjuration and her putting on of the female clothes that were given to her in prison, it was reported to the judges on the Friday or Saturday following that Joan was somewhat sorry she had put off male and put on female clothing. Therefore, my lord of Beauvais, the judge, sent me with Master Nicolas Midy in the hope that we should speak to Joan and induce and admonish her to persevere and continue in the good resolution she had made on the scaffold, and that we should warn her to beware of a relapse. But we could not find the man who had the key of the prison, and while we were waiting for the prison guard, certain Englishmen who were in the court of the castle uttered threatening words against us, as Midy reported to me, saying that it would be a good job if someone were to throw us both into the river. So on hearing this, we turned back, and on the castle bridge Midy heard, as he told me, more or less the same words uttered by some other Englishmen. This frightened us, and we came away without speaking to Joan.

As for Joan's innocence, she seemed to me to be subtle with an altogether feminine subtlety; and I never learned through any word of hers that she had lost her virginity.

As for her final penitence, I can say nothing. The Monday after her abjuration I left Rouen to go to Basel on behalf of the University of Paris; and she was condemned on the following Wednesday. Therefore I was not informed of her condemnation until I heard about it at Lille in Flanders.

Jean de Mailly

(Bishop of Noyon—aged seventy)

Ex-counselor to the King of England. He had taken part in the anointing of Henry VI in Paris, together with Louis de Luxembourg and Cauchon. He went over to Charles VII when that King entered Paris.

He took an active part in the trial and, like a prudent man, signed the letters of safeguard that the principal judges obtained on June 12, 1431 (a fortnight after Joan's death), from the King of England. But on this day, like Nicolas Caval, he finds his memory strangely defective.

> I well remember that on the day after the sermon at Saint Ouen I was present at an exhortation made to Joan. But I do not remember what was done or said....
>
> I do not remember the words of the preacher on the day of the abjuration. But I do remember that Joan said on that day or the previous one that if there was any evil in what she had said or done, or if she had said or done well or ill, that arose from herself alone, and that her Lord had directed none of her acts. After the sermon, I saw them command Joan to say or do something, and I think that was the abjuration. They said to Joan, "Joan, do as you are advised. Do you want to go to your death?"

It was probably owing to those words that she made her abjuration. After her abjuration, many said that it was nothing but a farce and that she had done it out of mockery. Among others, an Englishman, a doctor and priest belonging to the Cardinal of England's train, told the Bishop of Beauvais that he was showing too much partiality in this affair and that he was favoring Joan. The Bishop of Beauvais answered that he lied, and then the Cardinal of England told this doctor to be quiet. Later on, many of those present said that they did not attach much importance to the abjuration, and that it was just a farce. In my opinion, Joan did not attach much importance to it herself and did not think about it. She made it in response to the urgent prayers of those who were present.

The witness was questioned about the letters of safeguard that the King of England gave to the Bishop of Beauvais and the others who had taken part in the trial. It is clear from these letters that the Bishop of Noyon had been included in the guarantee given.

I certainly believe that there was one, but I do not remember very well. I do know, however, that the Bishop of Beauvais did not conduct the trial at his own expense, but at the King of England's, and that the outgoings incurred were put to the English account.

Thomas de Courcelles

(Canon of Paris and master of theology—aged fifty-six)

A model scholar, an excellent Latinist, and the perfect example of a "well-formed mind". He and Nicolas Loiseleur were two of the very few assessors who voted in favor of torture during the condemnatory trial. Having been entrusted, a long time after Joan's execution, with the drawing up of the records and with translating them into Latin, he took advantage of this fact to expunge his name from the list of those so compromised. This allows him to affirm at present with imperturbable assurance "that he never took part in any discussions about inflicting any sort of punishment on Joan".

He too had been one of the luminaries of the Council of Basel, where, beside Jean Beaupère, he constantly led the battle against the power of the Pope. He took an active part in the election of the anti-pope Felix V, who rewarded him by making him a cardinal. This was an ephemeral honor, but that very cool customer nevertheless found means of keeping himself constantly in office. It was he who was to be entrusted in 1461 with the reading of Charles VII's funeral oration at Notre Dame.

His deposition is a veritable masterpiece. See in particular the argument he puts up when asked whether he adjudged Joan a heretic, and on the examination as to virginity.

> I believe that the Bishop (Cauchon) accepted the task of prosecuting Joan for heresy because he was a counselor of the King of England, because he was Bishop of Beauvais, and because she had been taken and arrested on his territory. I heard that a gift had been sent to the Inquisitor through one Soreau,[1] a collector, for his part in the trial. But as for the Bishop, I do not know whether he received anything. As soon as Joan was brought to Rouen, I was summoned (I was then in Paris) by the Bishop of Beauvais, to go to Rouen for the trial. I went there in company with Master Nicolas Midy, Master Jacques de Touraine, Master Jean de Rouel, and others whom I do not remember now. We traveled at the expense of those

---

[1] Pierre Surreau, general revenue collector for Normandy.

who brought us there, among whom was a certain Jean de Rivel (secretary to the King of England). I do not know whether any preliminary information was collected at Rouen or at Joan's place of origin. I never saw any. At the beginning of the trial, when I was mixed up with it, it was only a question of reports that she had said she had heard voices and that she affirmed these came from God.

Thomas de Courcelles was then shown the report of the case, and it was pointed out to him that certain information had been read in his presence.

I do not remember ever having heard any of them read. Master Jean Lohier came here to Rouen, and orders were given that he should be shown the reports. He told me that he did not think there ought to be any prosecution of Joan for heresy without preliminary inquiries as to her reputation, and that legally such inquiries were necessary. I well remember that in my first opinion I never adjudged Joan a heretic, except conditionally; that is to say, if she should persist in affirming that it was not her duty to submit to the Church. In my last opinion, as I can conscientiously affirm before God, I believe I said that she was as she had been; that if she had been a heretic before she still was one. I am certain that I never said that she was a heretic. At the first deliberations, there was a great discussion and a great clash of opinion as to whether Joan should or should not be considered a heretic. I never gave an opinion about any punishment to be inflicted on Joan.

(*On her lack of an advocate*)

I do not remember anything.

(*On her prison*)

Joan was in the castle prison under the wardenship of one Jean Grilz and his men, and she had fetters on her legs. But I do not know whether she always wore them. Many of the assessors considered and greatly desired that Joan should be handed over to the Church and put in an ecclesiastical prison. But I do not remember that the question arose during the deliberations.

I never heard it discussed whether Joan ought to be examined to find out whether she was a virgin or not. But it seems to me probable that she was, since I heard from the Bishop of Beauvais that she had been found a virgin. If she had been no virgin but debauched, I do not believe that they would have kept quiet about it at the trial.

(*On the interrogations*)

They put a lot of questions to Joan, but I do not remember any of them except one. They asked her once whether the men of her party kissed her hands. I do not remember that Joan complained about the questions that were asked her.

I well remember that on one occasion, after Joan had been interrogated several times, instructions were given that in future the interrogations should take place before a small number of persons. But who decided this and for what purpose I have no idea. I think, however, that Master Jean de la Fontaine was one of those selected to question her.

(*On Joan's submission to the Church*)

I know nothing about it.

Joan was examined several times on the subject of her submission, and she was asked whether she was willing to submit her acts and words to the Church's decision. To this she made several replies that are contained in the report of the proceedings, to which I refer you. I can say nothing more about it.

(*On the sentence and the articles of condemnation*)

I know nothing about it.

Certain articles, to the number of a dozen, were extracted and compiled from Joan's admissions and answers. They were drawn up, in all probability and as far as I can guess, by the late Master Nicolas Midy. It was on these twelve articles, extracted in this way, that all the deliberations and opinions were based. But I do not know whether there was any discussion about correcting them, or whether they were corrected.

I only know that I heard several times from Master Nicolas Loiseleur[2] that he had talked with Joan on various occasions in borrowed clothes. But I do not know what he said to her. All I know is that he told me he went to see Joan and said he was a priest. I believe he heard Joan's confession.

(*On the circumstances of the relapse and the execution*)

A little before the first sermon, which was preached at Saint Ouen, Master Jean de Châtillon gave Joan some exhortations in my presence. And I also heard from Master Pierre Maurice that he exhorted Joan, as a brother, to submit to the Church. I remember nothing else.

... After the first preaching, the rumor went round that Joan had put on men's clothes again. For that reason, the Bishop of Beauvais went to her prison, and I went with him. He questioned her, asking her why she had resumed male clothes; she answered that she had done

---

[2] He had died suddenly at Basel in 1442.

so because it seemed more suitable to her to wear a man's clothes than a woman's when among men.

I was present at the last sermon read at the Vieux Marché, on the day of Joan's death. But I did not see Joan burned, for I retired as soon as the sermon was preached and the sentence read. Before that sermon and sentence, she had received the Eucharist, or so I believe, for I was not present when she received it. And I know nothing more.

The most extraordinary thing for us is to see Joan's former judges, Cauchon's accomplices or at least his tools, return comfortably home after making their depositions.

Philip of Bergamo, an Italian monk who wrote the history of Joan and her rehabilitation at the very end of the fifteenth century, relates that prosecutions were instituted against the surviving judges, and that Louis XI (to whom he attributes the credit for the rehabilitation) had the remains of those who were dead dug up to be thrown on the dunghill. This is pure invention, but it corresponds better than the reality to the reactions we should expect.

However, one should not be too hasty in attributing this absence of reaction, as has sometimes been done, to mere indifference. Charles VII had proclaimed a general amnesty; that he strenuously kept his word counted no doubt for much in the rapid pacification of the country. It must be said to his credit that no deed of vengeance came to stain his victory. His policy was entirely one of "moderation, clemency, and reconciliation". Besides, crimes against public opinion and reasons of state had not the significance for that age that they have since attained.

CHAPTER 10

The Upright Souls

Given the not very resplendent collection of judges, it is restful to find some sympathetic figures. Unfortunately they are few. Certainly the chapter of canons at Rouen, as a whole, proved rather shy during the condemnatory trial. Cauchon would have wished them to approve the completed case, but though there were several attempts at a meeting, these proved fruitless; the canons slipped away. Finally there was a discussion on April 14, 1431, and this reached negative conclusions; the chapter declared itself incompetent to judge because the question should not have been referred to the University of Paris and because Joan had not received the explanations and counsel that she should have had. The record of this discussion met the same fate as all the other compromising documents: Cauchon failed to have it transcribed in the official account of the case.

We know, from the deposition of Friar Isambart we are about to read, of the courageous attitude of Jean de Saint Avit, Bishop of Avranches. In the following year, 1432, this prelate was to be imprisoned, despite his great age, for the crime of having tried to deliver Rouen up to Charles VII.

Guillaume Manchon had mentioned in his first deposition, made during the royal inquiry of 1450, the attitude and replies of another "member of the resistance", Jean Lohier.

Jean Lohier (As seen by Guillaume Manchon)

When the case had begun, Master Jean Lohier, a solemn Norman cleric, came to this town of Rouen, and all the documents were submitted to him by the Bishop of Beauvais. Lohier asked for a delay of two or three days to look them through. The answer was that he must give his opinion on the spot, and this he was compelled to do. When he had glanced at the papers, Master Jean Lohier said that the case was invalid for several reasons:

Because the procedure was not that of an ordinary case;

"It was conducted in an enclosed and private court, in which those taking part were not at full and complete liberty to express their full and complete thoughts;

"Because the King of France's honor was impugned, she being of his party, and neither he nor anyone to represent him was called;

"Because neither written charges nor heads of charges had been submitted, and this woman, who was a simple girl, had replied to all these lawyers and doctors without counsel, and this on serious issues, especially on those referring to the revelations that she claimed;

"For these reasons the case appeared to him to be invalid."

My lord of Beauvais was most annoyed with Lohier; and although the Bishop ordered him to stay and see the case through, Lohier said that he would not stay. Then my lord of Beauvais, who was lodging in the house where Master Jean Bidault lives at present, just beside Saint Nicolas le Paincteur, rushed to the lawyers; that is to say, to Master Jean Beaupère, Master Jacques de Touraine, Master Nicolas Midy, Master Pierre Maurice, Master Thomas de

Courcelles, and Master Loiseleur, and said to them, "Here is Lohier trying to lodge a lot of interlocutories in our case! He is trying to vilify everything and says that it is all invalid. If we are to believe him, we ought to start it all over again, and what we have done so far is valueless." Then, when he had reported Lohier's reasons for demanding an annulment, he said, "It is easy enough to see which side he is on. By Saint John, we will do nothing of the sort. We will go on with our case as we have begun it." It was then the Saturday afternoon, in Lent. The next morning I spoke to Lohier in the Church of Notre Dame at Rouen and asked him his opinion of Joan's case. He answered, "You can see the manner of their procedure. They will catch her out, if they can, with her own words, that is to say, in her assertions concerning her visions when she says, 'I am sure about them.' If she were to say, 'It seems to me' instead of 'I am sure', in my opinion, no one on earth could find her guilty. They seem to me to be acting chiefly out of hatred, and for that reason I will not stay, for I want to take no further part in the business." And indeed he remained at the court of Rome ever after, and he died a dean of the Rota.[1]

Finally, there was to be summoned before the court one of the "upright souls" who had had the courage to resist their threats.

Nicolas de Houppeville

(Bachelor in theology—aged sixty)

The rest of the witnesses have been unanimous in attesting to his proud attitude and to the dangers he ran.

---

[1] The Roman Court of Appeal.

(On the pressure from the English)

I think that article is correct. I never supposed that it was out of zeal for the faith or to restore her to the good path that the English did what they did. That was everyone's opinion throughout the town.

I know very well that Joan was brought here to Rouen by the English and that she was imprisoned in the castle of Rouen. The case was conducted at the English expense, as I believe. As for fear and pressure, I do not believe in it in the judges' case. I think, on the contrary, that they acted voluntarily, and especially the Bishop of Beauvais. I saw him when he came back from fetching her, reporting his mission to the King and the Earl of Warwick, and he spoke exultingly with great joy, though I did not hear his words. After that, he had a secret conversation with the Earl of Warwick. What he said to him I have no idea.

(On the threats to the judges)

As I see it, the judges and the assessors acted for the most part voluntarily. As for the rest, I think that the majority acted out of fear, and my particular reason for thinking so is something that I heard from Master Pierre Minier. He told me that he had given his opinion in writing, and that it had displeased the Bishop of Beauvais, who had rejected it, saying that in delivering his opinion he must not confuse law and theology, but must leave law to the lawyers. Furthermore, I have heard that threats were uttered by the Earl of Warwick against Friar Isambart de la Pierre of the Dominican order, who took part in the case. My lord of Warwick told him that if he was not silent he would have him drowned. This was because he advised Joan and prompted her with words that she afterward repeated to the notaries. I think that it was from Friar Jean Lemaître, then sub-Inquisitor, that I heard this.

As for myself, I was called one day at the beginning of the case and did not appear since I was prevented by other reasons. When I came on the second day, I was not admitted. In fact, I was turned out of the door by the lord Bishop of Beauvais. This was because I had previously said in conference with Master Michel [sic] Colles that this prosecution was a dangerous one for several reasons. This statement was repeated to the Bishop, and for that reason the Bishop had me put in the royal prison at Rouen, from which I was released on the petition of my lord abbot of Fécamp, as he then was. I have heard that on the advice of certain men whom the Bishop had called together for this purpose, it was decided to exile me to England or elsewhere, which would have been done but for the intervention of the abbot and some of my friends. I am absolutely certain also that the sub-Inquisitor was in the greatest fear, and I saw him several times greatly troubled in the course of the trial.

(*On the interrogatories*)

I was not in court, but I heard from Master Jean Lemaître that Joan once complained of the difficult questions put to her, and of being unduly harassed by being questioned on matters that had nothing to do with the case.

(*On the threats to the notaries*)

I heard—and these were current rumors—that the notaries were prevented from writing down certain of her words. That article is true; that is what was said in the city of Rouen.

(*About the prison*)

I know that Joan was in the castle prison and that she was guarded only by Englishmen. As for the rest, that was the public rumor.

(*About Joan*)

I think that Joan was of the age set down in that article, and that all it says is true. The steadfastness that Joan showed caused many to say that she had spiritual aid.

It was rumored in this city of Rouen that certain persons pretending to be soldiers of the French king's party had been secretly introduced into her prison and had persuaded her not to submit to the Church's judgment. The rumor ran that it was owing to this persuasion that Joan subsequently wavered in her submission to the Church....

In my belief, according to the feelings I had then and still have, the whole thing could more properly be described as a deliberate and passionate persecution than as a judicial trial....

I saw Joan, bathed in tears, leaving the castle to be taken to the place of execution and to the final sermon. She was surrounded by about a hundred and twenty soldiers, some of whom carried maces and some swords.[2] I was too much moved by pity to go to the place of execution.

(*On the circumstances of the execution*)

That is true, according to public fame and rumor in this city of Rouen. But I heard nothing, since I was not present at the execution.

---

[2] See note 33 on p. 254.

(*On the English hatred of Joan*)

I think that the article is true. That is what was said throughout this city of Rouen; that is, that the English acted out of hatred and fear and also in order to defame the King of France.

(*On public opinion*)

That is the truth, and on this point there was not even one discordant voice.

In the course of another deposition, he gives this exact description of the dangers he himself ran.

Toward the beginning of the case, I took part in certain deliberations in which I stated the opinion that neither the Bishop of Beauvais nor those who wished to perform the office of judges had the right to be judges. I said that it seemed to me an improper method of procedure for members of the opposite party to be judges, considering that she had already been examined by the clergy of Poitiers and by the Archbishop of Rheims, who was the Bishop of Beauvais' own superior. This opinion earned me the great indignation of the Bishop, so much so that he summoned me before him. So I appeared before him and informed him that he was not my superior, and that not he but the Church court of Rouen had the right to try me; and with this I retired. Finally, however, when I insisted on defending myself before the Church court of Rouen, I was arrested and taken to the castle, and from there to the royal prison; and when I asked the reason for my detention I was told that it was at the request of the Bishop of Beauvais.

THE WITNESSES OF JOAN'S LAST MOMENTS

We will end with the depositions of the two Dominicans who assisted Joan on the scaffold. They appeared several times before the commissioners of the rehabilitation, and we have already quoted them at length. But here we turn back to their first deposition of all, which they made before Guillaume Bouillé when he was conducting the royal inquiry of 1450. As this inquiry made use of no questionnaire, and as the witnesses were only invited to recount their memories, the tone is here more personal. Moreover, it has come down to us in French, which makes the evidence more direct. There is good reason, therefore, for putting it before the reader.

Martin Ladvenu

Many appeared at the trial rather for their love of the English and their partiality toward them than out of zeal for justice and the Catholic faith. This I would particularly say of the zeal and excessive partisanship shown by Messire Pierre Cauchon, then Bishop of Beauvais. I would accuse him of two signs of partiality. Firstly, when the Bishop appointed himself judge he ordered that Joan should be kept in a secular prison and in the hands of her mortal enemies, although he could easily have had her kept and guarded in an ecclesiastical prison. Nevertheless, from the beginning of the trial to its conclusion, he permitted her to be tormented and ill-treated in a secular prison. Moreover, at the first hearing or instance, the said Bishop asked for and demanded the opinions of everyone present as to which was the more suitable, to keep her in a secular prison or to hold her in the prisons of the Church. On this point, it was decided that it was more proper to keep her in the Church prison than in any other. But the Bishop answered that he would not do that for fear of displeasing the English. The second sign is that on the day when the Bishop and some others declared her a heretic, lapsed and returned to her sin because she had resumed male clothing in prison, as he left the prison he said to the Earl of Warwick and a great crowd of Englishmen around him, "Farewell, farewell, it is done. Be of good cheer!" This, or something like it, he said in loud and intelligible tones, and laughed as he did so.

They put questions to her that were too difficult in order to catch her out by her own words and opinions. For she was a poor, rather simple woman who scarcely knew her *Pater noster* and *Ave Maria*.

This simple Maid revealed to me that after her abjuration and renunciation she was violently tormented, worried, beaten, and ill-treated in her prison, and that an English lord had done her violence. She openly said that this was the reason why she had resumed male clothing; and toward her end she said to the Bishop of Beauvais, "Alas, it is through your fault that I am to die. For if you had had me kept in a Church prison, I should not be in this plight."

When her last sermon was preached to her in the Vieux Marché and she was handed over to the secular arm, although the secular judges were seated on the platform, she was not sentenced by any of those judges. Without sentence, she was compelled by two sergeants to come down from her scaffold, and she was led by these sergeants to the place where she was to be burned, and there handed over by them to the executioner. In contrast to this, shortly afterward, a man called Georges Folenfant, who was arrested on a religious charge and prosecuted for heresy, was similarly handed over to the secular arm. But in this case, the ecclesiastical judges, that is to say, Messire Louis de Luxembourg, Archbishop of Rouen, and Friar Guillaume Duval, vicar to the general Inquisitor, sent me to the bailiff of Rouen to warn him that this same Georges must not be treated as the Maid had been when she had been burned without final sentence and definitive judgment.

After the burning, at about four hours after Nones, the executioner said that he had never been so much afraid in officiating at the death of any criminal as he had been at Joan's, and this for several reasons:

Firstly because of her great name and reputation.

Secondly, because of the cruel way in which she was tied and made a show of. For the English had a tall scaffold of stone built, so that, as the executioner reported, he could not easily reach her or hasten her end. This grieved him greatly, for he was much upset by the cruel form and manner in which she was brought to her death.

As for her great and wonderful contrition, repentance, and repeated confessions, she called continuously on the name of Jesus and devotedly invoked the aid of the saints, male and female, in Paradise, as Friar Isambart, who accompanied her to her death and spoke to her of her salvation on the way, has testified above.

Isambart de la Pierre

On one occasion, I and several others were admonishing and begging Joan to submit to the Church. She replied that she would willingly submit to the Holy Father, to whom she asked to be led, but that she would not submit to the judgment of her enemies. And at that time I advised her to submit to the Council of Basel, and Joan asked me what a general council was. I replied that it was an assembly of the whole universal Church and of Christendom, and that in this council there were as many of her party as of the English. When she heard and understood this, she began to cry out, "Oh, if there are some of our party there, I will willingly surrender and submit to the Council of Basel." Then suddenly, in a great fury and indignation, the Bishop of Beauvais began to shout, "Be quiet, in the devil's name!" And he told the notary to be sure not to record the submission she had made to the Council of Basel. On this account and for several other reasons, the English and their officers threatened me horribly that if I did not keep quiet they would throw me in the Seine.

After her renunciation and abjuration, when she had put on male clothes again, she excused herself for having done so in the presence of myself and several others. She said and publicly affirmed that when she put on women's clothes the English had done her great wrongs and violence in her prison. And indeed I saw her weeping, with her face running with tears, and so outraged and disfigured that I felt pity and compassion for her.

When she was labeled an obstinate and relapsed heretic, she publicly answered before the whole court, "If you, lords of the Church, had taken me and kept me in your own prisons, perhaps things would not be like this with me."

After the final conclusion of that session and of the suit, the lord Bishop of Beauvais said to the English, "Farewell, be of good cheer. It is done."

They put such difficult questions to poor Joan and framed such subtle and tricky interrogatories that the great clerks and men of learning there present would have found it very hard to know how to answer. Several of those present grumbled about this.

As for myself, I was summoned in person before the Bishop of Avranches,³ a good cleric but very old, who had been asked and entreated to give an opinion on the case. The Bishop asked me, therefore, what the worthy Saint Thomas said on the subject of the proper form of submission to the Church. I gave the Bishop Saint Thomas' ruling in writing. It says: "In all doubts as to faith, one should always resort to the Pope and the General Council." The Bishop subscribed to this opinion, and seemed most unhappy at the decision that had been reached in defiance of it. This opinion of his was not recorded, but omitted out of malice.

After her confession and her taking of the sacrament of the Host, sentence was pronounced on her, and she was declared an excommunicated heretic.

I well saw and clearly perceived—for I was present throughout and watched the whole summing up and conclusion of the case—that the secular judge did not condemn her to death or to be consumed by the fire. And although the lay and secular judge appeared and was present at the very place of her last sermon and her transfer to the secular arm, nevertheless, she was handed over to the executioner and burned without any judgment or conclusion by that judge. The executioner was told, "Do your duty." She received no other sentence.

Joan showed such great contrition and such a fine repentance in her death as was a wonder to see. The words she uttered were so devout, pious, and Christian that all who watched her—and they were a great multitude—wept warm tears. Even the Cardinal of England (the Bishop of Winchester) and several other Englishmen were constrained to weep and were moved to compassion.

---

³ Jean de Saint Avit, who was to be imprisoned at Rouen in 1432, under suspicion of having tried to surrender the city to the French.

The pious woman asked, commanded, and begged me, since I was near her at the end, to go into the nearby church and bring her the crucifix. This she made me hold up, right before her eyes, until the moment of her death, so that the Cross upon which God hung should be continually before her eyes so long as her life lasted. Moreover, when she was surrounded by flames she continued to cry aloud and acknowledge the sacred name of Jesus and ceaselessly to implore and invoke the aid of the saints in Paradise. And, what is more, as she gave up the ghost and bowed her head, she pronounced the name of Jesus. This was a sure sign that she fervently believed in God, as we read in the case of Saint Ignatius and many other martyrs.

Immediately after the execution, the executioner came up to me and my companion, Friar Martin Ladvenu. He was struck and moved by a marvelous repentance and terrible contrition; and he was desperate with fear that he would never be able to obtain God's pardon and indulgence for what he had done to that saintly woman. He said and affirmed that, notwithstanding the oil, sulphur, and charcoal that he had applied to Joan's entrails and heart, he had not found it possible to burn them or reduce them to ashes. He was astonished at this as at a patent miracle.

CHAPTER 11

The Last Act

The hearing of witnesses was concluded at Rouen on May 14, 1456. It was now necessary to collect and classify all the facts that the inquiry had established. This task was entrusted to Jean Bréhal. At the end of May, he returned to Rouen, where the hearings were resumed on the thirtieth. Henceforth, however, they were nothing but simple formalities. A last appeal was made for any contrary evidence, which was not forthcoming, and on June 2, the testimonies gathered during the course of the inquiry were accepted by a declaration of the tribunal. On the fifth, the counsel for the d'Arc family, Guillaume Prévosteau, put all the documents that he possessed into the hands of the tribunal. Several of these had already been produced during December. Finally, on June 10, after a final session, the documents of the case were all collected into the hands of the Inquisitor.

As soon as he was back in Paris, he applied himself to the classification and examination of the complete case, a work to which he gave the name of the *Recollectio*. This forms a bulky volume (208 pages of close type) in which the "Joan of Arc case" is methodically discussed, testimonies in hand. The *Summarium*, Bréhal's first work on the case, was no more than an examination of the facts, a comparison of Joan's answers with the judges' allegations. But here is the voice of the inquirer, the jurist, and the theologian. Point by point, he refutes the original case. First he clears Joan of the accusations leveled against her. That is the object of the first part, in which her visions, revelations, and predictions are examined, each in turn, then her behavior toward her parents, her male clothes, her submission to the Church, and her alleged relapse. Next it attacks the Rouen judgment, both for its findings and its procedure: the judge's incompetence and partiality; Joan's imprisonment in a lay prison; objections to the tribunal raised by Joan herself; the role of the sub-Inquisitor; the tendentious or deliberately mendacious editing of the articles that served as a basis for the court's deliberations; the false abjuration that led to a false relapse; the form of the interrogatories; the absence of a counsel for the defense; the irregularities in the sentence. On this last point, in particular, Bréhal picked out the paradoxical decision whereby an allegedly excommunicated heretic was allowed to receive the sacrament of the Eucharist.

Bréhal's work has not always been accepted at its true value. Quicherat did not include it in his edition of the documents dealing with the case,[1] and Anatole France thought himself justified in dismissing it in a few words.[2]

[1] The *Recollectio* was printed by the Reverend Fathers Belon and Balme in an appendix to their work on *Jean Bréhal, Grand Inquisitor of France* (Paris, 1893), from which we have borrowed everything concerning the Inquisitor's activities.

[2] He quotes in mockery the page in which Bréhal speaks of the role of numbers in Joan's life (an altogether characteristic feature of the age, which is not without its appeal). But he omits all mention of the 207 pages in which the author's arguments are based on the teachings of Saint Thomas and Saint Augustine, which have not the reputation of being so naïve.

In reality, if one takes the trouble to read it through even cursorily, one sees that one is dealing with a work perfectly satisfying to the intellect in its rigorous logic. Every doubtful or controversial point, either in Joan's answers or in the judges' allegations, is made a subject for methodical discussion based on the teaching of the fathers and doctors of the Church, from whom the work contains more than nine hundred quotations; and the same holds true for points of law and procedure. From our distance in time, we may feel almost astonished that a case as clear as Joan of Arc's should have required such thorough labors. But it is precisely after Jean Bréhal's labors that its clarity became apparent. Before the *Recollectio*, Joan was still a heretic and no more; when that work was concluded she was already a saint.

What is more, penetrating the reasonings of the jurist and theologian, there is here an obvious emotion—which was, it must be observed, totally absent from the first work dedicated by this same Bréhal to Joan, the *Summarium* mentioned above. Plainly he was conquered bit by bit by this heroine whom he never knew, and to whom he devoted five years of his life. At the end of the chapter in which he examined the evidence concerning the visions, he did not conceal his admiration for Joan's answers: "On all these points she answers with such wisdom and prudence that not only do her replies dispel all suspicion of error or artifice, but every word of them testifies to the most devout piety." And again, at the moment when he concludes his study of the fundamentals of the case, he exclaims, "She had very good reason always to trust in her voices. For in very truth she was delivered, as they promised, from the prison of the body by martyrdom and a great victory: the victory of patience."

The commissioners devoted the month of June to the study of the documents and the *Recollectio*. On the eighteenth, they received a visit from Jean d'Arc, accompanied by Guillaume Prévosteau and the promoter Simon Chapitault. The plaintiffs were losing patience; they were reassured. The dates of the final hearing would be fixed at any moment. In fact, on the twenty-fourth, summonses for July 1 were posted on the church doors of Rouen, inviting, for the last time, any possible objectors to the rehabilitation to come and reveal what they knew of the case. As no one appeared on the day fixed, the civil parties were called to speak at a solemn session on July 2. Simon Chapitault, and after him Guillaume Prévosteau, begged the judges *to let their reason have way* and, in the name of the Holy See, to pronounce Joan's rehabilitation.

On July 7, 1456, at eight o'clock in the morning, Jean Jouvenel des Ursins, Archbishop of Rheims, took his seat in the presidential chair in the great hall of the archiepiscopal palace of Rouen. At his side were ranged the two other commissioners, Guillaume Chartier, Bishop of Paris, and Richard Olivier, Bishop of Coutances, also the Inquisitor, Jean Bréhal. On the promoter's bench was Simon Chapitault, and at the bar Jean d'Arc, supported by his advocate Pierre Maugier and the devoted Guillaume Prévosteau. An imposing crowd of clerks and laymen filled the hall, and in the front row appeared the friar who had received Joan's last confession, Martin Ladvenu. Once the customary formalities had been dispatched, the Archbishop of Rheims pronounced sentence in the name of the pontifical commission: "We, sitting on our judgment seats and with our thoughts only on God ... say, pronounce, decree, and declare the said trial and sentence (of condemnation) to be contaminated with fraud, calumny, wickedness, contradictions, and manifest errors of fact and law, and together with the abjuration, the execution, and all their consequences to have been and to be null, without value or effect, and to be quashed."

One of the copies of the articles of accusation that had served as a basis for the trial was symbolically torn up. The findings having been pronounced, they were promulgated on the same day on the open space of Saint Ouen, where the famous "abjuration" had taken place, and on the next day at the place of the burning, in the Vieux Marché. Solemn processions marked this day not only at Rouen but throughout the kingdom.

All that remained was to go and officially to inform the authorities in the case—that is to say, the King and the Pope—of the conclusion of the affair. Jean Bréhal set out, accompanied by the faithful Guillaume Bouillé. On their way, both presided at the feasts that took place amid great joy at Orléans on July 21. The municipality went to some expense in their honor. The city accounts have preserved the memory of the banquet that was given to them, and for which there was a purchase of "ten pints and half-pints of wine ... a dozen chickens, two young rabbits, a dozen pigeons and two leverets". From Orléans they went to Rome, after having rendered an account of their mission to Charles VII, who in his joy ordered five hundred livres to be granted to them to cover their labors and their traveling expenses.

Two years later, in 1458, Isabelle Romeé died at Orléans. She had fulfilled her maternal task to the end. On the day her daughter had set out on her incredible adventure, she had mingled with the crowd and gone on the pilgrimage to Puy; and, in the end, it had been she who had helped Joan on the last stage of her journey, her solemn reentry into the Church from which the wicked doctors had thought they had expelled her.

> In the trial that pronounced her guiltless
> There are many things strange and rare,
> And it gives one a great pleasure
> The two trials to compare.
> This trial hangs enchained in Paris,
> At Notre Dame in the library,
> The gift of the Bishop—may his soul
> Find peace in Jesus and Mary.[3]

Thus Martial d'Auvergne concludes with the rehabilitation suit the long passage of his work, *The Vigils of King Charles VII*, which he devotes to Joan.

It is indeed not without "great pleasure" that one follows the development of Joan's cause throughout her rehabilitation suit. Even if it was instituted—as so many modern historians have chosen to repeat—for a purely political purpose, and to please the King, it irrefutably passed beyond that aim and carried the inquirers themselves further than they suspected. They believed that they had only to solve a question in the legal, or at most in the theological, realm; but in the end they found themselves confronted with a problem on the scale of the Divine.

Today we honor Joan of Arc as a saint. But at the time when Jean Bréhal undertook his first inquiry very few people knew with any certainty the details of Joan's arrival at Chinon or those of the siege of Orléans. No one, except the former judges, knew of her appeal to the Pope, which to a Catholic mind effectively transformed the whole case and was sufficient to acquit her of all suspicion of rebellion

---

[3] Bishop Guillaume Chartier, one of the commissioners of the rehabilitation, had made a gift to the library of Notre Dame of one of the authentic transcripts of the case, the one that is to be found today in the *Bibliothèque Nationale* and that formed the basis of Quicherat's edition.

against the Church. Up to that point, for convinced Christians, however admiring they might be of the heroine's exploits, a certain shadow would always remain. It was the rehabilitation suit that permitted the light to shine; and that required no less than five years of labor and fifteen hundred witnesses, drawn from every corner of France.

On the day when the Archbishop of Rheims pronounced the sentence that rehabilitated Joan, however, he must have had the feeling that, instead of concluding the affair, he was throwing it open to new developments. For whatever limits ecclesiastical caution tried to impose, popular veneration had already joyfully anticipated the formalities of a final case, the case for Joan's beatification and canonization.

This was to be delayed for nearly five centuries. Why? Joan's posthumous history is another story. But without attempting to trace it, one can ask whether the ages that followed were capable of appreciating her. Could Joan really be understood in the classical age—an age in which the stained-glass windows of cathedrals were smashed so that they might be replaced by clear glass, and when the word "Gothic" was the equivalent of "barbarous", when everything preceding Ronsard belonged to an "age of coarseness"? Whatever this argument is worth, the facts are clear: from Chapelain's *Maid* to Voltaire's, Joan does not appear to have aroused the slightest feeling of intelligent sympathy in the centuries of classicism.

When Joan's beatification was proclaimed in 1909, and at her canonization in 1920, it was to the rehabilitation case, to the work of Jean Bréhal, to the precious collection of inquiries and testimonies gathered by him, that men turned. Answers to every question were found there; everything had been said already. This fifteenth-century drama had become more living and more immediate than ever, and it had found a solution that conformed with popular belief.

APPENDIX A

The First Interrogatory of the Rehabilitation

This is the interrogatory of twelve articles drawn up for the ecclesiastical inquiry of 1452. This first interrogatory of twelve articles was only used for two days: May 2 and 3, 1452. Immediately afterward, an interrogatory of twenty-seven articles was drawn up, which will be found in Appendix B, and which served as the real basis for the inquiry (see Introduction, p. 30).

The interrogatory is not composed in the form of a questionnaire, but, according to custom, in the form of articles on the subject of which the deposing witness is called to give his opinion.

Here follows the tenor of the articles upon which the undermentioned witnesses were examined by the most reverend father in Christ, the lord Cardinal d'Estouteville, cardinal-priest bearing the title of San Martino de Monti, apostolic legate of the Holy See in the kingdom of France, and by the venerable friar Jean Bréhal, professor of theology, one of the inquisitors for heresy in the kingdom of France, touching the case of Joan called the Maid:

I. That the late Pierre Cauchon, then Bishop of Beauvais, was activated by immoderate zeal in prosecuting the late Joan, commonly known as the Maid; and that because Joan had fought in the army against the English, he pursued and hated her, seeking her death by every means that he could discover;

II. That the said Bishop sent to the lord Duke of Burgundy and to the lord Count of Ligny (Jean de Luxembourg) letters of demand, in which he required Joan to be delivered in the first place to the King of England, the Church herein taking only second place. And that he once more demanded that she should be given and delivered to him: and this with a promise to those who kept or guarded her that he would pay them six thousand francs, and later ten thousand francs; taking no heed of the sum he offered provided he might have her;

III. That the English had a lively fear of her, and therefore sought to deliver her to death, and by ending her life to put an end to the terror which she inspired in them;

IV. That the Bishop favored the English party; and that before he was acquainted with the case, he allowed Joan to be placed, from the very opening of her trial, in a secular prison and in the hands of her enemies, although there were good decent ecclesiastical prisons in which she might have been lawfully guarded and kept, as are criminals guilty of religious offenses;

V. That the Bishop was not a competent judge, as Joan herself often protested in declining to accept him;

VI. That Joan was a simple girl and a good Catholic, eager to confess her sins often and to hear the Mass, so much so that in her death she clearly appeared to those present to be a faithful Christian;

VII. That Joan declared several times during her trial that she submitted all her actions and all her sayings to the judgment of the Church and of our lord the Pope, and that what she said seemed to proceed rather from a good than from an evil spirit;

VIII. That Joan did not understand what the Church was when she was questioned about her submission to the Church, and that she did not take this term to mean the assembly of the faithful, but believed and understood the Church on the subject of which she was questioned to be the ecclesiastics there present, who favored the English cause;

IX. Therefore she was condemned as relapsed although she was willing to submit to the Church;

X. That after being ordered to resume and wear female clothing, she was compelled to put on male clothing; which was the reason why the self-styled judges pronounced her relapsed, they seeking not her repentance but her death;

XI. That although it was clear to the judges that Joan had submitted to the judgments and decisions of our Blessed Mother the Church, nevertheless the judges, in their excessive partiality for the English, or not daring to resist their terrorization and pressure, condemned her most unjustly as a heretic to the pains of fire;

XII. That each and every one of the aforementioned facts—that is to say, Joan's condemnation and the hatred and excessive partiality of the judges—were and are matters of public fame and popular report, commonly said and known in the city and diocese of Rouen, and throughout the kingdom of France.

APPENDIX B

The Second Interrogatory, or the Twenty-seven Articles Which Served as a Basis for the Rehabilitation Inquiry

(See Introduction, pp. 30–36)

I. That because she had come to the aid of the most Christian King of France and fought with the army against the English, Joan was pursued by a mortal hatred and was hated by the English, and that they sought her death by every means. And so it was and that is the truth.[1]

II. As Joan had inflicted numerous defeats on the said English in the war, they greatly feared her, and therefore sought by all possible means to deliver her to death and to put an end to her days so that she could harm them no longer.

III. That in order to give this some color and semblance of justice, they brought her to this city of Rouen, then laboring beneath the tyrannical power of the English; and that they caused to be instituted against her in the castle,

---

[1] Each article concludes with this affirmation, which the witness is asked to confirm or deny.

where she was imprisoned, a false prosecution for heresy, and this under fear and pressure.

IV. That neither the judges, confessors, and consultants, nor the promoter and others intervening in the said trial, because of the very severe threats made to them and the terrorization of the English, dared to exercise free judgment; but that they were constrained to suit all their actions to their fear and to the pressure of the English if they wished to avoid grave perils and even the peril of death.

V. That the notaries recording this trial, because of the same fear and the threats directed against them by the English, could not follow the truth or faithfully set down the true version of Joan's replies when writing and editing their account.

VI. That the notaries were prevented by this fear, and also expressly forbidden, to insert in their account words pronounced by Joan that told in her favor. Furthermore, that they were constrained to omit them and to insert certain things that told against her and that she never said.

VII. That because of the same fears and terrors, nobody could be found to advise Joan, or conduct her case for her, or instruct her, or direct her, or protect her in any other way. Moreover, those who sometimes put in some words for her suffered very great danger to their lives. For the English sought to throw them in the river as rebels, or to deliver them to some other form of death.

VIII. That they kept Joan in a private or lay prison, her feet fettered with irons and chains; and that they forbade anyone to speak to her so that she might not be able to defend herself in any way, and that they even placed English guards over her.

IX. That Joan was a girl of nineteen or thereabouts, simple and ignorant of the law and of judicial procedure; and that alone, without direction or advice, she was not capable or clever enough to defend herself in so trying and difficult a case.

X. That the English, desiring her death, went by night to her prison, pretending to be inspired by some revelations and exhorting her not to submit in any way to the judgment of the Church if she wished to escape death.

XI. That, in order to catch her out by her own words, the examiners plied her with difficult and insidious interrogations and questions, and that for the greater part of the time they interrogated her about things that she did not in the least understand.

XII. That they wore her out with their long interrogations and examinations, so that when she was finally exhausted they could seize on some unfortunate word in her replies.

XIII. That often, in court and elsewhere, Joan stated, affirmed, and protested in her answers that she wished to hold no belief contrary to the Catholic faith; and that if anything in her words or deeds had diverged from that faith she herself wished to retract it and to obey the judgment of the clerics.

XIV. That also, in court and elsewhere, Joan several times affirmed that she submitted herself and all her acts to the judgment of the Church and of our Holy Father the Pope; and so it was and that it is the truth; and that she would have been sorry if there had been anything in her that was in opposition to the Catholic faith.

XV. That although her words of submission to the Church were often repeated by her both in the court and elsewhere, the English and those who favored their cause did not permit but rather forbade them to be inserted or written in the acts or in the record of the so-called trial. And that they caused them to be written down in another form, although this was a perversion of the truth.

XVI. That if Joan ever affirmed that she would not submit to the judgment of our Holy Mother the Church, even the Church Militant, it was not proved by the previous article.

XVII. In any case or instance in which it might appear that Joan pronounced words implying her non-submission to the Church, the promoter says that she did not understand what the Church was, and that she did not understand by this term the assembly of the faithful, but believed and understood the Church of which her interrogators spoke to consist of those ecclesiastics there present, who had embraced the English cause.

XVIII. That the alleged report, originally written in French, was translated into Latin with no great accuracy, many things having been suppressed that told in Joan's favor and even more having been added, in defiance of truth, that prejudiced her case, and therefore that the said record disagrees with its original in numerous and substantial points.

XIX. That, the preceding truths having been recognized, the said trial and sentence does not deserve the name of a judgment and sentence, since there can be no question of a judgment where the judges, consultants, and assessors are not at liberty to exercise judgment owing to fear.

XX. That, for the preceding reasons, the alleged record is in many parts untrue, vitiated, corrupt, and neither perfectly nor faithfully written; and that it is moreover so defective that no trust can be put in it.

XXI. That the preceding and other points being weighed, the case and the sentence are both null and most unjust, since they were conducted and passed without due observance of legal formalities by judges who were not the rightful ones and who had no jurisdiction in such a case or over such a person.

XXII. That, moreover, the said trial and sentence are both null and tainted with manifest injustice for the additional reason that on so grave a charge Joan was given no facilities for defending herself. Furthermore, that defense itself, which exists as a natural right, was totally denied her by manifold and insidious means.

XXIII. That although it was abundantly apparent to the aforenamed judges that Joan had submitted to the judgment and decisions of our Holy Mother the Church, and that she was so faithful a Catholic that they allowed the Body of our Lord to be administered to her, nevertheless out of their excessive zeal for the English, or not wishing to extricate themselves out of fear and pressure, they most unjustly condemned her as a heretic to the pains of fire.

XXIV. That without any further sentence from the secular judge, the English, inspired by a sort of rage against her, immediately led her to the stake under a large escort of armed men.

XXV. That Joan continuously, and notably at the moment of her death, behaved in a saintly and Catholic manner, recommending her soul to God and invoking Jesus aloud even with her last life's breath in such a manner as to draw from all those present, and even from her English enemies, effusions of tears.

XXVI. That the English perpetrated and caused to be perpetrated against Joan each and all the preceding acts, in deed and against the law, by means of pressure, because they had a lively fear of Joan, who supported the party of the most Christian King of France, and because they hated her and pursued her with a mighty hatred; and this in order that the most Christian King might be discredited for having availed himself of the aid of a woman so utterly damned.

XXVII. That each and all the preceding facts were and are of public fame and popular report, and that they are commonly said and known in the diocese of Rouen and throughout the kingdom of France.

APPENDIX C

The Interrogatory Taken in Lorraine

I. Her place of origin and her parish?

II. Who were her parents and what was their station? Were they good Catholics and of good reputation?

III. Who were her godfathers and godmothers?

IV. In her youth, was she properly educated in the faith and in sound morals?

V. What was her way of life in adolescence, from the age of seven till her departure from her father's house?

VI. Did she go to church and to the holy shrines often and gladly?

VII. What were her activities and what her occupation in the time of her youth?

VIII. At that time did she confess gladly and often?

IX. What did popular report say of that tree which is called the "Ladies' Tree"? Were girls in the habit of gathering there to dance? And what of this fountain that is near the tree? Did Joan go there with the other girls, and for what reasons and when did she go?

X. In what way did she leave her country, and what were the stages of her journey?

XI. Was there any information collected by the authority of the judges in her native country at the time when she was a prisoner at Compiègne and held by the English?

XII. On the occasion when Joan once fled from her native village to Neufchâteau because of the soldiery, was she always in her father's and mother's company?

APPENDIX D

List of Witnesses at Orléans

We have thought it would be of interest to give a list of the witnesses who testified at Orléans on March 16, 1456 (see chap. 5).

Jean Luillier, burgher, aged 56.
Jean Hilaire, burgher, aged 66.
Gilles de Saint Mesmin, burgher, aged 74.
Jacques l'Esbahy, burgher, aged 50.
Guillaume Le Charron, burgher, aged 59.
Cosma de Commy, burgher, aged 64.
Martin de Mauboudet, burgher, aged 67.
Jean Volant, burgher, aged 70.
Guillaume Poustieau, burgher, aged 44.
Denis Roger, burgher, aged 70.
Jacques de Thou, burgher, aged 50.
Jean Carrelier, burgher, aged 44.
Aignan de Saint Mesmin, burgher, aged 87.
Jean de Champeaux, burgher, aged 50.
Pierre Jongault, burgher, aged 50.
Pierre Hue, burgher, aged 50.
Jean Aubert, burgher, aged 52.
Guillaume Rouillart, burgher, aged 46.

Genien Cabu, burgher, aged 59.
Pierre Vaillant, burgher, aged 60.
Jean Coulon, burgher, aged 56.
Jean Beauharnais, burgher, aged 50.
Robert de Farciaulx, priest, canon of Saint Aignan, aged 78.
Pierre de la Censure, priest, canon of Saint Aignan, aged 60.
Raoul Godart, priest, prior of Saint Samson, aged 50.
Hervé Bonnard, priest, prior of Saint Magloire, aged 60.
André Bordes, priest, canon of Saint Aignan, aged 60.
Jeanne, wife of Gilles de Saint Mesmin, aged 70.
Jeanne, wife of Gui Boileau, aged 60.
Guillemette, wife of Jean Coulon, aged 51.
Jeanne, widow of Jean de Mouchy, aged 50.
Charlotte, wife of Guillaume Havet, aged 36.
Réginalde, widow of Jean Huré, aged 50.
Pétronille, wife of Jean Beauharnais, aged 50.
Massée, wife of Henri Fagoue, aged 50.

BIBLIOGRAPHY

Fabre, Joseph. *Procès de Réhabilitation de Jeanne d'Arc, raconté et écrit d'après les textes officiels latins.* Paris, 1888, 1912. 2 vols, 12°.

O'Reilly, Eugène. *Les Deux Procès de Condemnation, les Enquêtes et la Sentence de Réhabilitation de Jeanne d'Arc.* Paris, 1868. 2 vols, 8°.

Quicherat, Jules. *Procès de Condemnation et de Réhabilitation de Jeanne d'Arc, dite la Pucelle, publiés pour la première fois d'après les manuscrits de la Bibliothèque royale.* Paris, 1841. 5 vols, 8°.

(The first two works are only mentioned formally, since they could not serve as a basis for a serious study of the rehabilitation suit, for which the only valid source except the MSS is still Quicherat's edition.)

As for the condemnatory trial, at present the most recent and the most complete account is

Doncoeur, The Reverend Father Paul. *La Minute française de l'Interrogatoire de Jeanne la Pucelle, d'après le réquisitoire de Jean d'Estivet et les manuscrits d'Urfé et d'Orléans.* Melun, 1952. Text established with the collaboration of Yvonne Lanhers.

For the manuscripts of the rehabilitation suit, consult the following:

Champion, Pierre. *Notice des Manuscrits du Procès de Réhabilitation de Jeanne d'Arc*. Paris [n.d.], Volume 37 of the *Bibliothèque du XVe Siècle*.

On the suit as a whole see the following source:

Belon, The Reverend Father M-J, and Balme, The Reverend Father François. *Jean Bréhal, grand inquisiteur de France, et la Réhabilitation de Jeanne d'Arc*. Paris, 1893. 4°.